ONE DAY THREE AUTUMNS

LIU ZHENYUN

Translated by
Howard Goldblatt and **Sylvia Li-chun Lin**

SINOIST

Published by Sinoist Books (an imprint of ACA Publishing Ltd)
London - Beijing
www.sinoistbooks.com
info@alaincharlesasia.com ☎ +44 20 3289 3885
www.sinoistbooks.com

Published by Sinoist Books (an imprint of ACA Publishing Ltd) in association with the China Translation and Publishing House
Author: Liu Zhenyun **Translators:** Howard Goldblatt and Sylvia Li-Chun Lin
Editor: David Lammie **Cover Art:** A. Bodrenkova
Production Manager: Dawn Bailey

Original Chinese Text © 一日三秋 (yi ri san qiu) 2021, Guangdong Flower City Publishing House co. Ltd, Guangdong, China

ALL RIGHTS RESERVED. NO PART OF THIS PUBLICATION MAY BE REPRODUCED IN MATERIAL FORM, BY ANY MEANS, WHETHER GRAPHIC, ELECTRONIC, MECHANICAL OR OTHER, INCLUDING PHOTOCOPYING OR INFORMATION STORAGE, IN WHOLE OR IN PART, AND MAY NOT BE USED TO PREPARE OTHER PUBLICATIONS WITHOUT WRITTEN PERMISSION FROM THE PUBLISHER.

English Translation text © 2023 ACA Publishing Ltd, London, UK. A catalogue record for *One Day Three Autumns* is available from the National Bibliographic Service of the British Library.

This novel is entirely a work of fiction. The names, characters and incidents portrayed in it are the work of the author's imagination. Any resemblance to actual persons, living or dead, events or localities is entirely coincidental.

Hardback ISBN: 978-1-83890-584-2
Paperback ISBN: 978-1-83890-583-5
eBook ISBN: 978-1-83890-582-8

ONE DAY THREE AUTUMNS

LIU ZHENYUN

TRANSLATED BY
HOWARD GOLDBLATT & SYLVIA LI-CHUN LIN

SINOIST BOOKS

Foreword
Sixth Uncle's Paintings

Having finished this novel, I look back and feel like saying something about its origin.

I wrote it for Sixth Uncle, for his paintings.

Sixth Uncle once played a stringed *sanxian* in Yanjin County's Henan Drama Troupe. He was the sixth child in the family. In his youth, he was called Little Six or Sixth Brother. As an elderly man, he became Sixth Uncle to the village youngsters. The drama troupe put out a call for new blood when I was eight, and I went to give it a try. I'd barely opened my mouth to sing when the director jeered me off the stage. "You've got talent," he said, "the talent of sounding like a chicken being slaughtered. It would be hard to learn to sing that badly."

At the time, my mother was selling soy sauce at the Foodstuffs Store on East Avenue. When Sixth Uncle went to buy soy sauce, he said to her, "Big Sis, I tried my best when your kid was auditioned. I even tuned my *sanxian* to the lowest key for him."

"You can't support a wall with mud," was how my mother responded.

In the troupe, in addition to playing the *sanxian*, Sixth Uncle also painted the sets.

People stopped going to the theatre once all families owned TV sets, and the troupe disbanded. Sixth Uncle got a job in the foundry of the county's state-owned machinery shop. After that folded, he maintained machinery at the county cotton mill and stopped playing music, even after coming home from work. Instead, he went back to his old craft of painting sets and began painting at home. During the Spring Festival, he also wrote celebratory couplets, which he sold in the market to supplement his income.

I went back to Yanjin on a family visit one year during the Mid-Autumn Festival and bumped into him on the street. When I mentioned my failed audition, he said, "Lucky for you you didn't make it. Otherwise, you'd be out of a job now." We had a good laugh over that.

"I hear you're a novelist?" he said.

"I took the wrong path, Uncle. I hear you're a painter now."

"Your aunt is unhappy with me, calling me crazy," he said. "So, I'm crazy. I don't care. I'd be bored to death without something as a diversion."

"I'm with you on that. It's why I write, a diversion. It's nothing special." We laughed over that too.

I gave him a few of my novels, and he offered to show me his paintings. As time went by, it became a routine for us. I'd go to see his works on my visits home over Tomb-Sweeping Day, the Dragon Boat Festival, and the Mid-Autumn and Spring Festivals. He painted off and on, and I saw them off and on. Yanjin was his main subject matter, but not the city he lived in. Yanjin is not by the Yellow River, but the Yanjin he painted is, with roiling, surging waves and a ferry landing. The real Yanjin is an open flatland, whereas his Yanjin backs to towering mountains, beyond which are more mountains, all snow-capped the year round. Once, during the Dragon Boat Festival, one of the paintings I saw was of a moonlit night with a pretty young girl doubled over laughing beside a persimmon tree overladen with fruit as big as lanterns.

"Who is she?" I asked.

"An immortal fairy who landed in Yanjin by mistake."

"What's she laughing about?"

"She's laughing over jokes she'd heard in people's dreams. We residents of Yanjin love to tell jokes."

In another, a painting of men's and women's heads, all laughing, their mouths wide open, was in stark contrast to the next one, which featured similar heads but with long faces, their eyes shut. I understood the former, because, as he said, Yanjin people loved to tell jokes. But why were the people's eyes shut and their faces unsmiling in the latter?

"Crushed to death because of jokes," he said. "There are people who like hearing jokes and others who prefer to be serious. You might say their seriousness crushes them to death."

In another painting, a man in a cafe was lying under a table surrounded by a crowd. Leftovers on the table included a smiling fish head.

"What happened to him?" I asked.

"He was eating the fish," Sixth Uncle said. "When someone at the next table told a joke, he died laughing, a fish bone caught in his throat. You could even say he was killed by a joke."

I checked the title: "Public Space, No Joking".

"You're quite postmodern, Sixth Uncle," I said.

"He waved me off. "I don't know anything about those things. I just paint whatever comes to mind."

"Painting whatever comes to mind is a frame of mind all its own."

He shook his head. "I don't know how to express what I mean."

His wife was in that day. She'd been a performer in the troupe when she was young, playing female leads in martial arts dramas. After the troupe disbanded, she found a job wrapping sweets in the county sweets factory.

"Why don't you paint something useful if you like it so much?" she said.

"Like what?"

"Like blooming flowers bring wealth and riches, or good luck magpies on a branch or a phoenix bowing to the sun. Even portraits of guardian deities for doors. You can get paid for those too, like the New Year's couplets. You've spent a lot of money on brushes, ink and paper, not to mention paints."

He didn't respond, and I didn't try to argue his case. It wasn't something that could be easily argued.

During another Dragon Boat Festival, in one of his paintings I saw a woman dancing in the sky over the Yellow River, like a fairy taking flight, or Chang'e flying to the moon.

"Who's she?"

"A ghost," he explained. His wife wasn't around that day.

"Who is she, anyway?"

"She used to be a performer in the drama troupe," he replied, almost whispering. "A kind of confidante for me. She married someone else and later hanged herself over a handful of chives. She entered my dream a few days ago, dancing over the river like that. Dancing and dancing." Then he whispered, "Don't tell your aunt."

Later, during the Mid-Autumn Festival one year, I saw a painting of a man on a train carrying a woman in his belly.

"Who's that?" I pointed to the woman.

"Another ghost."

"What's she doing in a man's belly?"

"Taking possession of him so she can travel a long distance to search for her family."

I saw the underworld he painted one Tomb-Sweeping Day, featuring a cluster of little demons – one having his nose cut off, one having his eyes gouged out, one being sawn in half, one roasting over a fire and one tossed onto a hill of knives. It was just a painting, but I could almost hear their agonised howls. Yama, King of Hell, on the other hand, was laughing.

"It's so gory. Why's he laughing?" I asked.

"One of the ghosts told a joke before he died," Sixth Uncle replied. "Yama said, 'You must be from Yanjin.'"

I had to laugh when I heard his explanation.

"Overall, Yanjin should be considered a city of laughter," he added.

In yet another painting, a shaman-like woman is mumbling something while nailing paper figurines onto a board. It was entitled, "No Rancour, No Enmity".

"If there's no rancour or enmity, why's she nailing those figurines?"

"To her, it's just a job."

I saw what he meant and broke out in a cold sweat.

He also painted people from daily life, like Big Mouth Wu, who sold tripe soup in Beiguan, Old Zhu, who stewed pigs' feet in Xiguan, blind Old Dong, who told fortunes on East Avenue, Guo Baochen, who swept streets, and so on. They were rendered true to life, but sketches nonetheless.

"There was no one better at making tripe soup in all of Yanjin," he said, pointing to Big Mouth Wu. "What a shame he was barely forty when he died.

"Ate too much and got too fat," he continued.

"This one was the brooding type, crushed to death by too many thoughts," he said, as he pointed at the blind fortune-teller. "Old Dong spewed nonsense all his life. Sighted people had to go to a blind man to solve their problems. Anything that couldn't be resolved was pinned on a man who spewed nonsense."

"Guo swept the streets all his life," he said, moving on to Guo Baochen. "But the fortune-teller said that in his previous life he'd been a prime minister who'd killed countless people. So he was reborn to clean himself up."

"Guo had mush for brains, but his son went to study in England," he continued. "That's what I call two negatives making a positive."

Sixth Uncle once painted a large canvas, some six feet wide, sketching his co-workers at the troupe, everyone with their own unique expression and demeanour.

"This one's Chen Changjie," he said, pointing. "After the troupe was disbanded, his wife swallowed pesticide and he moved to Wuhan to be a stoker on the trains. And this is Sun Xiaobao. He played the clown role, but ended up in Daqing as an oilfield driller."

He then moved to a boy who looked to be about five. "This is Chen Changjie's son. Mingliang's his name. He stayed backstage, playing all alone. He grew up and went to Xi'an, for some strange reason."

"And her," he said, lowering his voice as he pointed to a woman, "she's the one dancing over the Yellow River."

Ah, I thought, she must have been his confidante.

"What a beauty," I said after a closer look.

"It's history," he said, "not worth a backward look. Most of them are gone by now. I forgot quite a few of them when I painted this, so they didn't make it in."

Later, over New Year, I saw the drawing of a boy running along railway tracks, a kite floating over his head and an old cow following behind.

"Why's he running along the tracks?" I asked.

"He took a train going in the wrong direction."

"What a careless child," I said after reading the title, "Wrong Direction".

"So many things in life are like that," he said.

I nodded my understanding.

He even painted a thirty-foot-wide scroll, like the famed *Qingming Festival by the River*, with the same meticulous attention to detail. The market along the Bian River had been replaced by the Yanjin ferry landing, and the figures were all dressed in the style of the Song dynasty: waves surged in the Yellow River; figures played a flute and a *sanxian* under willow trees along the bank; in the middle of the river, a man stood in the bow of his boat trawling for fish, catching not a grass carp, a crucian carp nor a big-head carp, but a mermaid; figures pushing a cart, carrying things on a pole or herding livestock, all crowded onto a bridge by the ferry landing. A shop beneath the bridge had a plaque above its door: "One Day Three Autumns".

"No shop would put out a plaque like that, Uncle," I said. "It's always something like 'A Rousing Business', or 'Money Rolling In'."

"I'd had too much to drink that day," he said with a laugh, "and didn't leave enough room for a phrase that would take up a lot of space. I had to settle for 'One Day Three Autumns', with fewer strokes."

He added detailed sketches of animals – dogs, cats, foxes, weasels – all with different faces. There was even a monkey leaning against a willow tree by the ferry landing, hugging its belly, fast asleep. Around its neck was a metal ring attached to a chain fastened to the tree. A section of the chain was draped over its body. Wounds were visible on its head and body, still scabbing.

"Look at the calluses on its rear end and its feet," I commented. "Thick as coins. It must be an old monkey."

"A self-portrait."

"Why the beatings?" I pointed at the wounds on its head and body.

"The monkey's too old to perform tricks, but its master can't allow that, so it got a beating."

When I returned for the Mid-Autumn Festival a couple of years ago and went to look at his paintings, I heard that his wife was suffering from depression. It turned out to be true. Most people with depression don't talk much, but not her; she couldn't stop talking, bringing up a litany of unhappy events in her life, each and every one of them because of her husband. His head lowered, Sixth Uncle mutely pointed to his paintings. Looking at his works amid non-stop chatter was too much for me. I quickly lost interest and, after looking at a few, walked out under the pretext of expecting a guest at home at noon.

When I went home for the Spring Festival last year, I heard that Sixth Uncle had died. Heart attack. Over a month already. When I went to his house, he'd become a picture on the wall. I chatted with his wife about him.

"He was slurping spicy soup when his head tilted to one side and he stopped breathing." She went on about taking him to the ER, where they failed to revive him. He didn't say a word before he died. Then she talked about how she notified friends and family and took care of the funeral. She talked fast, with no hesitation, like a stage performer reading lines, and that told me she'd been saying the same thing to too many people to count. I interrupted her when something occurred to me: "What about his paintings?"

"Burned them all the day he died."

"They were so good." I was stunned. "How could you burn them?"

"They were worthless. No one but him liked the stuff he painted."

"I did, Auntie."

"I forgot about you." She clapped her hands. "I'd have kept them for you if I'd remembered."

"The dead can't come back to life and you can't retrieve paintings once they've turned to ashes. That's that, then."

And that was that. I have no idea where the ashes from the paintings went. I dreamed about Sixth Uncle that night.

As snow flurries fell on the Yanjin ferry landing, he was there, dressed in a long white robe, apparently performing opera on the riverbank. As drifting snow turned into his paintings, he spread his hands and sang to me, "What to do? What to do? What shall I do? What shall I do?"

I couldn't go back to sleep after that. A month later, I decided to restore his burned paintings. I can't paint, but I could create a novel by connecting all his works. Put differently, since I'd never see him again, I was left with creating a novel to commemorate our friendship and to retain the Yanjin he painted.

When I got down to do it, I realised that turning paintings into a book is anything but easy. His works recreated scenes in real life, but they weren't necessarily connected, while a novel must have linked characters and a storyline. Besides, some of his work seemed quite postmodern, with exaggerated or altered people and backdrops, transcending life and death, including supernatural elements, while others were highly realistic, focusing on daily life and common people going about their business, the continuation of routine existence. The two forms are radically different; that can be accomplished with paintings, one by one. But a novel must have a unified narrative technique and writing style. After finishing two chapters, I was tempted to give up, but then I reminded myself that I'm a writer with no great talent to make a masterpiece. I write to provide readers with a diversion. I silently promised Sixth Uncle that I would, with whatever skill I have, retrieve my friend's emotions and inner thoughts, forgotten by everyone.

I did my best while writing about the postmodern, the exaggerated or altered personages and backdrops, as well as elements transcending life and death, and supernatural aspects that serve as a foundation and for contrast. Most of the chapters focus on daily life, while others feature supernatural postmodern components to elicit laughs from readers, who, I hope, will not take them seriously. I selected a few actors from the scroll as characters who appear throughout the novel. Uncle's confidante naturally was one of the female protagonists. My decisions were based on the characters' proximity to him. Most of them had left Yanjin because I think only people who leave know a place best, whereas Uncle's paintings never deviated from the city. Such is the distinction between fiction and painting. I hope he won't be upset that my rendition moves beyond Yanjin, away from his paintings. In the meantime, expanding the geographical location provides the novel with room to develop. Moreover, my memory of his work belongs to the past, since the paintings are all gone now, and comprises only recollections of what I remembered about what he'd shown me. If I were just to recreate what he painted, I could miss something tiny and yet end up with a major flaw, failing to restore the tenor of his work. If I commit the proverbial error of trying to draw a tiger but ending up with a dog, I hope he won't angry. In short, some parts of the novel are faithful representations of Sixth Uncle, while others are betrayals, something I did not anticipate when I began. Heaven and Earth can vouch for my pure heart and noble motive. Sixth Uncle once said that Yanjin was best known for laughter, so let's treat this as a joke.

I'd like to thank everyone for reading this book and express my gratitude on Sixth Uncle's behalf.

PART I
HUA ERNIANG

One

Hua Erniang loved jokes. When asked where she came from, she said Mount Wanglang. When asked where she was going and why, she said off to look for jokes. When asked why there was frost on her brows, she said the snow on Mount Wanglang hadn't melted. A basket hanging from the crook of her arm held red lantern-shaped persimmons.

She searched for jokes at night, never during the day.

Hua Erniang wasn't born in Yanjin. She'd come from far away to wait for someone at the Yanjin ferry landing. It was a man called Hua Erlang. After more than three thousand years, he'd yet to make an appearance. She told everyone she saw that they'd agreed to meet, and did not know if he'd changed his mind or might have died along the way, owing to incessant wars and other calamities. When she was tired from standing at the landing, she sat on the riverbank to wash her feet and praise the flowing water for being so faithful, coming unfailingly every day.

The water replied, "It wasn't us you saw yesterday, Erniang. We just got here."

"I'm glad the river hasn't changed," she said with a sigh. "I wouldn't have anywhere to go otherwise."

"The river is different when the water changes," the water said.

"You're the punctual ones, Geese," she said when a large flock flew over. "You left last year and here you are, back again."

"We're not the flock you saw last year, Erniang," the geese said. "Those died in the south."

Some cranes flew by, followed by several golden pheasants, all during Song Emperor Hui's reign when Erniang sensed that her waiting had become a joke. She turned into a mountain that evening; it was named Mount Wanglang, or Swain Waiting Mountain.

People later came to understand that she was a rock, not a real person, which was how she could become a mountain. But rocks are supposed to be hard and unfeeling, while Erniang was filled with tender affection, and that was the root of her troubles. During the passage of a thousand years, from the Song dynasty to the present, longing and resentment had gained for her immortality. Immortality *and* eternal youth, actually. She still had the pretty face of an eighteen-year-old, even after all those years.

Some said she died from crying too much when the man failed to show. Unwilling to tolerate the sight of tears after returning to life, she entered people's dreams in search of jokes.

Not everyone is good at telling jokes. Rather than being upset if she came into someone's dream for jokes and they could not make her laugh, she'd say, "Carry me on your back for a bowl of spicy soup."

Is there anyone strong enough to carry a mountain on their back? When they tried to pick her up, she flattened them. Put differently, they were flattened by jokes. If they made her laugh, however, she'd give them one of the persimmons from her basket.

A loafer who was terrific at telling jokes once made her roar with laughter. They should have parted ways once they'd shared a laugh and the man finished his persimmon. But her face had a rosy glow when she laughed, which made her more fetching than ever. The young man was bolder in dreams than in life, so he flirted with her, aiming to get further. She laughed even harder, for a man wanting to have sex with a rock was truly laughable, and she was so amused she said yes. They undressed and the man went to pieces from pleasure the moment they came into contact. The next morning, his family found him sprawled across the bed, naked and dead. When his body was moved, the sheet was sticky wet, but his death had nothing to do with the sexual encounter. He'd died of a heart attack. To be sure, she was not responsible for every fatal heart attack in Yanjin; some of the deaths were in fact caused by unhealthy hearts.

There was yet another bold man who, after making her laugh at a joke, said, "Erniang, you're always asking people to tell *you* a joke. Can you tell *me* one?"

Being in a good mood, she said, "Sure. I recently gave my house a new name. It's been called Mount Swain Waiting since the Song dynasty. It was time to change it."

"What did you change it to?"

"I changed 'Swain Waiting' into 'Swain Forgetting'. I've

waited for him for more than three thousand years, like a rock. Time to forget that turtle spawn."

"You are so wrong, Hua Erniang," he ventured. "Why do you say you want to forget him since you cannot get him out of your head?"

"Isn't that funny?"

He laughed.

After that, she'd ask whoever told her a joke if it would be all right for her to tell them one.

People all knew she'd bring up the story of waiting and forgetting, so they'd say, "I won't trouble you with that, Erniang."

There was one man who could make her laugh with a one-liner instead of a long-winded story, and that pleased her. "What a talent," she said, giving him two persimmons, as well as the privilege of a three-year joke waiver for the whole family. Naturally, not too many talents like that emerged over the centuries.

"The world is so vast you should go see what other places are like, rather than spend all your time in Yanjin."

"It's too late for me. The world is vast, and I would like to see it. I could have done that before I became a mountain, but not now, not any more. Call it whatever you like, Waiting Mountain or Forgetting Mountain, it cannot be shaken or moved. I'm here to stay. I'm not hanging on to Yanjin, I'm stuck here. The way things are with me now, I can only stay put and imagine the world beyond, or worse, forget about it."

For safety's sake, most Yanjin residents memorised a few jokes when they reached adulthood and repeated them once or twice before bedtime, just in case. Which was why

Yanjin people were endowed with a great sense of humour. It was with them at night, not to mention during the day. Some reckless residents thought there was little chance they'd be picked out of a population of half a million, and had no jokes ready. One can be heedless in the safety of a crowd. As a result, they lost their lives the moment she made a surprise visit to their dreams. Served them right for being heedless.

There were interludes, of course. She let the Yanjin residents off the hook during holidays. They did not have to tell jokes during the Dragon Boat Festival, the Mid-Autumn Festival or a New Year's celebration. The locals had a stern approach to holidays, pulling long faces when they were out on the streets. The frosty stares they exchanged when meeting someone familiar did not mean they were hostile. On the contrary, they were being warm. Acting frosty was being cordial, and looking stern was being easy-going. That's why.

I'd had an encounter with Hua Erniang in a dream the previous winter during a family visit. She'd forced me to tell her a joke. Caught unprepared and flustered, I had to come up with something fast, so I said, "I've found that after leaving Yanjin, people often treat jokes as real. Does that count as a joke?"

"For instance?"

"When someone said there was a moon in the water, people jumped in to grab–"

"A stale joke. It's the one about the monkey trying to fish out the moon. Don't try to fool me," she warned, "that's the same as fooling yourself."

"It may be a stale joke," I defended myself, "but people

keep telling it, and people keep trying to grab the moon in the water. Isn't that funny?"

She laughed, and I made it out alive. I was grateful that people outside Yanjin took jokes seriously, for that was my salvation. She then asked if I'd like a joke from her. I'd heard about her age-old joke about waiting and forgetting, so I said, "I won't trouble you with that." But I did wonder why she hadn't given me a persimmon after I told her a joke, like she did with everyone else. Then it occurred to me that my joke might have barely made the grade, and that I was lucky to be spared from having to carry a mountain. That possibility made me shudder. Truly:

In a dream, a vague sense of Hua Erniang,
Slurping spicy soup all day long,
Too bad a day like three autumns is short,
Tears spatter my shirt as I sing this song.

PART II
YINGTAO

One

Chen Changjie sent Li Yansheng a letter from Wuhan, inviting him to his wedding. "Please make sure to arrive by 8 July. We'll catch up when you're here. Looking forward to it."

Li and Chen had been members of the Fenglei Henan Drama Troupe from Yanjin ten years earlier. In their best-known piece, *Legend of the White Snake*, Li Yansheng played the role of the main character Xu Xian, Chen Changjie played the sorcerer Monk Fahai, and Yingtao the White Snake. On reflection, the play's success rested on a comment by Chen Changjie: "The dramatic highlight of *Legend of the White Snake* is the misfortune caused by the body's lower half." That proclamation was then expanded into an exposition.

"You see, the snake became an immortal, after a thousand years of ascetic practice," Chen said. "Mortals want to go to fairylands when they die. 'Early Ascension to Fairyland' is always inscribed on mourning sheds at funerals. But this snake changes itself into a woman after becoming an immortal and being involved with a man. It wants to be an immortal both ways. So greedy. Before getting involved with a mortal, it considered carefully. It wouldn't have a poor man – a dockside porter knows nothing of romance. It wouldn't have a rich man either, for he would be encumbered by a wife and concubine and would not care for a woman he meets on the street. Which is why it has its eye on the fair-skinned Xu Xian, a scholar with a nice face. In the daytime, he apprentices at a herbal shop to earn his keep, and at night he is alone at home. When a beauty drops into his lap in such a manner, it's like dry kindling coming in contact with a burning flame. A scholar surely knows about romance. The snake is spot on. As for Fahai, he's a monk and thus forbidden to have involvements with women. Or put differently, he's a man in name only. How can he not be jealous when a snake is causing trouble in the human world? So he strikes out and turns her from a woman back into a snake, before placing a pagoda on top of it. If I can't do it, neither can you. Don't you agree that's what he's thinking? Those are his thoughts, wouldn't you say?"

Li Yansheng agreed that Chen Changjie was making sense, so did Yingtao. Bearing Chen's comments and explication in mind, the three of them put on regular lively performances. Each line they sang came from the depths of their hearts, with additional insinuations lurking beneath their sincere and credible acting. Their performances made an exceptional play exceptionally sorrowful and stirring. Ah, amazing how a man and a snake can develop such deep feelings, an emotional bond that can be found only in dramatic plays, never in the mortal world.

In the play, Fahai sings to Xu Xian,
You love her because she's lovely as a flower,
Knowing not there's a snake in the bower

Xu Xian replies,
I did not know she was a snake at the start,
To give her up would break my heart

The White Snake sings to Fahai,
With no bad feelings, old or new,
Why must you separate us two?

To which Fahai replies,
I separate only what I cannot fix,
For humans and demons should never mix.

The three of them spread their hands and sing,
What to do? What to do?
What shall I do? What shall I do?

Legend of the White Snake became the Fenglei Henan Drama Troupe's signature play, which in turn earned the actors some renown in Yanjin. But the play sowed the seeds of trouble, and they all had issues in their daily lives, leading them to say, "What to do? What to do? What shall I do? What shall I do?"

In the play, Yingtao, the White Snake, gets together with Li Yansheng, who is Xu Xian on the stage, but in reality, she is married to Chen Changjie, who plays Fahai. She had a willowy waist, an oval face and almond eyes that cast oblique glances before she spoke. After spending so much time together on and off the stage, Li fell for her, but was aware of how Chen was given to explaining the plays to her. And he told her jokes that made her giggle, a giggle after each joke. Li knew she'd end up marrying Chen, who, with his talent to make a play come alive, could surely win over a woman's heart. Later, Li Yansheng married Hu Xiaofeng, who was a product wrapper at the county's sweets factory. She had an ample bosom and big eyes. A theatre-goer when she was off work, she was taken with his Xu Xian character, a handsome, fair-skinned scholar. One night after the show, he walked out through the stage door after removing his makeup and saw Hu Xiaofeng standing there. She offered him a handful of sweets.

"Have some." She added, "Not your run-of-the-mill sweets."

"How's that?"

"Take a closer look."

He did and saw red hearts on every wrapper.

"That's the advantage of wrapping sweets in a factory."

"Thanks, but no thanks. I've got cavities, I can't eat sweets."

"Where are you going now?"

"I'm always tired after a performance. I'm going home to sleep."

"Aren't you hungry after a night of singing? It's bad sleeping on an empty stomach." She continued, "Old Hu's spicy soup stand at the crossroads is still open. Let's go have some."

"I need to rest my vocal cords. No spicy food."

"Big Mouth Wu's tripe soup in Beiguan is open too. Let's try that. Soup is gentle on the teeth."

So they went and then they went again, on and off, for about a month. She wore a new outfit every time. On this night, as they enjoyed the soup, she said to him, "I'm a straight talker, Yansheng. You don't find that offensive, do you?"

"Your offence is forgiven," he replied with a common line from plays.

"Which do you prefer, falling in love with a snake or with a woman?"

"It's a stage play." He looked up from the steaming bowl. "In real life, no one would go looking for a snake at the base of the city wall. That would be insane. Of course, a man falls for a human."

She laid down her spoon and said, "Then come to me when you want to fall in love with a human."

"Why's that?"

"I'm better than the White Snake."

"How so?"

"I have breasts. She doesn't."

He thought it over, recalling that, despite her bewitching look, Yingtao was indeed flat-chested. Hu Xiaofeng was on the heavy side, but she did have breasts. Sitting across from her, he could see those two mounds nearly bursting through her blouse, and he laughed.

During their first two years of marriage, she often asked him to paint his face at night, the face of Xu Xian in the stage play.

"Who do you like, me or the character Xu Xian?"

"I'm the White Snake when I do this with you," she said, as she moved her body on top of him.

So she wanted to be a slithering snake.

Later, once every family owned a TV set, people stopped going to the theatre, and the Fenglei Henan Drama Troupe was disbanded. The hundred or so members of the troupe dispersed, like monkeys fleeing a fallen tree, going into various lines of work, depending on their skill set. Li Yansheng, Chen Changjie and Yingtao got jobs at Yanjin's state-run machinery shop. The head of the plant, Hu Zhankui, was a theatre buff, his favourite being *Legend of the White Snake*, which was why he took on the three actors. Li Yansheng worked in the foundry, Chen Changjie became a panel beater and Yingtao made steamed rolls for the dining hall. He asked them to perform *Legend of the White Snake* for holiday celebrations and when entertaining visitors to the plant. They sang without musical accompaniment and performed only the highlights, mostly the segment with "What to do? What to do? What shall I do? What shall I do?" As the three of them sang away on stage, Hu would rub his bald pate and roar with laughter. They finally put the three roles to rest when the plant folded, and they went looking for other ways to make a living. Chen and Yingtao went to the county cotton mill, where he worked in maintenance and she tended the looms. Li Yansheng got a job with the county's Foodstuffs Store, selling soy sauce, vinegar and pickled vegetables at the retail outlet on East Avenue. A stall to his left was tended by Xiao Bai, who sold peppercorns, anise and fermented tofu. Li took over the sale of her offerings when she followed her husband to Gansu with his army unit.

Now that they worked at different places, Li and Chen could no longer meet daily, as they had before. Sometimes they ran into each other on the street and stopped to chat awhile. Or they'd arrange to have pigs' feet at Marshal Tianpeng's Cafe in Xiguan, where they'd often gone for a sip and some pigs' feet back when they worked together. They'd gone whenever they felt like it then, but now, working in different places, they had to arrange a get-together. At first, they met once a week, later once a month. Then they got busy over making a living and taking care of daily necessities, and slowly lost interest in meeting altogether. If one of them felt like having pigs' feet, he'd go to the diner, buy them and take them home to enjoy. The two families got together, though, when Chen's baby was a hundred days old. Chen and Yingtao named their son Hanlin. Li knew why; the White Snake in the play had a son called Hanlin, who had passed the Imperial Exam. The couple had given their son the same name, obviously hoping he'd amount to something, like his namesake in the play.

"She named the baby," Chen said, pointing to his wife.

"A good name. A wonderful name," Li and Hu responded in unison. "Look at his broad forehead. That's the sign of an impressive future."

Chen and Li began to see each other on and off after the gathering. But since they didn't meet often enough, they usually heard about their friends from other people. Li heard that when Chen's son was a year old, the boy kept saying everything was dark in front of him, so his grandma renamed him Mingliang – Brightness. Two years went by, and Li learned that Chen and Yingtao weren't getting along, fighting all the time. The two men ran into each other now and then, but a long time had passed since they'd shared their innermost thoughts, so brief, chance encounters could only be perfunctory. Li refrained from asking

Chen about his family life, until one day when he heard that Yingtao had hanged herself. Why? Over a bunch of chives, he was told. She and Chen had fought over chives, when Chen said, "Go hang yourself if you think you're so hot," and he walked out the door, not expecting her to do just that.

Li Yansheng offered his condolences at her funeral. Following the Yanjin custom that the mourning family was lower in status, Chen Changjie knelt and kowtowed to Li Yansheng when the latter arrived. As Li helped his friend up, Chen burst into tears, still holding Li's hand.

"It's a long story."

"The dead can't come back alive," Li tried to console Chen. "No need to say anything now."

"I shouldn't have fallen for her. We were so different. I caused her death."

"Don't say that."

"Why not? We were mortal enemies in the play, White Snake against Fahai."

"That was just a play, not real life."

Li spotted "Early Ascension to the Land of Immortals" inscribed on the mourning shed. Before Yingtao's picture stood her three-year-old son, Mingliang, dressed in mourning garments, sniffling and looking over at him.

"That's all in the past. You need to focus on the boy."

"Now everyone in the county knows I caused her death. I can't stay in Yanjin."

"You're the only one who thinks that."

"We spent every day together in the troupe, then at the machinery shop. You know the real me, don't you?"

"Of course, I do. Anytime you need to talk to someone,

come see me, won't you? We'll go have pigs' feet at Marshal Tianpeng's."

"You're the only person in Yanjin I can really talk to," Chen said with a nod.

Li did not expect that, a month after Yingtao's funeral, Chen Changjie would pack up and leave Yanjin. He had an uncle in Wuhan working as a pointsman for the railway bureau, so he'd taken his three-year-old son to stay with his uncle. He hadn't even said goodbye.

Another three years passed before Chen wrote to say he was getting married again and invited Li to his wedding in Wuhan. The letter was sent to Li's workplace. After reading the letter, Li recalled the time he'd spent with his friend, in the troupe, at the machinery shop and enjoying pigs' feet meals together. The letter brought back all those forgotten memories. He knew he had to go. When he got home after work, he talked to his wife about the upcoming trip. By this time, Hu Xiaofeng had puffed up all over, not just her chest, and she no longer asked him to paint his face as Xu Xian at night, nor did she writhe on top of him. Her response came as a surprise.

"You're not going!"

"He's an old friend. I have to go. At his wife's funeral, he told me I'm the only person in Yanjin he can really talk to."

"His wife died and now he's remarrying. I don't care about that. I just want to ask you one question. Who'll pay for your trip?"

"Me, of course."

"Will you give a wedding gift?"

"I will, of course."

"Wuhan is miles from Yanjin. You make less than seventy

yuan a month. It'll cost you two months' pay for the trip and the gift money. As you know, I haven't been feeling well these past couple of months, sweating heavily whether I'm sitting or standing, but I can't bring myself to spend the money on a doctor's visit. Apparently, you don't care about your own wife, but do care about someone else getting a new one, is that it?"

Li hadn't expected his plan to lead to something like that, the sort of thing that happened all too frequently now that they'd been married several years. Worried that she'd bring up more complaints, he abruptly changed his tune.

"I just thought it would be a good idea to talk to you about this. But he invited me, and I'm the one who decides if I go or not."

After getting off work the next day, Li asked Xiao Meng, who sold tobacco and alcohol in the stall to his right to watch over his own stall, where he sold soy sauce, vinegar, pickled vegetables, peppercorns, anise and fermented tofu. Then he looked up some of his former fellow actors in the drama troupe as well as his co-workers at the machinery shop and asked them if they'd heard about Chen Changjie's impending wedding in Wuhan, and if so, whether they planned to attend. Not only had none of them heard about Chen's marriage, several of them had already forgotten the man. Chen Changjie? Who's he?

He saw he'd have to refresh their memory. "Oh, I see, he, uh, he's the one who drove his wife to suicide." To all appearances, Li Yansheng was the only person in all of Yanjin who had been notified of Chen Changjie's wedding. If so, then there didn't seem to be any need to go. But precisely because he was the only one to be informed, his absence would be noted. Now that was no big deal, but his being the only invitee meant that he was Chen's only Yanjin friend, and not going would be an act of disloyalty. And besides, the invitation included the statement, "We'll catch up when you're here." What was it he wanted to catch up on? But to go, he'd have to find his way around the obstacle that was his wife. He checked the price of a round-trip train ticket to Wuhan. More than a hundred yuan. Then there was the cost of the wedding gift, bringing the total to nearly two hundred yuan, for a man whose monthly wages were sixty-five yuan. In other words, a trip to Wuhan would cost more than two months' income. Hu Xiaofeng knew what she was talking about. What to do? What to do? What shall I do? What shall I do? Li Yansheng heaved a long sigh.

So as not to complicate matters, he replied to Chen's letter. After the requisite congratulations on his forthcoming wedding, he wrote, "I ought to be there to congratulate you in person, and would be if I hadn't suffered a twisted ankle last week. I have to stay off my feet." He signed off with, "There will be time in the days ahead for us to catch up." A simple lie took care of the matter.

Two

Li Yansheng was unhappy, moody even, for a whole week. A song called *Go Eat, Go Drink* had won over residents all across Yanjin. The song went:

> *Go eat, go drink, don't let things get you down.*
> *Fate controls our lives, don't let your thoughts go wild.*
> *Heaven and Earth, nothing to fear;*
> *If the sky falls, it'll get us all,*
> *So go eat, go drink, there's nothing you can do to me.*

Everyone was singing it, even Li Yansheng. If something's bugging you, try the song, was how people felt. Sing your troubles away, and be happy. But Li had been singing the song for a week, and his funk got worse. The reason? No reason. He went to work every day at the Foodstuffs Store, had his three meals a day, as regular as clockwork. There were no arguments with his wife and no disputes at work. Old Meng, who ran the tobacco and alcohol stand next to him, said it best: "It's all in your head." But it sure felt real. Never much of a talker, Li was more close-mouthed than ever, uttering no more than a handful of comments a day, preferring to be alone to stare into space. At work, if a customer asked for soy sauce, he might give her vinegar, or pepper for anise. At home, in the middle of a meal, he'd lay down his chopsticks and stare out the window.

"What's on your mind, Yansheng?" his wife would ask.

With a shiver, he'd snap out of his daze. "Oh, nothing."

If Hu Xiaofeng woke up in the middle of the night, there'd be her husband, sitting up, legs dangling over the side of the bed as he stared into the darkness beyond the window. One night, she was abruptly awakened by babbling from Li, who was staring into the darkness and softly singing that aria from *Legend of the White Snake*: "What to do? What to do? What shall I do? What shall I do?" Then he started to cry.

"You're scaring me, Yansheng," she said.

She took him to the hospital for a check-up. They checked his blood pressure, drew blood, gave him an ECG and an abdominal CT scan. They found nothing wrong. Next to the mental hospital, for more tests. Everything normal.

"Nothing's wrong," Hu said, "but something's definitely wrong. Now I'm really worried."

"I don't want to be like this," he said, "but I can't help it. Whatever happens, Xiaofeng, whether I live or die, don't worry about me."

That made her cry. "You're scaring me, Yansheng. Are you trying to put me in my grave before you die?" Then something occurred to her. "Has Hua Erniang come into your dreams?"

He shook his head. "If she had, since I'm as tongue-tied as Big Mouth, I'd wind up flattened. Would I be talking to you if that happened?"

That gave her an idea. "If you think she might come to you tonight, why not prepare some jokes? Armed with memorised jokes, maybe you'll be your old self again."

Li shook his head a second time. "I did that, I even sang *Go Eat, Go Drink*, but nothing worked."

"Then what's wrong?"

"I wouldn't be like this if I knew."

His worried wife's penchant for heavy sweating was cured by worrying about him.

But then, Li lost his appetite, and within a month, he was noticeably thinner, his eyes were sunken, which made his eyes look bigger, and his cheekbones were the most prominent feature of his face.

"Yansheng," Old Meng said to him, "you can't keep on like this."

"I'm getting more and more depressed, Old Meng, and I'm not sure I want to go on living."

"Then what you need to do is see Old Dong. I'll go with you."

Three

Big Mouth Wu ran a cafe in Beiguan, where he sold tripe soup. When Li Yansheng and Hu Xiaofeng were dating, they ate there every day for more than a month. It was more successful than any of the other fifty or sixty Yanjin restaurants that sold tripe soup. Wu also sold mutton kebabs, mutton cakes, boiled mutton and mutton noodles. All the other places were open during the day and closed at night. Wu's cafe was closed during the day and open at night, staying open till dawn, with customers flocking in as late as four and five in the morning. They came because his soup was the freshest, his meat the tenderest. How had he managed that? By slaughtering a new sheep every day.

The slaughtering took place during daylight hours, around three or four in the afternoon. A short, clean-shaven, stocky man with a round head and bulging belly, Wu would fetch an animal from the sheep pen. *Baa-baa*, the sheep would bleat; *baa-baa*, the other sheep would bleat. He'd drag the chosen animal over to the butcher's block.

"Stop bleating, it won't help. If I don't slaughter you, somebody else will."

And: "I opened my cafe to earn a living. I bought you out of those earnings. I can't feed you forever."

And: "It's not my fault, and it's not yours either. Just your bad luck to have been born a sheep. But I'll put you to good use tonight. Now, no more wild thoughts. Off you go to paradise. You were fated to meet your end at my hand."

The knife made its entry, the sheep stopped bleating, and so did the others in the sheep pen. Blood spurted from the sheep's neck and straight into a bucket under the butcher's block. Sheep's blood was one of his customers' favourites.

Except for the brief monologues with sheep that died under his knife, Big Mouth Wu had little to say. Smooth talking was alien to him. As we've seen, Chen Changjie and Yingtao ate a lot of soup at Wu's cafe. Chen talked up a storm while they were eating, telling Yingtao one joke after another. She giggled after every joke, no exception. When that happened, Big Mouth Wu would give them a look before going out back. Then, as we've seen, when Li Yansheng and Hu Xiaofeng were dating, they too came for Wu's tripe soup. Wu paid no attention to Li Yansheng, assuming that as an actor, he'd be a master of smooth talking. He did not know that people who earn their living with their mouths aren't all the same. The real chatterbox was Chen Changjie, not Li Yansheng.

The local street sweeper was a man named Guo Baochen. Despite his occupation, Big Mouth Wu counted him as a friend. Why was that? Because both were taciturn men not given to shooting their mouths off. What was accomplished by talking about things you know all about?

Do what you were supposed to do, and save the chatter. Was the world really so funny that people could not stop laughing? The only attention Big Mouth paid to his diners was to take their money. But when Guo Baochen walked in, he would sit down with his friend to enjoy a few drinks and a meal, usually boiled peanuts, cold beefsteak plant, fried eggs in scholartree petals – lots of scholartrees in Yanjin – and shredded mutton. The mutton was for Guo alone since Wu no longer ate it. The tables around them would be filled with raucous diners, while the two of them would hardly say a word as they finished off two bottles toasting each other. Most people might assume that they were drowning their sorrows, while in fact they could not have been happier. For them, a silent table always won out over a noisy one. That comment was uttered by Li Yansheng when he was enjoying a bowl of soup at Big Mouth's cafe one day.

Guo Baochen came over one night to silently share two bottles with Big Mouth. In the morning, Wu was found dead in bed. His body was taken to the hospital, where it was determined he'd died of a heart attack.

Wu's sister hand-cut sweets in Yanjin's factory, where Hu Xiaofeng was a wrapper. They considered each other coworkers, even though they were in different workshops. Big Mouth's sister notified Hu Xiaofeng about her brother's funeral services. On the day of the funeral, Hu Xiaofeng told her husband she wanted him to go with her to the funeral banquet at the Wu residence.

"Will we have to give them something?"

"Of course."

Reminded that only days before, his wife had told him he could not attend Chen Changjie's wedding, he complained, "So it's OK if it's *your* friend, but not if it's *my* friend."

His wife knew he was talking about Chen Changjie's wedding in Wuhan.

"Those aren't the same," she said angrily. "Your friend is getting married in Wuhan, Big Mouth Wu died right here in Yanjin. And not only that. You can't compare a wedding congratulatory gift and a funeral sympathy offering."

The custom in Yanjin was to give more for a wedding, say, fifty yuan, and less for a funeral, say, twenty yuan.

Afraid where this was headed, Li Yansheng stopped her from saying more: "That was just a bunch of talk, and here you took me serious. I think you're afraid that if you go to the funeral alone, you won't be able to eat twenty yuan's worth of food."

That got a laugh out of her.

Big Mouth's funeral banquet was held at the cafe, where ten invited guests sat at each of eighteen tables. Seated at Li Yansheng and Hu Xiaofeng's table were people they knew and others they didn't. Three rounds of good cheer made friends of them all. They were all talking about Big Mouth's abrupt passing.

"He and Guo Baochen were sitting at that very table," one guest said.

"He looked so healthy, but a heart attack is a heart attack," said another.

"He drank too much, him and the street sweeper, two whole bottles."

"He was overweight, that didn't help. Five-three, over two hundred pounds."

"He killed too many animals," one guest volunteered softly. "That's retribution."

Big Mouth's brother, Second Mouth, walked up to toast the table on behalf of the family. "I heard the mutterings at this table," he said. "I want you to know that my brother did not die of a heart attack and he did not die over retribution."

"Then how did he die?" they asked.

"Over a joke."

Big Mouth Wu hardly ever spoke and never laughed. His younger brother, on the other hand, talked non-stop, the recipient of all the talk that should have gone to his brother, according to some people. Big Mouth was fond of calling his brother a moron. When this talkative brother was performing odd jobs in the cafe, the moment he saw Big Mouth Wu coming, Second Mouth would shut up and get to work. The death of Big Mouth hit him pretty hard, and yet it thrilled him. How could it not, since now he could talk as much as he wanted?

"Did you say a joke killed him?" they asked. "By that you mean–"

"It's clear as can be. He met Hua Erniang that night. He went to bed after he and Guo Baochen finished off two bottles. That had never bothered him before, but that night it did, for some reason. He was surprised by Hua Erniang's visit to his dream, where she asked him to tell her a joke. A mulish, closed-mouth man like my brother, how could he tell a joke? That set her off. She told him to carry her on his back to get a bowl of spicy soup. And just like that, he was flattened."

Hua Erniang had been hanging around Yanjin for three thousand years, and during that time had flattened many residents with her joke demands in their dreams, which the community found acceptable, more or less. Of the hundred or more sudden deaths in Yanjin each year, which ones were caused by Hua Erniang and her demand for jokes was impossible to determine.

"No way to be sure," people said.

"Who's willing to put the blame on Hua Erniang?"

With a wave of his hand, Second Mouth volunteered, "My brother had a round head, didn't he? Well, when we laid him in his coffin, his head was flat. He also had a big belly. Now he's paper-thin. Obviously flattened under a mountain. I explained this to Sima Niu when he came to investigate my brother's death, and he confirmed that Hua Erniang had killed him."

Sima Niu lived in Nanguan. A chemistry teacher at Yanjin's Number One High School, he was also a fan of supernatural tales from the Wei, Jin, and Southern and Northern dynasties. He even wrote a biography of the visitor who had already been in Yanjin three thousand years ago. He stated he planned to write "A Biography of Hua Erniang", not just to paint a picture of her stay in Yanjin, but also to do research on the chemical reaction between her and Yanjin over jokes. Little by little, for thirty years he had unearthed everything she'd done in the city. All this is to say that he was a Hua Erniang expert. He stated with authority that Big Mouth Wu's death was indisputably caused by Hua Erniang.

Second Mouth Wu added, "I heard the sound of a little whirlwind in the yard that night. He was forever calling me a moron, so why wasn't he more cautious?" He, being Big Mouth Wu.

"He gave everyone he met a sullen look, ignoring the importance of jokes."

With that, he encouraged the diners to drink up and moved to the next table.

They nodded as he walked off. "That settles it, it was Hua Erniang if Sima Niu says so. He didn't just croak for no reason."

The conversation moved to a discussion of Hua Erniang's search for jokes.

"That Erniang," they said, "she deliberately sought out mulish Big Mouth Wu."

"Nothing unfair about that. It can happen to anyone. When the sky falls, we all die, no one is immune. Hua Erniang has stuck around Yanjin for three thousand years. She's such a force, nothing can move her."

"Generations of Yanjin folk have been stuck with her, no way around it."

"Say that if you want, but her presence hasn't been all bad. She's forced us to become people with a sense of humour."

"Without it, you'll be off to drink spicy soup."

"Big Mouth should have said, 'Erniang, don't drink any of that spicy soup. Come to my place for some tripe soup.'"

They all laughed, including Hu Xiaofeng and Li Yansheng.

"Second Mouth was right to fault Big Mouth for being careless," another man said. "As a resident of Yanjin, he should have prepared a joke before going to bed."

"Why did he have to be so opposed to jokes in the first place? See what it got him?"

Again they laughed, including Hu Xiaofeng and Li Yansheng.

"We need to be more watchful from now on," they said.

As they were all talking at once, Li Yansheng got up and went out to empty his bladder in the outhouse next to Big Mouth's sheep pen, where the occupants were obliviously grazing. The sight of the penned animals drew a sigh, as he contemplated how Big Mouth, who had slaughtered so many of the sheep, had died at the hand of Hua Erniang. How ironic that a man who was as sombre as the day is long died from the lack of a joke. Hua Erniang had never entered one of Li Yansheng's dreams, although, like Big Mouth, he was anything but a chatterbox. If she did come one night, he could not expect to make out any better than Wu had. So, to guard against that unlikely occurrence, he needed to learn a couple of jokes and commit them to memory. Taking his thoughts further, as someone not given to laughing, loading up with a bunch of jokes might be so difficult that not being flattened by Hua Erniang would be a joke in itself. Then again, he was thinking, there are half a million people in Yanjin and only one Hua Erniang. What were the odds she'd come to him? He knew he must be neither overconfident nor overly concerned, for if he was on tenterhooks day in and day out, he'd die of fright before Erniang and jokes had a chance to flatten him, that was yet another joke in itself. Like the sheep in the pen, when Big Mouth killed one of them, the others would *baa-baa* out of fright a time or two, and then go back to grazing. If, before one of them was taken, it could only graze quietly, there was no need to be afraid. That, in a nutshell, was Yanjin. Now that Big Mouth was dead, Li Yansheng wondered whether Second Mouth would take over the cafe. If he did, mutton soup sold by someone who seldom talked and then by someone who never stopped talking could not possibly be the same. If the man chose not to take over, Li would have to take his business to Marshal Tianpeng's Cafe.

Four

Old Dong was a Daoist master who told people he was blind, had been since birth, so had never seen what the world or its people were like. He could tell what a person looked like by feeling their bone structure while telling their fortune. But according to some folk, he was only partially blind and could make out blurry outlines of men and women. They'd seen him walking along with a bamboo cane when it started to rain; he tucked his cane under his arm and trotted home. One day, back when Li Yansheng was working in the machine shop foundry, he and Chen Changjie were enjoying pigs' feet at Marshal Tianpeng's Cafe when Old Dong walked in, cane clicking on the floor, and sat at their table, where he ordered a pig's foot.

Li and Chen had finished their pigs' feet before Dong had eaten only half of his. To play a prank, Chen took Old Dong's half-chewed pig's foot off his plate when he laid it down to lick his fingers and replaced it with his finished bone. Dong picked it up and began to gnaw, muttering as he did, I sure ate fast today, I don't remember finishing this. Li Yansheng was ready to believe his eyes, not his ears, that Dong was completely blind.

All or partially, it made no difference. When sighted residents encountered problems they could not understand or deal with, they sought the help of Old Dong. If a pig or a dog went missing, or a tractor, or a family member, they'd ask Old Dong where they got off to and if they'd ever get them back; if a family member was stricken with cancer or a child was scheduled to take an advancement test, they'd ask if a cure or a passed exam was in their future; if their business was struggling or their official position was in jeopardy, they'd ask if the business could rebound or the official could remain free from prison. Whatever the matter or situation, anyone coming to see Old Dong was facing trouble; no one else would take the time. You went to see a doctor because you were sick; everyone else stayed away.

After you told Old Dong why you'd come to see him, he'd ask for your birth details – year, date and time of birth. He'd then make a calculation on his fingers, and if that didn't produce an answer, he'd feel your bones. By bones, he meant all 206 of them, which would create a picture of your fortune. He had felt the bones of thousands of people, and the more he felt, the sadder it made him. That was because the bones of so few of those thousands were human; most were pig or sheep bones, crawling on the street, their backs to the heavens. With all those people crawling along, they'd ask, were there none in previous lifetimes with positive fortunes? Yes, he said, the street sweeper Guo Baochen, who'd enjoyed great good fortune in his previous life: a military governor in the early years of the Republic who became prime minister and was responsible for the deaths of thousands, in his current life he was relegated to the role of a street sweeper by means of sweeping himself clean.

In addition to his skill in calculating fortunes from birth dates and bone structures, Old Dong was also able to message between realms. If someone wanted to speak to a dead relative or a dead relative had something to tell the living, when he received the precise birth dates and times of both the living and the dead and the date and time of the death, with a magic incantation he would pass on whatever was asked, ghostly words to the living and human words to the dead. He could even create living transmissions, allowing the living to see their deceased loved ones. As an acolyte of Celestial Master Zhao, for transmission between the living and the dead, he needed to pay homage to Zhao. When the Celestial Master appeared, he permitted the deceased to briefly occupy Old Dong's body to meet with a living descendant. People who had recently lost their parents wanted to see them again to say things that had been left unsaid before the parting or might want to ask where they could find everyday things, something they could do thanks to Old Dong. "I never imagined we'd ever meet again," a man would sob as he held Dong's hand to reach his parents. Or they might say, "Dad, where the devil did you put the bank book?"

Other people sought to see what the future held. With a firm shake of his head, Old Dong refused all such requests. "Heaven's secrets cannot be divulged," he'd say. "That not only serves the fortune-teller but the seekers of fortunes as well. If you know what life is now and what it will be the next time, what's the point of living?" "I want to understand what life is all about," they'd reply. "If I told you that," he'd respond, "you might not want to go on living."

"Rubbish," they'd say. "You can't see the world we can see, so how do you expect to see things we can't see?" "I can see things you can't see precisely because I can't see the world you can see." More rubbish. But when people run up against something they can't explain in traditional ways, rubbish is their only recourse. Without Old Dong's rubbish, there would have been a lot of bottled-up people in Yanjin and at least a third more depressed residents.

Old Dong never demanded that people believe the fortunes he told for them. That was up to them. There was a postscript tacked on to every fortune he told. "It's all made up, so don't take it too seriously." He had named his fortune-telling studio "Cosmic Land of Illusion". Old Dong: "A void, the cosmos, can only be a land of illusion, no need to take any of it seriously."

The scrolled couplets on the sides of his door read:

Life's Solvable Riddles are not Welcome Here

Rubbish from a Blind Man is Yours to Fear

Above the door:

Relieve Your Melancholy

Old Dong was in Yanjin, and so was Hua Erniang. "You can't see a thing, Old Dong," someone said, "eyes open or shut. Has Hua Erniang come into your dream looking for jokes?"

"The jokes she seeks are rubbish," said Old Dong, "so are the fortunes I tell. Rubbish has no business looking for rubbish."

Again: "Is this 'two negatives make a positive'?"

Again: "Or how about, 'well water does not mix with river water'?"

It's probably rubbish. If not, by relying on rubbish, Blind Old Dong was the only resident who never suffered the calamity of Hua Erniang coming to him for a joke.

Five

Li Yansheng decided to look up Old Dong and get his fortune told. His depression had become so bad he had no desire to go on living. Like everyone else, now that he'd run up against something he couldn't explain in traditional ways, rubbish was his only recourse. He did not ask Old Meng, the tobacco and alcohol seller, or his wife Hu Xiaofeng to go with him. There was nothing wrong with taking someone along when seeing a fortune-teller, and his wife had accompanied him when he'd gone to two hospitals. But not this time. He did not want anyone to be there when Old Dong told his fortune.

Old Dong lived in Grasshopper Lane off East Avenue. A blind man will have little luck finding a wife. But from his fortune-telling and other-worldly activities, Old Dong took in many times the income of a seller of condiments like Li Yansheng and did not worry that women were unwilling to marry him. It was only natural that sighted and unafflicted women were uninterested, but one named Kuai was. Blind in one eye, her marriage to a totally blind man was considered marrying down, but she presented Old Dong with a daughter and a son, both fully sighted. Li Yansheng came to see Old Dong, the first time he'd been to the fortune-teller's home. There he encountered Dong's daughter, a girl of seven or eight who was running around the yard chasing chickens with a stick. She stopped when she saw him and, with a suspicious look, asked, "What do you want?"

"I want to see your father about something."

"Have you registered?"

Apparently, registering to see Old Dong was required, like at a hospital. "No. I didn't know I had to."

"You do. Register today and come back another day."

"But this is urgent."

"Not following procedures will cost you."

He had to laugh at that, and was struck by the realisation that it was the first time he'd laughed in more than a month. He also felt that the moment he stepped into the compound, he sensed a cordial atmosphere, and knew he was right to look up Old Dong. "If I'm supposed to pay, that's what I'll do," he said to the girl.

That was when he noticed a dozen or so people lined up under the eave outside the house. Crouching, standing, one even sitting on a stump and staring blankly into the sky. As he perceived from the girl, there was no shortage of people wanting to hear Old Dong's rubbish. Clearly, there were many things that begged explanation, and he was not the only person suffering from depression. He went over and joined the queue.

The sun travelled from the east to due south as those in front went inside and came out, one after the other until it was his turn. By now there were already four or five people in line behind him. The first thing he saw was a painting of the Celestial Master hanging on a wall in the centre of the room. He had heard that Old Dong was an acolyte of a Celestial Master named Zhao, so that must be him. Wearing a red monastic gown and holding an iron staff, he was seated on a Qilin, the mythical creature, under the words: "Cosmic Land of Illusion". Smoke rose from three sticks of incense in a burner on the table in front of the painting, beside which sat Old Dong. A man in front of Old Dong was gesturing. "This was my fault," he said, "but was that other thing my fault too?"

When Old Kuai, Dong's wife, saw Li Yansheng part the door curtain and walk in, she went up to him, pointed to the man and whispered, "Wait a moment. There's something else he wants to ask."

Li backed out and waited under the eave, where he listened to what was happening inside. The man said something, followed by Dong saying something and then the man crying. "Don't cry," Dong urged, "don't cry, it doesn't help." Soon, the man walked out, eyes red and puffy. "Next," Old Kuai called out. Li's turn. He parted the curtain, walked in and sat on a stool in front of Dong.

"May I know the visitor's name?" Dong said.

"I'm Yansheng, Old Dong. I run the condiments stall in the market at East Avenue."

"Ah, Yansheng, I know you. You sang opera. You were Xu Xian in *Legend of the White Snake*. I remember hearing you."

So he's heard me sing opera, though he couldn't have

seen my performance, of course, which is why he said "heard".

"That's been seven or eight years already."

"What can I help you with?"

"So many things have been bothering me that I'm about to lose my mind, and I don't know the cause. I was hoping you could get to the bottom of this and rid me of what's weighing me down."

Kuai interrupted him at this point and replaced the previous seeker's three sticks of incense in front of the Celestial Master Zhao portrait with three new ones. Starting anew. Kuai lit the incense as Old Dong stood up and walked to the burner, where he muttered something and bowed three times to the Zhao portrait. Then he knelt and bowed three more times. Getting to his feet, he bowed three more times, returned to his seat and said to Li Yansheng, "Tell me the year, month, date and precise time of your birth."

Li did as he was asked. Old Dong began calculating on his fingers, and when he was done, he stopped and reflected. Finished, he calculated once more. Back and forth, until he abruptly smacked the table.

"Good!"

"What does that mean?" a surprised Li wondered.

"You're not depressed, you're carrying another person."

Astounded, Li jumped up from the stool. "Carrying another person? Who?"

"Someone deceased, of course."

That compounded his amazement. Carrying a deceased person? "How can you be sure?" he stammered.

"Easy, your body has been occupied by a dead soul. The trouble in your heart is that person's, not yours."

Even more amazed, Li stood there like a zombie. "Who is it?" he managed to ask.

Old Dong called Li Yansheng up and began feeling his bones – his arms, his legs, his front and back, and then his neck and head.

"Can you tell who it is?" Li Yansheng asked.

"Too deep to reach, I can't get there."

"A man or a woman, can you tell me that?"

Dong felt him from head to toe a second time. "A woman."

Li could hardly believe it. "A woman, which one? It's not Hua Erniang, is it?"

"Since the woman has been in you," Old Dong replied, "has she demanded jokes?"

Li shook his head. "No, that she hasn't."

"If it's not about jokes, then it isn't Hua Erniang. It's someone else."

"Who?"

"I can't tell."

"Is there some way to find out?"

"Yes."

"What is it?"

"Messaging."

"Then let's do it."

"Time for unpleasant business," Kuai interjected. "There's one fee for fortune-telling and another for messaging."

"Of course, that makes sense."

Old Dong stood up and walked to the incense burner, where he muttered something and bowed three times to the Zhao portrait. Then he knelt and bowed three more times.

Getting to his feet, he bowed three more times, returned to his seat and settled into deep thought. That went on for some time before he opened his eyes and said to Li Yansheng, "It failed."

"Why?"

"She cried with her head down, but wouldn't say who she was."

"What do I do? There must be something."

"There's living transmission. She wouldn't have anywhere to hide if we did that, and we could see her face."

"Then let's do it."

Again, Kuai stepped up. "I need to say that there's one fee for messaging and another for living transmission."

"Don't worry, I brought enough money."

Li Yansheng noticed that Old Dong dressed differently for messaging and for living transmission, everyday clothes for the former and a monastic robe like the one in the painting, as well as the same hat, for the latter. Old Dong's wife brought out the red robe and black square-top Daoist hat, which he put on. Then she brought over a bowl of clean water for him to wash his hands and face, after which he knelt in front of Zhao's portrait, coughed twice, cleared his throat and began muttering an unintelligible chant. Then he was on the move, making three complete revolutions one way and three the other, before quick-stepping around the room, around and around, until Old Dong was no longer Old Dong, but had become a woman. One look at the way she walked around the room and moved her body, Li did not wait for Old Dong to say anything.

"I know who she is," he blurted out.

"Who am I?"

"You're Yingtao."

Yingtao, his fellow actor in the Fenglei Henan Drama Troupe. Back when he was in the role of Xu Xian in *Legend of the White Snake*, Yingtao had been the White Snake, husband and wife. In the opera this was how she walked and, as she sang, she made serpentine movements, writhing and twisting her hips, like a snake. After he'd performed with her for eight years, he was all too familiar with her. She wound up marrying Chen Changjie, who'd acted in the role of Fahai. One day, they'd argued over some chives, and in a fit of pique, she'd hanged herself. That had happened three years before. What puzzled Li was why she had suddenly taken up occupancy in his body a month ago since neither her suicide three years earlier nor any cross-realm relationship later had involved him.

"Why have you come to me, Yingtao?" he asked.

"I want you to pass a word on for me," Old Dong/Yingtao said.

That answered his question, bringing an end to the living transmission. Old Kuai helped Old Dong out of his monastic robe and removed his Daoist hat. He was sweat-soaked, as if he'd been in a steam bath. "That tires me out," he said as he towelled off. "It's why I so seldom do it."

Li Yansheng wanted to get to the point. "Who did Yingtao want me to pass a word to?"

The fortune-teller was himself again. He handed the towel to his wife, sat down and began calculating on his fingers. "Ah," he said after a few moments. "It's someone down south."

"Where down south?"

Dong went back to finger calculations. "Thousands of *li* from here."

"Thousands of *li*? Did you say *thousands*?" Li Yansheng was beside himself. "I don't know anyone thousands of *li* from here."

"I wouldn't know. That's just what the symbols say."

On second thought, thousands of *li* down south could refer to Wuhan, where there was someone who was tied to both Li Yansheng and Yingtao, and that would be her former husband, Chen Changjie. Only a month earlier, Chen had invited Li to the ceremony for his remarriage in Wuhan. When he revealed that bit of information, Old Dong nodded.

"That must be it."

"But I'm not planning to go to Wuhan, so I can't pass on her message."

"But you must have said you'd go at one time or another, and she heard you. That's why she took occupancy in you."

Li did in fact recall that a month earlier he'd said he'd go to Wuhan to attend Chen's wedding but was stopped by Hu Xiaofeng over the cost, travel and gift.

"That's true, I did say I'd go to Wuhan a month ago, but how could Yingtao have heard me?"

"There cannot be waves without wind. Think hard, there has to be an explanation."

Then it hit him. On the wall behind the stall where he sold soy sauce, vinegar and pickled vegetables hung a poster advertising a performance of *Legend of the White Snake* by the Fenglei Henan Drama Troupe. The image portrayed the scene involving "What to do? What to do? What shall I do? What shall I do?" The poster dated from the time when they were performers in the troupe and had been put up by his neighbour Xiao Bai when she was still operating her stall. Seeing it always caused him to shake his head and sigh over how a good opera singer could wind up selling condiments in the marketplace. Xiao Bai then followed her army husband to Gansu, and the poster remained where it was, slowly fading and dust-covered, one corner hanging and flapping in the wind, but no one paid any attention to it. Li Yansheng was reminded that the invitation to attend Chen Changjie's wedding had reached him in the marketplace, where he'd torn open the envelope and read the contents. He'd then struck up a conversation with Old Meng, who ran the tobacco and alcohol stall next to him, and all this might have been heard by Yingtao, up on the poster. Who could have imagined that a poster left by Xiao Bai would be where the spirit of Yingtao would be hidden and then one day appear?

"Old Dong," Li Yansheng said, "forget about going to Wuhan for the moment. Is there some way you can drive Yingtao out of my body?"

"Come here, I'll see what I can do."

He went up to Old Dong, who felt him all over. "Can't do it," he said, shaking his head.

"Why not?"

"Driving her out is no problem, but within a couple of hours, she'll be right back. It's such a powerful obsession that if you don't do what she asked, she'll never leave. You can find someone else to do it for you, but she'll keep coming back, time and time again. Every instance will cost you money, won't it? I won't lie or cheat you. And not just for your benefit. I've had a glimpse of my next life, and I won't be blind, so I need to accumulate good karma till then."

Li nodded, he understood.

"It looks like you'll be going to Wuhan," Old Kuai said.

"But that was a month ago. I didn't go then, and I have no reason to go now."

"I have no control over that."

"What I don't understand is why me? We were never related or otherwise involved."

"How can you say that? When you were in the role of Xu Xian and Yingtao was the snake, you were man and wife."

"That was on the stage. It wasn't really me. It was make-believe."

"Real or not, a relationship was there in form, at least."

Finally, the important question occurred to Li Yansheng. "Old Dong," he said, "exactly what was it she wanted me to pass on?"

"I'm not even going to guess. From here on out, it's between you and her."

His wife stepped in and concluded the talk between Li Yansheng and her husband. "That ends the session," she said, indicating she wanted Li to leave, which he did, after settling up with Kuai, who turned and shouted into the yard, "Next!"

Li made it to the door before he stopped and said to the next seeker, "Would you mind holding up for a moment? I need to ask one more question."

The man walked back outside as Li returned to Old Dong.

"Old Dong, there's one more thing I'd like to know."

Before the fortune-teller could open his mouth, his wife said with a scowl, "You already got what you came for and more."

Her husband stopped her. "Back then, he was one of Yanjin's cultural stars, not just anyone."

"Does the message Yingtao wants me to pass on have anything to do with how she died? Chen Changjie actually drove her to killing herself."

Old Dong told him to come closer, so he could feel his bones. After a moment, he shook his head. "It's too deep, I can't feel it."

With that bit of news, Li walked outside. The entire session, given the extra fees for urgency and living transmission, had cost him more than twenty-five yuan, about what he earned selling soy sauce, vinegar and pickled vegetables for a week and a half. That was a lot of money, but now he knew why he was feeling bad. On his way home, he realised that the idea to go see Old Dong had come from the one who'd taken up occupancy in his body – Yingtao. Only by looking up Old Dong had he been able to find her. He also understood that not taking his wife or Old Meng along to Dong's house had been her idea.

"Yingtao," he said to himself, "now that it's come to this, what's the message you want me to pass on?"

To his surprise, the living transmission brought Yingtao's spirit to life inside him, but only after leaving the fortune-teller's house. Probably something Old Dong would not have anticipated.

"Wait till we're on the road, and you'll know," she said from inside.

"If it's only a simple message, why do we have to get on

the road? Won't writing Chen Changjie a letter take care of it?"

"No, you have to give it to him in person."

"In person or in a letter, what's the difference?"

"A big difference. When you tell him face to face, he'll have to deal with it. If you sent a letter, you'd have to wait till he wrote back, which would give him time to come up with a response. There are lots of issues you can't dodge if you're told in person. With a letter, you can invent excuses. A month ago, he invited you to his wedding in Wuhan. If you'd been face to face with him, you couldn't have said you twisted your ankle. Letters give you the chance to make things up."

That made sense, at least as far as he could tell. "If I agree to go to Wuhan, when will you leave my body?"

"As soon as you get on the road."

With a sigh, Li Yansheng realised he'd have to go to Wuhan.

Six

So, Wuhan it was. The only way Yingtao would leave his body was if he got on the road. It was his only chance. But how was he going to manage that? The first obstacle to clear was his wife. Chen Changjie's wedding had been held a month earlier, and he had said he wouldn't be going. If he suddenly changed his mind, he'd need a reason to go. Obviously, he couldn't tell the truth, that a woman had taken up residence in his body. And not just any woman, but Yingtao, his former stage wife. Hu Xiaofeng would go berserk if she heard that. Either she'd send him to a mental hospital or check herself into one. Because Chen's wedding had been held in Wuhan, the city was a sensitive topic. Li and his wife had had words over the wedding during Big Mouth Wu's funeral. If they hadn't, no problem. But since they had, to have words again would be rehashing the issue. So if he wanted to travel, it would have to be somewhere other than Wuhan. And this place would have to be where he might reasonably be expected to visit.

He had a sudden inspiration. The commodity market sent someone to the city of Luoyang once a month to buy pickled vegetables. Based on the season and the sales of the previous month, they determined what needed to be replenished: pickled turnips, pak choi, ginger, potherb mustard, chives, green beans, sweetened garlic, raw peanuts, cucumbers, a variety of black vegetables or fermented soya paste. After the order was filled, the purchases were delivered to Yanjin by truck. Old Meng was the person sent to fill the order. One would think that, as a tobacco and alcohol pedlar, he would not be the logical choice for the job. But his cousin was a supervisor in the Luoyang pickling plant, which made it possible for him to purchase substandard products, those damaged during the chopping and slicing process, which affected the appearance but not the quality. In Luoyang, substandard products, which sold for half the price of unspoiled items, must be sold as such. But in Yanjin, they could be sold at full price.

Li talked to Old Meng about going to Luoyang in his place. He could say family business would keep him from going this month, and he'd asked Li to help him out since he sold pickled vegetables and was an ideal choice. Once he was on the road, he would not go to Luoyang but would head to Wuhan instead.

Yingtao would not let Li Yansheng deliver her message to Chen Changjie via a letter, but Old Meng could compile an order and send it to his cousin in Luoyang. Having worked together in the marketplace for four years with no disagreements, Li assumed that Old Meng would go along with the plan. And Hu Xiaofeng would not be suspicious about a business trip to Luoyang. It was the only plan he could come up with. The problem was the difference in distance between the two cities. Yanjin to Luoyang, a distance of three hundred *li*, was a two-day roundtrip by bus. Yanjin is two thousand *li* from Wuhan, around six hundred miles, requiring a ride on a slow train, with lots of stops, many with long layovers, a four-day round trip. Then, once he reached the station in unfamiliar Wuhan, he would need to find Chen Changjie's house and explain the situation to him, and after he finished, return to the train station; that would take another day. When he arrived at the station, he might not find the right train to board at once, which would require waiting at both ends, another half day. All told, a roundtrip to Wuhan would take five and a half days.

A two-day trip had become a five-and-a-half-day trip. How was he going to explain away the extra three days? Here's what he thought he'd do: two days into his trip, he'd phone Hu Xiaofeng at the sweets factory, telling her he'd run a fever in Luoyang and would have to rest a couple of days before returning to Yanjin. Who's to say that couldn't happen? Fortune is as unpredictable as the weather. He didn't think his wife would give him a hard time over that. He must be clear on the phone that he was suffering from a fever, not a consequence of his recent troubled mind, or his wife might rush to Luoyang, and his trick will have backfired.

Now that he'd settled on a plan, he had to worry about how to pay for it. The Luoyang travel would cost twenty yuan, Wuhan was a hundred and twenty. How would he make up the extra hundred? Beyond the ticket cost, there would be other expenses. Such as food. And then unanticipated needs for money. The popular adage said it best: A thousand days at home and all is well; one day away from home is pure hell. Even a hundred yuan might not be enough. The trip to Luoyang would be for government business, meaning the costs were reimbursable. The cost of the trip to Wuhan would all be on him. As for the private stash he'd accumulated from his marketplace wages, after giving twenty-five yuan to the fortune-teller, he was left with slightly more than ten. Where would he get the rest? He'd have to borrow it. But from whom?

As he was selling spices and oils in the market, he pondered possible sources of money for the trip. He had two conditions. First, the lender must be someone with plenty of disposable cash. What did that mean? It meant money left over after all the monthly expenses at home. Second, it must be someone he knew, a good friend willing to lend him the money.

His first thoughts centred on family: uncles, aunts, grandparents, cousins, all close enough, but none with the spending money he was looking for. In simplest terms, these were all poor people, and considering them was a waste of time. As for friends, he could boast at least a dozen in town, but the friends of someone who sold soy sauce, vinegar and pickled vegetables at a market stall would not be the type to have extra cash. He spent all morning thinking and came up with no one. Then he added another consideration: since Xiaofeng must not learn of the trip to Wuhan, whoever lent him money had to be tight-lipped. Having no alternative, he thought first of his tobacco and alcohol neighbour Old Meng. But his wages were roughly the same as Li's, and he had a family to support. He'd have no extra cash. His cousin in Luoyang was Li's excuse to be away, and Li would be embarrassed to hit him up for a loan as well. So Old Meng was out. Friends, family and Old Meng constituted the sum total of possible lenders. After a morning of frustration, Li Yansheng headed home for lunch. On the way, he passed by the public baths on North Avenue and was reminded of Old Bu the bathhouse employee who scrubbed backs. Maybe he'd lend him the money.

Back Scrubber Bu, a man in his fifties, lived alone. He'd married young but had no children, and the year he turned thirty, his wife had run off with his cousin and was never heard from again. People had tried to line him up with other women, but the cousin, a childhood playmate who'd inexplicably stolen his wife, had left a dark shadow on the institution of marriage for him. During the first two years after his wife walked out, he gestured and said they were always too tall, too short or too something else, and couldn't make up his mind. By the time he was fifty, he'd given up hope. Living alone had its advantages, he said. If a bachelor has eaten his fill, no one in the family goes hungry. Where money was concerned, he was not stingy with his needs or wants, but he was not a spendthrift either. He did not spend money if he didn't have to. Other people may not care to save up money, but he did, money he earned by scrubbing backs for a pittance. Men with children can manage without saving up since the children are a hedge against old age. But not a bachelor. "That's what savings do for me. Does that make sense?" he'd ask people. It does, they'd agree, including Li Yansheng, who realised that the man did have money.

The two men had become friends due to the fact that Li always asked for Old Bu, one of five scrubbers, when he went to the public bath. He appreciated more than just the work;

he also loved to hear Old Bu talk. There was substance in the man's tales, which included logic. For instance, take the worst thing in the world that can happen: two people associate with one another, but only one of them treats the other as a friend; so they talk like friends but act like strangers. If all goes smoothly, well and good. But if a problem crops up, that can sour the relationship, which made perfect sense to Li Yansheng. Or another case: Old Bu talked about grocery shopping when you're hungry, and you wind up buying too much food. Again, very sensible. Li knew that when people who shopped before mealtime came to his stall to buy soy sauce, vinegar, pickled vegetables, peppercorns, anise or fermented tofu, they always bought more than they needed. Business fell off after mealtime, with only an occasional customer, who would buy salt when they'd run out and vinegar if they needed vinegar. What he found puzzling was how the wife of a sensible man like Old Bu could run off with another man. His own cousin, to boot. Well, they became friends after many bathhouse visits, and now that Yansheng had a problem, he thought of Old Bu.

At noontime, after asking Old Meng to watch his stall, he strolled to the bathhouse; he'd take a bath before broaching the issue with Old Bu while his back was being scrubbed. Better that than come straight out and ask for a loan.

At the entrance, he was reminded of Yingtao, who had taken up residence in his body. "Yingtao," he said, "you can't go in there with me, it's men only."

"All right," she said, "I'll wait for you outside."

She removed herself from his body, making him feel

comfortably lighter. But only until he was reminded that she'd be right back as soon as he walked out of the bathhouse. He was stuck with her.

As always, having got undressed, Li tied his clothes up with rope and hung them from a rafter before slipping into the bathwater. After soaking until he was sweating, his skin nice and red, he got out and walked over to Old Bu's table to let him go to work.

They chatted for a few minutes. "How's business, old friend?" he asked.

"Not bad, winter weather. Pretty soon, it'll be summer, when people can wash at home and won't care to waste money on a public bath. I'd say it's been at least a month since the last time you were here. Quite an accumulation of dirty, flaky skin, like you just climbed out of a mudhole."

Yansheng reflected on how, owing to his troubles over the past month, he'd forgotten even to take a bath. "You're right, and it hasn't been a good month for me. I got so itchy and uncomfortable, I just had to come today." With that, he turned to the subject at hand.

"How would you say the two of us get along?"

"Not bad," Old Bu said as he worked. "You always come to me when you visit the bathhouse."

"I'd like to talk to you about something."

"Go ahead."

"Can I borrow some money?"

Old Bu stopped scrubbing. "How much?"

"A little more than a hundred yuan."

"What for?"

Li could not tell him the truth. "My second aunt and uncle are doing up their house," he said, "and have asked me to help financially. They've always been good to me, even lent me a hundred when I got married. I can't say no to them now."

Old Bu went back to work. "Too bad you didn't come yesterday."

"Why's that?"

"I lent money to my uncle, who was admitted to the hospital. For your relatives it's a house, for him it's his life. You know the saying 'help the starving but not the poor', I assume. When you compare the two, I had to lend it to him, and won't be able to help you out."

Li saw through his excuse. Even if true, since he'd lent his uncle the money the day before, there was no way he could have "compared the two". The key was in the weight of the two matters that would decide who got the loan. For a man who dealt with events rationally, to hem and haw like this made it clear that he needed a reason to not lend the money. Maybe it wasn't even about the money, but an indication that their friendship had its limitations, which was in line with the man's frequent reference to "the worst thing in the world: two people associate with one another, but only one of them treats the other as a friend; so they talk like friends but act like strangers. If a problem crops up, that can sour the relationship."

Old Bu himself knew the flaw in his excuse and tried to soften the blow: "If it's eight or ten yuan you need, no problem. A hundred's a lot of money. I told my aunt how hard I worked to save up what I have, one scrubbing at a time. You can use the money, I told her, but you have to pay it back, and early."

"It's too much trouble," Li said. "I was just talking."

"But since you brought it up, and I can't lend you the money, today's scrubbing is on me."

That's not the way it works, Li was thinking. When he went up to pay for the bath, he handed in Old Bu's tally and paid for the scrubbing, as always.

Yingtao returned to Li Yansheng's body as he walked out of the bathhouse, making him suddenly heavy in body and nettled in his mind. But so what, since the real issue was how and where to borrow the money to make a trip to Wuhan? Once he had the money, he could send Yingtao packing. But just wracking his brain thinking about who he might go to would not bring in the money he needed.

Just then he spotted Butcher Bai, his bamboo hamper chock-full of pigs' feet in a wheelbarrow he was pushing down the street. Li knew the supply was headed for Marshal Tianpeng's Cafe, which was the destination for almost all the pigs' feet produced by Yanjin's three slaughterhouses. Seeing the load of pigs' feet reminded him of Old Zhu, the owner of Marshal Tianpeng's. Maybe he'd lend him the money. In recent days, Li Yansheng had been preoccupied with his worries. He'd let too much time pass between visits to the bathhouse, just as he'd not been to the cafe lately, and had neglected to consider the possibility of hitting up the owner for a loan.

Old Zhu, whose business flourished, would have to be considered a member of Yanjin's moneyed class. He also loved opera. And because he loved opera, much in the manner of Old Dong the fortune-teller, he considered Li Yansheng a star even though he was no longer performing. That had also been the case with the head of the state-run machinery shop, who had hired Li Yansheng, Yingtao and

Chen Changjie because he was an opera fan. Old Zhu even took pleasure in screeching a few notes on his own before each day began, belting out an aria or two on the riverbank behind the restaurant, a cornfield as his audience. He knew how to stew pigs' feet, but not how to sing. He was off-key, so any time Li Yansheng was in the cafe, Old Zhu would ask him what he had to do to improve. Despite knowing that Zhu was not opera material, he didn't mind giving a few pointers between bites of food. Sometimes that earned him a free meal. But that was then. Now Li had a problem, the solution for which Zhu might be the answer.

So he went to Marshal Tianpeng's Cafe, but he avoided going at what he imagined was the busiest time. If there were loads of people there, he'd be embarrassed to ask for a loan in front of all those diners, and anyway, Zhu would obviously be too busy taking care of business to deal with a friend's request. So he waited till midway through the afternoon to stroll into the cafe for the first time in over a month. A tent had been thrown up beside the entrance, outside of which a row of large metal tubs containing pigs' feet were being prepared by half a dozen workers, all of them debristling with knives. Once the feet were scraped clean, they were tossed into another tub. Inside the tent, crackling firewood sent flames up the sides of a huge cookpot in which the feet were stewing in boiling water.

Li Yansheng parted the curtain at the entrance, walked into the cafe and saw the owner's wife sitting at the counter working her abacus.

"How come you moved the cookpot outside?"

She looked up. "It's just temporary, we're redoing the kitchen."

"Business must be good."

"Not bad," she said as she went back to her abacus.

"Where's Old Zhu?"

"What do you want with him?"

"I wanted to ask him something."

"That'll have to wait."

That was a surprise. "What happened?"

"He went to Daqing."

"What for?"

"His aunt accompanied her husband to the Daqing oil fields and settled there. She just died, so he went for her funeral."

Not expecting that, Li paused and then asked, "When's he coming back?"

"Hard to say. Could be seven or eight days, maybe a couple of weeks. They have to let a week pass before the burial. Getting to Daqing takes two trains, four thousand *li* or more, so there's no way to predict how long it will take him."

Another case of bad timing. Li could not reach Old Zhu, no matter how good a friend he was. That was before mobile phones, and Li barely knew Zhu's wife. She did not sing opera and did not ask for singing hints, so he had no chance to hit her up for a loan. Not wanting to make the same error he'd made with Old Bu, mistaking an acquaintance for a good friend, he left the cafe shaking his head. It was Zhu's aunt's fault for choosing the wrong time to die.

After a whole day, he had not found a single person who might lend him the money he needed, and he could not think of anyone else in the city he could approach. A good night's sleep was out of the question for days. He'd wake up in the middle of the night and not be able to fall back asleep. Sitting on the edge of the bed, he'd stare into the dark night and fret.

"Yingtao," he'd say, "getting to Wuhan for you is too hard."

"I expected more from people."

Li's wife awoke abruptly, frightened by the sight of her husband talking to the window. "Is your problem acting up again?"

"No," he quickly replied.

"Who were you talking to?"

More cover-up needed. "No one, I was thinking out loud about something at work."

He spent all the next day at the marketplace, thinking so much his head hurt, and still he could not come up with anyone who might lend him money. On his way home that evening, he ran into Guo Baochen, the street sweeper who was spearing scrap paper with a bamboo spike under a streetlight.

"Ask him, Yansheng," Yingtao said. "He'll lend you the money."

That sounded to him like total nonsense. A street sweeper earns half my wages, he reasoned. With five kids at home, he doesn't make enough to get by. Picking up scrap paper, he might earn a little extra selling it at the recycling station. But how could he have any surplus money? Yet, since Yingtao said so, he might as well give it a try. He'd run out of options. If it worked, well and good. If not, what had it cost him? It would give him a good excuse to vent with her. Going to Guo Baochen for a loan had one advantage: being tight-lipped, he wouldn't tell anyone.

Guo may have been a street sweeper, but according to Fortune-Teller Dong, he'd been a military commander and prime minister in a previous life. He was a stocky man with a ruddy face and had the booming voice of a military commander addressing his troops or a prime minister with officials. But like Big Mouth Wu, who'd owned the cafe in Beiguan, that booming voice was heard no more than ten times a day. Some people just don't talk much, Dong had said.

People in Yanjin often made fun of Guo. If they encountered him out on the street, they'd ask, "Is the prime minister busy today?" or "Has the prime minister's office been moved out onto the streets?"

The street sweeper did not let that bother him – at first. But the more he ignored them, the more they made fun of him, and as time went by, he'd stop what he was doing and respond sternly, "Since you know this is the prime minister's office, where important work is done, show some respect, and go away!"

They'd laugh and walk off.

There were also people who asked him who he'd met when he was an official, and what he did. Again, he ignored them at first. But that just encouraged them to intensify their mockery.

"I recall one thing that really annoyed me when I was prime minister," he'd say.

"What was that?"

"What a failure in bed your little sister was as a concubine. Go home and tell her not to come tonight."

"Like hell!" they'd say. "*Your* sister's no good in bed."

When Guo Baochen was alone, he was given to private

monologues: "If I was prime minister, I'd slaughter every last one of you bastards. There'd be no more of that nonsense from you."

Sometimes he'd even recite a famous line of poetry from children's textbooks: "The nation is lost, but the mountains and rivers remain."

He had been drinking with Big Mouth the night before Wu woke up dead.

"You had a hand in Big Mouth's death, Guo," they'd say.

When he heard this, he laid down his broom, crouched down and wailed.

"Cry all you want, you killed a friend."

"I'm crying for him, and I'm crying for myself. I'll never have another friend in Yanjin."

"Boo-hoo." When he was finished crying, he looked up and saw that the teasers had left. He dried his eyes, blew his nose, picked up his broom and went back to work.

Li Yansheng, prodded by Yingtao to go up to Guo Baochen, did so. "Baochen, there's something I'd like to talk to you about."

"What is it?" he asked as he stopped spearing paper.

"Think you could lend me some money?"

"How much?"

"A hundred or so."

"Sure."

Surprised and elated, Li said, "Really, you've got the money?"

"But there's a condition."

"What is it?"

"Before I lend you money, you'll have to lend me some first."

That was something new. "What does that mean?"

"I don't have anything on me, but I can gamble with yours."

Hopelessly poor though Guo was, he loved to bet. Maybe a bad habit from his prime minister days. He'd been wanting to supplement what he made sweeping streets and selling scrap paper for his family, but most of his earnings went to an underground gambling house, leaving his wife and children always on the verge of starvation. He had borrowed from just about everyone he knew in Yanjin, but, strangely enough, never from Big Mouth Wu, because that would have meant he wouldn't have a place to drink.

When he borrowed money from someone, he'd say, "Don't worry, lend me what I need, and you'll get it back in a few hours."

People eventually got used to his routine. "Since you'll have money in a few hours," they'd say, "why not just wait that long for what you need?"

Li Yansheng was stopped short by Guo's response. "I asked you for a loan, and you asked me for one to gamble with. Isn't that turning things on their head?"

"No. I checked my horoscope. I was born in the year of the pig, which means this is a good month for getting rich, something that happens only once every thirty years. I don't have any money to make money, and you're here asking for a loan. Fate has brought us together. Lend me the money, I'll gamble and win, then I'll return the loan plus a hundred yuan, and won't consider that a loan."

"What if you lose?"

"Losses are on me, wins are on you. If you're not daring

enough, then I'll just have to say I don't have any money, and you won't get a loan from me."

Li Yansheng was in a quandary. He could not discount Fortune-Teller Dong's assertion that Guo Baochen had been a prime minister in a previous life, a position favoured with good fortune. If this was his good month, would he be lucky at the gambling table? If Li didn't lend Guo the money he asked for, there'd be no other road to a loan open to him. Why not just go ahead? So he returned to his stall in the marketplace, where he retrieved the stash of a little more than ten yuan from where he'd hidden it between the shelves. He put the spare change back and returned to the intersection with the ten yuan, which he handed to Guo Baochen. With a sombre look, Guo took the money and said, "Let's meet here tomorrow morning at eight o'clock."

He tossed down his bamboo spike and took off.

When Li Yansheng arrived at the intersection at eight the next morning, Guo was already sweeping the street, yawning as he worked.

"Did you win or lose last night, Baochen?" an anxious Li Yansheng asked.

"I lost."

Before Li's temper erupted, Guo said, "I lost, but... I found someone who'll lend you the money."

"Who?"

"Last night's winner, Old Shang. He beat eight of us. I lost, but I didn't forget a friend who needed money. That's just the kind of person I am."

Li had no choice but to ask, "How much can Old Shang lend me?"

"He said he'd lend you a hundred. But here's the bad news, he wants thirty per cent interest."

Li Yansheng had no choice. "Go talk to him, but tell him I need two hundred."

As he walked off, Li said to Yingtao inside his body, "Thanks to you, Yingtao, I'm really screwed."

Seven

That night, Li Yansheng told Hu Xiaofeng he'd be going to Luoyang the next day to buy supplies from the pickling plant.

"How come you waited till now to say you're going tomorrow?"

"I didn't know myself this morning. Old Meng, the guy who runs the tobacco and alcohol stall, was supposed to go, you know. He goes every month. He has a relative who works in the Luoyang plant. But his stomach acted up at noon, and the people in Luoyang agreed that I could go in his place. I've been working there four or five years, and I really couldn't say no. Besides, since I sell pickled vegetables, I know exactly what needs to be ordered."

"I'll go with you," she said.

Oops. Going to Luoyang was only a ruse for him to travel to Wuhan. Now there was the danger that Hu Xiaofeng would turn pretence into reality.

Li was quite familiar with his wife's temperament. She

was quick to convert thought to action, and once she made up her mind to do something, you could try to talk her out of it, but not even a herd of cattle could manage that. His only option was to come up with a way to get her to change her mind and salvage the situation.

"Perfect, I won't have to travel alone," he said, pretending to be enthusiastic.

They were sitting in bed that night.

"Let's make our plans for the trip before we go to sleep. We'll leave early in the morning and be in Luoyang in the afternoon, where I'll go straight to the pickling plant. I have to be clear on what they're pickling, based on seasonal demands, what we sold out of this month, and what was left unsold, what sells well and what doesn't. Then I have to determine what pricing works and what doesn't, which are open to discounts and which aren't, all before I can place an order. We'll stay in Luoyang overnight and return home early the next morning. Will you go to the pickling plant with me or will you just do some shopping and looking around?"

"I'm not going to Luoyang to visit a pickling plant or just to take in the sights. It's a much bigger city than Yanjin."

"Sounds good. We'll each do our own thing. Any place in particular you want to visit or just go where your feet take you?"

"I'll go shopping at the Luoyang Marketplace."

"Shopping for what?"

Hu Xiaofeng began counting on her fingers. "Face cream, hair oil, osmanthus-scented soap, waterproof plastic sandals for the boy, a pair of Dacron trousers for me and some camel's hair thread to make you a turtleneck sweater."

"I hate to say it, but all those things are available right here in Yanjin and at thirty per cent less than what you'd pay in Luoyang. You said it yourself, Luoyang is a big city, one where everything is more expensive."

"What are you trying to say? Don't you want me to go along?"

"That's not what I'm saying. I just don't want you to be angry with me if the trip costs you more than you expected. Isn't that what happened the time you bought an enamel basin in Xinxiang? You knew you'd been cheated, but you blamed me for not warning you. You said that since I sell things in the marketplace, I should have told you upfront. I suffered by keeping my mouth shut."

Hu sat there speechless.

"I just did a quick calculation. If you bought all those things in Yanjin, you'd spend no more than twenty yuan. In Luoyang, they'd cost more than thirty."

After thinking it over, she said, "OK, then, I won't go shopping. As I said, I'll take in the sights."

"Then I need to tell you that taking in the sights in Luoyang isn't free. I'm going on business, so my travel expenses will be paid for by the department. For what you want, you'll have to pay your own way. A round-trip bus ticket costs twenty yuan, which by itself is enough to buy everything you want."

Speechless a second time, she paused a moment before saying, "I only make fifty yuan a month wrapping sweets at the factory. Twenty to travel to Luoyang, no way, you go by yourself. I'll buy everything here in Yanjin. Since I'm buying them locally, there's no hurry, I can wait."

With that, she lay back to go to sleep. He heaved a sigh in relief. But she sat up abruptly.

"What are you going to do if your problem recurs and I'm not with you?"

"I'm over that," he said. "Have you seen it act up recently?"

Three days had passed since his encounter with Yingtao at Old Dong's.

"No, I haven't," she said after reflecting for a moment.

"That settles it. I'll take advantage of this official trip to start feeling better."

"Be very careful," Hu cautioned.

"Don't worry, I won't do anything foolish."

She slipped back under the covers and fell asleep.

Eight

Early the next morning, Li Yansheng left for Wuhan. He couldn't go empty-handed. Recalling how, when they were both in Yanjin, he and Chen Changjie had often gone out for pigs' feet, before setting out, he went to Marshal Tianpeng's and spent five yuan on ten pigs' feet.

He assumed that once he was on the road, Yingtao would tell him what message to give to Chen Changjie. He'd take whatever it was to Wuhan, while she would depart his body and stay in Yanjin. But when they boarded the bus to Xinxiang, she didn't say a word, staying put in his body.

"Yingtao," he said, "I have to be going, so tell me what I'm to pass on to Chen, then you can get off."

"I'll stay with you till we get to Xinxiang, then I'll tell you."

"Is this going to be a performance of *Broken Bridge*, where two people stay together because there's only one umbrella?"

Like "What to do? What to do? What shall I do? What

shall I do?" In the aria *Broken Bridge*, the White Snake has just come down to West Lake in the human world from a fairy mountain. It's raining, so Xu Xian offers to share his umbrella with her. They see one another off, back and forth, holding the one umbrella, and slowly develop an emotional attachment.

"If you'd do it for an umbrella," Yingtao responded, "you really must do it to deliver a message."

"When we get to Xinxiang, how will you travel the hundred *li* back home?"

"Don't worry about that, I can manage."

The bus got underway. Li Yansheng had to do what she wanted. When they reached Xinxiang train station, he went in to buy a ticket to Wuhan, which would leave in two hours. Then he went out and sat on the station steps.

"You can tell me now, Yingtao. I'll be boarding the train in a little while."

"There's no need for that. I'll go to Wuhan with you."

Li froze for a moment. "Instead of wanting me to take something to Wuhan for you, now you're asking me to take you. That wasn't the bargain."

"Taking a message isn't enough. I have to see him."

"If all you want is to see him, why can't you go there Wuhan alone? Why involve me?"

"Tagging along in your body is the only way I can get there."

Li finally grasped what Yingtao was up to. Taking her, not just a message, had been her plan all along. Poised to have a verbal fight with her over being lied to, on second thought, since he was off to Wuhan one way or the other, he could take her as easily as he could take her message. Two days with her in his body was all it would take. She didn't need food or drink and she cost him nothing, but if he wrangled with her, she might turn unreasonable and stick around a lot longer, turning a minor annoyance into a fiasco. So, one ticket for two people. On the outside, it looked like one, but was in fact two, though if he said that to anyone, they'd think he was a madman. There certainly was something absurd about it, but that was the situation; he wouldn't believe someone else in a similar quandary, so why should anyone believe him? In a crowd, no one would suspect he was carrying anything strange inside him.

"Yingtao," he said with a sigh, "you're more devious than I am."

"I have no choice," she replied, feeling somewhat chagrined. "Who would attach themselves to someone else's body if they weren't desperate?"

"What I don't understand," he said, "is what in the world you want to say to Chen Changjie."

"That's my business."

"I won't go if you won't tell me. You can't keep me in the dark forever. I'd be a dumb fuck to just blithely carry you all the way to Wuhan, wouldn't I? If I don't go, you can't either."

"It's a long story," she said tearfully.

"Don't cry, take your time."

"I hanged myself three years ago, not a good death since I couldn't get into an ancestral cemetery. So Changjie buried my body among unmarked common graves in Nanguan. It was an uneventful three years, but six months ago, an executed rapist and murderer was buried nearby. He knew I'd been an opera singer, and wanted me to perform my role at night so he could sing Xu Xian. After we finished, he demanded sex. When I refused, he beat me, saying we're husband and wife. That was just for the stage, not real life, I told him. He wanted to make it real. After that, my mind was clear. I'd died, no argument there. But when I was still alive, I was imprisoned in the Leifeng Pagoda in the play, and I hanged myself in real life, so what was there to be afraid of? But after he climbed off me, that wasn't enough for him. He started letting others pay to climb on, money he collected. If I refused, he beat me. I couldn't keep on living – or dying, actually – so I have to get Changjie to move my grave."

Li was dumbstruck. Now he saw Yingtao's predicament and understood why she wanted him to take a message. "So that's what it's about," he said with a heavy sigh. "I didn't know this was so hard on you. Can't you find a relative in Yanjin to move your grave? Why go all this distance to see Chen Changjie?"

"He buried me. The last spadeful of dirt has his imprint on it, so he has to be the one to move me. Karma is important in the land of the living. It's even more important to us. Without it, nothing works. Since Chen tossed down the last spadeful, he has to move me. Just as in the play, Fahai put me under the pagoda, and he had to be the one to remove the seal on it. If someone else tried, my spirit would stay put. If I couldn't keep body and spirit together, I'd have been better off with the rapist. So, I repeat, only Changjie can move my grave, no one else can do it. Not only that, the rapist-murderer is turning play-acting into real action. In the opera, Changjie was Fahai, wasn't he? Fahai can subdue demons, so he could vanquish that malicious spirit and place him under a pagoda. That's the additional purpose."

Knowing what Yingtao wanted, he was sympathetic. He could see it was complicated. One question remained, however.

"If you're going to get Chen Changjie to move your grave and vanquish the demon, what's wrong with my giving him the message? Why is it so important for you to go with me?"

"What if he doesn't believe you? If I'm there, and he won't do what I want, I'll make a scene until he agrees to come back to Yanjin with me."

Once again, Li Yansheng understood that what she wanted was not only for him to take her to Wuhan, but that she also wanted Chen Changjie to return to Yanjin with her.

"If that's the case, once we get to Wuhan and see Chen Changjie, you can tell him what you want, and that'll end it for me."

"Of course. This time I mean it."

Suddenly reminded of why Yingtao had died, he said, "There's something I'd like to ask you. A casual question."

"How casual?"

"Three years ago, really, how did you die?"

"There's nothing casual about that question. How a person dies can never be a casual question."

"Sorry," he hurried to add. "I said that wrong, all wrong. I just wanted to ask if, like people say, it was over a bunch of chives."

Yingtao sighed. "You can say it was over a bunch of chives, and you can say it wasn't. Changjie and I did argue over chives that day. He walked out and slammed the door behind him, which made me so angry I fell onto the bed and started to cry. I actually cried myself to sleep, and in a dream

I encountered Hua Erniang, who wanted to hear a joke. What happened was all my fault. Erniang usually comes at night looking for jokes. Why did I have to fall asleep in the middle of the day? How was I supposed to have a joke ready after a good cry? Erniang, I said, I'm not much of a talker, how about I sing for you? She said she knew I'd been an opera singer. Go ahead, sing, she said. So, I started with *Broken Bridge* and sang all the way up to 'What to do? What to do? What shall I do? What shall I do?' I sang and I sang, giving voice to the snake's grievances and sadness, never imagining that my singing would bring out Erniang's grievances and sadness. I cried, so did she. When the aria was over, she got really angry. I came looking for jokes, and you made me cry. What are you up to? Take me for some spicy soup. I recalled why she was in my dream and was embarrassed. Erniang, I said, you don't have to do anything, I'll do it for you. I picked up a rope and hanged myself."

Li Yansheng was rendered speechless. Yingtao died over some chives, no argument. But over a joke as well. When he was troubled, his wife had asked him if it was because Hua Erniang had come into his dream looking for jokes. He'd said that wasn't it. How strange that instead of coming into his dream, Erniang had gone into Yingtao's, who was the cause of his troubles, and whose subsequent death came about because of Erniang and a joke. With everything turned upside down, Li Yansheng could only shake his head and sigh.

"Since Hua Erniang was a factor in your death, and you are now being tyrannised by a vicious demon, why not tell Erniang about it and get her to remove this evil spirit?"

"Hua Erniang can only enter living people's dreams, not

those of demons. She enters dreams in search of jokes. Is there a demon anywhere that hasn't suffered? Would she be amused if I told her about being tyrannised by a vicious demon?"

There was nothing he could say.

"After telling you all these upsetting things, I have some good news."

"What's that?"

"A month or more ago, Big Mouth Wu, who ran the tripe cafe in Beiguan, was flattened because of jokes. You heard, didn't you?"

"Yes. I attended his funeral. But how can someone's death be good news?"

"I'm talking about after he died, not before. She caused his death over jokes, just like me, and I sympathised with him when he came here. During last month's demon-eliminating day, I met him in the marketplace, and it was he who passed on the good news."

"What was it?"

"It's different for people who are flattened over jokes than for others, since they have trouble getting reborn. When he first arrived, a month or so ago, during his brief stay in King Yama's realm, Yama said to him, 'Better to come at the right time than to come early.' A veteran clan leader spoke to Yama for the humourless ghosts. Yama, showing his goodwill toward ghosts, announced a new policy: if those who are flattened because of a joke could make a fresh start by working to improve themselves and tell Yama fifty jokes, they would qualify for rebirth."

"That *is* good news," a surprised Li Yansheng replied. "Who was the clan leader?"

"Big Mouth didn't even ask," Yingtao said. "But they were not to be any old jokes. They had to be short and visibly amusing."

"Tough."

"Since then, ghosts of those who were flattened are on a frenzy, practising their joke-telling. In one short month, the mulish Big Mouth Wu had a complete makeover and is now a real smooth talker. This time, when I get to Wuhan, in addition to having Changjie go back to Yanjin with me and vanquish that evil ghost, I'd like him to teach me how to tell jokes. Before we were married, he could make me laugh with a single comment. He was good at telling jokes, I was not. When he teaches me fifty one-liners, I'll commit them to memory and tell them to Yama. If he laughs, I'll be up for rebirth, and we'll meet again in the world of the living."

Li Yansheng was surprised to learn that there was more to Yingtao's trip to Wuhan, and that was to learn fifty one-liners. Again, he shook his head and sighed.

"Yansheng," said Yingtao, "as a nod to all those years we were on the stage together, can you come up with some one-liners to help me?"

Li had never been a joke-teller, had in fact never told a single one. Of greater significance, if he did as she asked, she might use that as an excuse to keep hanging around.

"Back when we were in the drama troupe, Yingtao, you knew as well as anyone how inarticulate I was. If I couldn't even keep up a conversation, how could I be expected to tell jokes? Besides, one-liners are really asking a lot. I'd like to help, but I don't have what it takes."

Yingtao didn't press him, just sighed. The sound of a steam whistle signalled the arrival of the train at the station.

Li Yansheng took Yingtao up to the platform and, as he boarded, was thinking that whatever the reason to be going to Wuhan, whether over some chives or Hua Erniang or moving a grave and vanquishing a ghost or Yama and jokes, all Yingtao's affairs, the presence of her in his body was a burden that in itself was a joke. What a mess!

Nine

In order to get to Wuhan as quickly as possible, the train Li Yansheng took carrying Yingtao terminated in Wuchang, one of the three municipalities that make up the city of Wuhan. He had originally planned to take the train to Hankou, which was where Chen Changjie lived, but that train would not be passing through Xinxiang for nearly six hours. Xinxiang was one of the stops on the route, so when he and Yingtao boarded, all the seats and most of the space in the central aisle were taken. After passing through as many as six carriages and finding no seats in each one, he found room in the linking space between two carriages and sat down, back against the train, cradling his travel bag against his chest. After a tiring day, the rhythmic clickety-clack of the wheels put him and Yingtao to sleep.

They did not speak the whole trip. When they walked out of Wuchang train station, it was eight-thirty the following morning. Travel bag in hand, Li rushed across the square to the telephone and telegraph office to place a long-distance call to the sweets factory in Yanjin. Its only phone was in the reception office and was the responsibility of a man named Zhang. Workers were not permitted to receive phone calls during working hours, so Zhang received, answered and delivered all incoming calls to the person phoned. Li Yansheng told Zhang he was in Luoyang purchasing pickled vegetables and had awakened in the hostel with a fever. He could not get out of bed and would have to stay over a couple of days. He'd return to Yanjin as soon as he recovered. He asked Zhang to pass the word to Hu Xiaofeng. "Will do," Zhang replied impassively and hung up. The advantage of the telephone policy at the factory had not escaped Li. His wife could not take the phone call and would have no chance to ask questions, such as whether Li's problem had resurfaced.

Chen Changjie's Wuhan address was on the envelope of the wedding invitation he'd sent to Li Yansheng the month before. Li took the envelope out of his pocket as he exited the telephone office and carried Yingtao with him to Chen's flat at Room 433, Fourth Floor, Unit Three, Building Seven, Xinyi Lane, Dazhimen, Jinhang Road, Hankou. To get from Wuchang to Hankou, they'd have to cross the Yangtze River. They went straight to the ferry landing, where he bought a ticket. It was a warm, sunny day, though the river was choppy, with waves lapping against the bank. Ticket in hand, they boarded the ferry, which was rocking from side to side.

"Hold on, Yansheng," Yingtao blurted out.

"What's up?"

"I can't go on this ferry."

"Why not?"

"Water is my cosmic nemesis. Just looking at this river

throws my heart into panic mode," she said, taking her words from the opera.

"Why the hell didn't you say so before?"

"I never thought the Yangtze could be so choppy."

"If we don't cross, we won't be able to find Chen Changjie."

"We can go by land, take the Yangtze River Bridge."

"I already asked. It's a bus ride from here, adding miles to our travel. Force yourself to put up with the boat ride. After turning you over to Chen, I have to rush back to Yanjin as quickly as possible. If I'm late, my wife will find out what I was up to."

"But what if I die from panic on the boat? Spirits are weak to begin with and can't weather storms. I've already died once, so dying again would be no big deal. But if I die when I'm inside your body, I guess I'll be with you forever."

Visibly alarmed, Li said, "If you say go by bus, that's what we'll do. No need to scare me."

He carried Yingtao back onto the riverbank, where he returned his ticket and looked for the bus station. The bus they boarded made frequent stops. Combined with the many bicycles, the sudden stops to miss pedestrians crossing the street and the circuitous route, it took them two hours to reach the Yangtze River Bridge. Li held on to his travel bag with one hand and the overhead strap with the other, heaving long sighs.

Yingtao could tell he was unhappy. "Don't be angry, Yansheng. I know this trip to Wuhan has been hard on you, and costly. I'm aware that you're eager to get back to Yanjin. Well, so am I. Once we find Changjie, we can all go home."

"I'll give it to you straight, Yingtao. When we get back to

Yanjin, don't come looking for me if you ever need anything more. We live in two separate realms."

"Don't worry, I'll only bother you this once."

When they reached Hankou, they stepped off the bus and, envelope in hand, asked how to get to Chen Changjie's address. It was noon by the time they reached Xinyi Lane. The month before, Li Yansheng had begged off attending Chen's wedding, complaining of a twisted ankle. Now that they'd nearly reached their goal, he began a show of limping, in case they met up with Chen in the lane. He turned right and left before they found Building Number Seven's passageway and located Unit Three. He walked down the passageway, took the stairs to the fourth floor, checked the door number plate and saw 433 on the door to the right. He went up and knocked. No one home. He looked at the envelope to make sure it was the right number. Then he knocked at the door across the hall. When it opened, he was confronted by a middle-aged man who, by the looks of his mussed hair and sleepy eyes, had been in bed. He was not happy to see it was a stranger.

"What the hell do you want? I work nights, you woke me up."

"I'm so sorry," Li apologised, "I just need to know if Chen Changjie lives across the hall."

The man nodded.

"Do you know why no one's home?"

"Do you really have to ask? If they're not in, they must be at work."

"When will they be back?"

"They didn't make a point of telling me. He slammed the door shut. "Damn!"

Li let that go. He turned to Yingtao.

"I've delivered you to Chen Changjie's door, Yingtao. You can wait here for him, I'm going back."

He expected her to leave his body. She didn't. "I do want you to be on your way, Yansheng, but where am I going to attach myself if you're not here? Besides, I'll be worried until I actually see him."

Li had no choice but to sit and wait in the hallway with Yingtao. He kept checking his watch. At 12.30 they heard footsteps on the ground floor. He trained his eyes on the stairway, where, a moment later, a man came up the stairs, breathless, carrying a butane gas container over his shoulder. Who was it? Chen Changjie in the flesh.

"Yansheng, what are you doing here?" he asked, visibly surprised.

Naturally, Li couldn't say he'd brought Yingtao to Wuhan, so he said he'd been sent on business and had decided to look up Chen while he was in town. "I felt bad about missing your wedding last month."

Chen set down the gas container. "We were about to make lunch, and saw we were out of gas." He opened the door. "Come on in. What a surprise."

Li saw it was a small two-bedroom flat with a tiny entryway. They took a long look at one another and laughed.

"It's been three years."

"It sure has."

Li opened his travel bag. "I didn't bring anything for you, except these pigs' feet from Marshal Tianpeng's."

"What a nice surprise," Chen said as he accepted the package. "I've had pigs' feet here in Wuhan, but nothing compared to Marshal Tianpeng's. In your letter, you said you twisted your ankle. Is it all right now?"

Li sat down and stuck out his leg for Chen to see. "See, no more swelling, but I still limp a little. I can tolerate a short walk, but a long one is out of the question."

Now that he was in Chen Changjie's home, Li Yansheng experienced a sensation of lightness. He was once again the Li Yansheng of a month earlier, and he knew that Yingtao had left his body. He did not, however, dare mention any of this to Chen, and began a casual conversation about other things.

"Where's your wife?"

"At work."

Li spotted a framed family photo of four people on the opposite wall, two adults and two children. Noting that his friend was looking at the photo, Chen said, "My wife, she's from Jingzhou. Works at the Hankou Enamelware factory. This is Mingliang. The girl is my wife's daughter, a month younger than Mingliang." Now Li knew that it was Chen's wife's second marriage and that she already had a child.

Seeing the look on his friend's face, Chen quickly clarified the situation: "Her second marriage. Mine, too, wasn't it? She has a child, so do I. Seeing each other's situation, we knew we couldn't be picky."

"I agree. That's how things work out." Li studied the face of Mingliang, whom he'd seen three years earlier at the boy's mother's funeral. He'd worn a black armband. He was a head taller now. "Where's the boy?"

"In school."

"He'd only be six now. Isn't it early to start school?"

"I'm out every day, so there's no one home to take care of him. I don't have to worry if he's at school."

"Shouldn't you be working today?"

"I'm a freight train stoker. It's not my shift today, so I'm at home."

"Lucky me. If it had been, I'd have wasted my time."

"That's for sure."

Chen invited Li to lunch at a cafe, but Li was in a hurry to return to Yanjin. "Let's just see what you have here. I have a ticket for the three o'clock train, so I don't have much time."

"Since you've come all this way, don't be in a hurry to leave. Why not spend a few days in Wuhan? We can visit Yellow Crane Tower. There's been a shift change, so I have nothing to do for a couple of days."

Nothing to do, you say, Li was thinking. I've brought Yingtao with me, and she's going to want you to return to Yanjin with her to move her grave. She'll also ask you to teach her some jokes. But he couldn't say any of that, so he made up an excuse. "I'd originally planned to do that while I was here on business, but I phoned home and learned that Xiaofeng has run a high fever and can't get out of bed."

That news kept Chen from pressing the issue. "Since she's ill, I won't try to keep you. Unfortunately, there's nothing to eat here but some hot dry noodles."

"Sounds good to me. I've always wanted to try your Hubei speciality."

Chen hooked up the fresh gas container and started cooking the noodles. There was a knock at the door. Li went over and opened it. A boy with a book bag stormed in, his head steaming. His shirt was food-stained. He made no attempt to say hello to their guest, so Yansheng took the initiative: "You must be Mingliang. School out for the day?"

Chen Changjie stuck his head out from the kitchen. "Yes, it's Mingliang. Mingliang, say hello to Uncle Li. He's from our hometown."

Mingliang took a look at their guest and said "Hi, Uncle Li." He then laid his bag down on the cupboard, opened the drawer and took out a pack of instant noodles, which he crunched on as he leaned against the sofa.

When the hot dry noodles were ready, Chen filled three bowls and carried them to the table along with three of the pigs' feet Li had brought with him. He cut each of them into four pieces and put them on a plate.

"Since time is an issue, this'll have to do, noodles and pigs' feet."

He turned to his son. "Mingliang, don't eat those, come have lunch."

"Aren't we going to wait for your wife?"

"She doesn't come home for lunch. She eats in the factory cafeteria."

Li pointed to the family photo. "How about the girl?"

"Her school is by the enamelware factory, so she eats there with her mother."

As lunch ended, Li looked at his watch.

"It's nearly two o'clock. I've got to run to catch my train."

"This has been too rushed. If not for your wife's illness, I wouldn't let you leave."

"There will be other opportunities. I'll be back."

Li took twenty yuan out of his pocket and handed it to Mingliang.

"I didn't bring you anything, so use this to buy some school supplies."

Chen stopped him. "We've got money, you don't need to give him that."

"This is for him, not for you."

When he heard that, he let Li go ahead. "You can take that from Uncle Li, Mingliang."

The boy took the money, ran to the cupboard and put it into his bag.

Chen saw a limping Li to the end of the lane.

"You'd better go back, Changjie. Your son's home alone."

"Since you've come all this way, this is the least I can do."

"'I see my swain off, but the parting shall come,'" Li said, from the opera.

"Thank you, Yansheng, for coming to see me, even with a limp." He answered Li's quote with one of his own: "'As we say farewell, when shall we meet again?'"

It was a sentimental exchange. Li Yansheng knew that before long, Chen might return to Yanjin with Yingtao, and the two friends would meet again. But he couldn't say so. "Don't worry, it'll happen." Getting his friend to stop there, Li hobbled off, turning to look after he'd gone a couple of blocks. Chen was still at the lane entrance watching him. He waved to his friend, who waved back. Li turned right into another lane and could finally stop his fake hobble. He strode to the ferry landing.

When he reached the train station, he could only buy a ticket for the midnight train to Xinxiang. Ticket in hand, he checked his watch. Three-fifteen, more than eight hours to wait. Chen had offered to take him to the Yellow Crane

Tower. He was told there was a bus to the site, so he went. Back then, it cost fifteen cents to visit Yellow Crane Tower, so he bought a ticket, walked through the entrance and began climbing towards the tower, where he stopped to read the inscriptions on the two columns in front:

People of the past flew off on the back of a yellow crane

Here, there is an empty Yellow Crane Tower

Li was unaware of the poetic allusion but didn't care. He was wondering if Chen would be returning to Yanjin in a few days with Yingtao. He recalled what she'd said to him at Xinxiang train station, that if Chen refused to go with her, she'd give him hell.

It was the reason she'd come all this way. How would a living human stand up to the badgering of a ghost? Li Yansheng, an outsider, from Yanjin to Wuhan, certainly hadn't been able to. As her former husband, Chen Changjie could not possibly defy her. And so, Chen would have to return to Yanjin within the next few days. But then Li was reminded of what Chen had written at the bottom of the wedding invitation a month earlier. "We'll catch up when you're here." During lunch at Chen's place, he'd forgotten to ask what to "catch up" on. Now he'd have to wait till Chen returned to Yanjin to ask him in person.

Ten

The minute Li Yansheng walked in the door at home, his wife asked him about his fever. Luckily, he told her, Old Meng's cousin heard about his condition and asked his wife to prepare some ginger soup, which they'd delivered to his hotel. After sweating under a blanket for two days, the fever had abated.

"If he ever comes to Yanjin, I'll take him to dinner."

Hu Xiaofeng felt his forehead – cool, no fever and that was that. He went back to work in the market, selling soy sauce, vinegar and pickled vegetables. He also sold peppercorns, anise and fermented tofu. To his surprise, after several days, there was no sign of Chen Changjie back home with Yingtao.

A couple of weeks later, Yingtao appeared in one of his dreams.

"Yansheng, you'll have to return to Wuhan," she told him.

"What? Why?"

"Come pick me up. I can't stick around here any longer. You brought me here, so now you'll have to take me back."

As if he'd been the one who'd insisted on taking her to Wuhan, now it was his responsibility.

He was about to put up a fierce argument, but Yingtao was unrelenting. She rushed him, and in trying to get away, he banged his head against the bedside cupboard, which woke him up. His wife snorted in her sleep. He gazed out the window, through which moonlight shone onto the wall, where the shadows of trees danced. When he'd set out with Yingtao for Wuhan, they'd agreed that when they saw Chen Changjie, they'd part company, and she and Chen were free to do what they wanted. The days had passed, with no sighting of Chen back in Yanjin to move Yingtao's grave, and Li began to wonder if a problem had arisen between them in Wuhan. In his dream, he could see that she was still in Wuhan and was in some sort of trouble. He assumed the dream was caused by these thoughts. He got up and went to the toilet, where he relieved himself before returning to bed and back to sleep. Yingtao surprised him by returning to his dream the next night. But this time, she screamed, "It hurts, it hurts so much!" As if she was rolling around in a briar patch.

Li went to work the next morning. Feeling out of sorts, he walked to the local post office to place a long-distance call to Chen Changjie in Wuhan and find out what happened to Yingtao. But, he reminded himself, she was a spirit, not a living person, one he'd personally delivered to Wuhan. If a dispute had broken out between her and Chen, he himself had set the scene, and he worried that Chen would be angry with him. He decided against the phone call. Still unsettled that afternoon, he asked Old Meng to watch his stall for him and took a stroll to Old Dong's house in Grasshopper Lane on East Avenue, wanting to ask what he should do. As on the first visit, he lined up under the eave outside the door. When his turn came, Dong's wife called out "Next!"

He entered and sat across from Dong, where he told him in considerable detail how he had delivered Yingtao to Wuhan, where they had separated and parted company for good, so he could return to Yanjin alone. But she then came into one of his dreams, wanting him to go to Wuhan to bring her back to Yanjin. This time, Dong did not feel his bones or message with her spirit and no living transmission. He merely said, "Since you agreed to each go your own way in Wuhan, she should not come into your dream to bother you again."

"You're right."

"Appearing in your dream is nothing to worry about. She can't attach herself to you now that she's in far-off Wuhan, so this is all she can do. Attachment qualifies as an illness, appearing in a dream means nothing, so just ignore her."

Li breathed a sigh of relief. He turned to Kuai to settle up, but Dong said, "He just asked a question, didn't involve the Master, so no charge."

Li knew he was getting this treatment because Dong still considered him to be an opera singer. At the same time, he did it also to accumulate merits so he would not be reborn blind. Li did not insist on paying.

Back in the marketplace, Li kept thinking about how tortured Yingtao had been in his dream. Obviously, she had encountered something terrible in Wuhan. At the very least,

Chen had refused to accompany her back to Yanjin. Why hadn't she been able to make him do so? She hadn't had any trouble forcing him to do her bidding, so why not Chen? It didn't make sense. If Chen would not come back to move her grave, and she'd asked Li Yansheng to go to Wuhan to fetch her and bring her back to her gravesite, the vicious spirit ghost would be waiting for her. By crying and asking to come back to Yanjin, she obviously no longer feared the vicious ghost. Her circumstances in Wuhan must be worse than what she'd face back in the Yanjin cemetery. But she could only return by attaching herself to someone. And that was the source of her difficulty.

He and Yingtao had once acted together, a stage husband and wife, and that thought had him thinking that he should bring her back home. But what kind of excuse to go to Wuhan could he make up this time for his wife? The trip would, of course, be expensive, and he had not yet returned the two hundred he'd borrowed from Old Shang at a high rate of interest. Was he going to borrow more? He only earned something over sixty a month, all above board and all known by Hu Xiaofeng; he had no means of putting something aside for himself.

Being in debt twice, how would he ever pay it back?

His enthusiasm for returning to Wuhan cooled. After two visits to his dreams, Yingtao stopped coming. Why? He couldn't figure it out, and after more days passed, she faded from his memory. He went back to work at the marketplace, selling soy sauce, vinegar and pickled vegetables, as well as peppercorns, anise and fermented tofu. But every once in a while, he recalled stranding Yingtao in Wuhan, with no hope of returning to Yanjin. Where could she go?

PART III
MINGLIANG

Way Back When

ONE

Chen Changjie's uncle, Jiang Dashan, was a pointsman at the Wuhan Railway Division. He'd greased the wheels for Chen Changjie to get hired in the division. Short and overweight, with a ruddy face, he loved to drink, and when he did, he was fond of saying, "Know how long I've been working at the Railway Division? More than thirty years. I'm what they call a veteran. I've definitely got some standing at the division."

He also liked to say, "There are two deputy division chiefs. A pointsman who started work the same time I did is one of them." As to why, after thirty years, one had become a deputy chief while he was still a pointsman, Chen Changjie did not dare state an opinion to his face. But he watched as his uncle travelled to and from work; if he met someone he knew, they'd call him Master Jiang or Old Jiang. He said hello to a lot of people; few people said hello to him, proof that there was quite a gulf between how he saw himself and the way other people saw him.

That is not to say he had no standing in the division; if that had been the case, how could he have found Changjie work as a stoker? And yet, just what standing did he have if he could only get his nephew a job as a stoker? When Chen started out, the trains were all steam-powered. They could hurtle down the tracks thanks only to the stoker flinging shovelfuls of coal into the furnace chamber, sending out clouds of steam to move the train forward. It was hard work, the hardest on the train. But when arriving at a new place, finding a job right away – any job – was worth it.

At first, Chen Changjie stayed in the division workers' dormitory. He had no choice but to live in a large community of twenty-eight men, all with a variety of jobs – pointsman, track walker, mechanic, apprentice engineer, stoker and more. All these jobs took workers up and down the tracks, usually four or five days away from the dormitory, where fewer than a dozen beds would be occupied at any one time, sometimes no more than five. There were even special times when the place was totally empty.

Chen Changjie had brought his three-year-old son, Mingliang, with him to Wuhan. Since he was not a worker, no bed was assigned to him, so he had to squeeze onto his father's bed. Happily, there was considerable fluidity of occupancy in the dormitory, with plenty of open beds most of the time, and no one said a word about the addition of a child. When Chen was out on one of the trains, he left Mingliang alone in the dormitory. From the age of three, the boy knew how to take his mess tin to the dining hall to get his meals. When Chen was away for up to five days at a time, the waking hours were no problem, but the nights threw a scare into Mingliang. "When will you be back, Pa?" was his constant refrain. "Don't ask that every time," Chen would reply. "This job is what keeps us fed."

The division employed more than five thousand people, of whom Chen Changjie knew but one – his uncle – when he arrived in Wuhan, though he gradually got to know some of his fellow workers. As a novice stoker, there was so much to learn: how to feed the furnace with coal, how much when the train started out, how much when it was at full speed, how much to shovel to meet the required speed, how much on level ground, how much in the mountains and how to economise as he worked. With father and son sharing a bed in the dormitory, they felt virtually homeless, and Chen gave no thought to starting a new family. A one-time talker of note, he now had little to say and was a jokester no more. Three years passed before he knew it.

On the night of 30 April, the division held a social gathering to celebrate International Workers' Day the next day. In this case, that meant each section – operations, ground personnel, security, depot, logistics and so on – was to design a performance by its workers to present in the auditorium. Chen Changjie's train had come in that afternoon. He worked on freight, not passenger trains. Owing to the greater weight, a five-day trip exhausted him, and he had no plans to attend that evening's festivities, preferring instead to get a good night's sleep. Mingliang, now six years old, was eager to have a good time and badgered his father to take him to the performance. Seeing no way to refuse, Chen changed into a clean shirt and took Mingliang to the auditorium to watch the show.

A man named Min was the boss of the division. He sometimes attended holiday celebrations and sometimes didn't, depending on how busy he was. He hadn't planned to show up for the May Day celebration, as a deputy minister of the Transportation Bureau was stopping over in Wuhan on his way from Changsha and needed to be accompanied by a responsible official. But late that afternoon, the deputy minister received a summons to return to Beijing and boarded a train to the capital without even stopping for dinner. After taking him to the station, Min returned to the division, took a few bites of food, and, seeing the bright lights outside, strolled over to the auditorium. His arrival did not go unnoticed – the performers redoubled their efforts on the stage, the audience of workers redoubled their applause. The opening act comprised a Hubei festive lantern dance by the Railway Division Office staff. That was followed by dragon-boat songs performed by the security section, humorous cross-talk by the depot section and a pantomime piece by two workers in the electrical section. When it was the operations section's turn, the performance broke down. They had prepared a skit from the drama *Yang Guifei Gets Drunk*. The emcee announced the section and the name of the skit, but no one took the stage, creating an awkward silence. A buzz of discontent spread through the auditorium.

Director Min stood up. "What's going on with the operations section? Where are they?"

The director of the Railway Division Club ran over from the stage. "Something's come up, Director Min."

"What do you mean?"

"The worker selected to play the Guifei role had a sudden intestinal episode and can't perform." He then turned to the administrative section chief. "How about doing something else, Chief Wu?"

Nothing else had been prepared, so they'd have to improvise. But how? Wu's face showed his embarrassment.

"A medical emergency didn't give us time to prepare anything new."

"This all happened so fast, Division Chief," the club director said to Min. "Logistics is ready with a musical *The Great Harvest*. Shall we move on to the next act?"

Chief Min surprised them by getting angry. "Absolutely not. This isn't just a matter of performances," he said as he pointed to Operations Section Chief Wu. "What the hell's wrong with you, Wu? You cover your head but forget to cover your arse. Why didn't you have a backup ready? If one of the engineers has a case of the runs, does that mean a train can't leave the station? Is this how things work around here? If we can't even get something like this done, how will our trains ever run?"

Wu was mortified, as was the club director. The crowd in the auditorium buzzed with opinions and reactions. As a stoker, Chen Changjie was a member of the operations section and, as a one-time opera performer, he did not know the meaning of stage fright.

Seeing all the discomfort around him, he stood up.

"I'm a member of the operations section. Would it be all right for me to perform something?"

"What can you do?" the club director asked.

"I'm from Henan and can sing some Henanese opera."

No one there was aware that Chief Min had come to Wuhan from Zhengzhou, where he'd served as deputy director of the railway division. Having lived in Henan for more than a decade, when he heard Chen say he could sing Henanese opera, his anger turned to delight.

"Which opera can you sing?"

"How about *Legend of the White Snake*?"

"That's a good one. I've seen it performed. Let him go up onto the stage," he said to the club director, before turning to Chief Wu. "Lucky for you your saviour came riding in. I don't know how you would have wriggled out of this if he hadn't. Don't let something like this happen again."

"It won't, Chief," Wu said as he wiped his sweaty brow. "Never again."

Chen Changjie sat Mingliang down and told him to stay there before mounting the stage. As a one-time professional actor, the moment he stepped onto the stage, he became a different person, no longer a train stoker. First, he pranced across the stage, then he spun around and struck a pose, drawing hoots of approval from the crowd. Lacking musical accompaniment, he sang the aria "What to do? What to do? What shall I do? What shall I do?" a cappella. He'd often sung it at the Yanjin Machinery Factory. It incorporated lyrics sung by Fahai, Xu Xian and the White Snake. The fellow actors from his Yanjin days, Li Yansheng and Yingtao, were not with him, so after singing the Fahai parts, he made visual changes to sing as Xu Xian, and then, with feminine moves and looks, sang in falsetto the role of the White Snake. When the snake wept, he moved his sleeves to dry his eyes.

You love her because of her fragile beauty,
Not knowing it masks a poisonous viper.

Xu Xian sings:
I did not know she was a viper when I
loved her,
Now as love cannot endure, my heart is cut
in two.

The White Snake sings to Fahai:
There is no enmity or hate between you and me.
Why must you keep us from being together?

Fahai sings:
I reject you not out of selfish claims,
But to keep separate human and spirit realms.

Chen then spreads his arms as the three characters sing, one after the other:
What to do? What to do?
What shall I do? What shall I do?

A hush fell over the auditorium as the audience had followed Chen Changjie's every word, every look, every gesture. As he sang, he was transported back to his days in Yanjin, when he shared the stage with Li Yansheng and Yingtao. They were at the peak of their careers. Yingtao was still alive, they were dating. He sang and he sang, and became so emotional he was in tears. When he finished singing the lines "What to do? What to do? What shall I do? What shall I do?" not a sound emerged from the audience. After a moment of stunned silence, the crowd burst into thunderous applause. Chen bowed once and stepped down off the stage. Chief Min signalled to him and indicated the chair beside him, inviting him to sit.

"Young man," Min said, "you are very talented. What's your name?"

"Chen Changjie."

"Why have you come here from Henan?"

"Because of my uncle."

"Who is your uncle?"

"A pointsman called Old Jiang."

"Old Jiang, you say. One of the older crowd. I think I recall him. Tall, acne scars."

Chen's uncle was short, about five-three and had no acne scars. Apparently, Chief Min had his personnel wires crossed, but Chen was not about to correct him.

"You were fine in Henan, so why come to Wuhan?"

Chen had to lie. "Everything was going fine in Henan, but my wife died from an illness three years ago. We had a wonderful marriage, but when she died, all the familiar spots brought me such sadness, I decided to move to Hubei."

Chief Min nodded. "Affection and faith go hand in hand. Have you found a new wife here?"

Chen shook his head.

"If that's the case," Min said, a thought forming in his mind. "This might work. I've got a niece who just went through a divorce. I think you two might hit it off. If so, I'll have done something good. If not, you can at least be friends." Then he whispered to Chen, "Her mother's hair has turned grey since the divorce."

Caught by surprise, Chen stammered, "This is pretty sudden, Chief."

"That was just off the top of my head," the chief said with a laugh. "I'm not trying to force you into anything."

Chen went to see his uncle when he was off the next day. He told him what the division chief had proposed. Even though the chief had described the wrong "uncle", Old Jiang was excited by the news.

"Why are you hesitating?" he exclaimed. "To become a member of the chief's family as a stoker would be your great good fortune. Do you think you'd keep shovelling coal? Bringing you here was a good move on my part, wouldn't you say?"

"Maybe he wasn't being serious."

"If so, there's nothing we can do. But if not, just play it by ear."

Chief Min was dead serious, it turned out, for the very next morning, the club director came to see Chen in the dormitory and handed him a cinema ticket. He was to turn up at the Changhong Theatre that night at seven to take in a film with Chief Min's niece. He learned that her name was Qin Jiaying. Divorced three months before, she had a six-year-old daughter.

When they left the cinema after watching *The Fairy Couple*, they strolled down the street.

"Did you enjoy the movie?" she asked.

"I did."

"Then why did you fall asleep?"

"A fairy descends from the heavens and links up with a cowherd is something you'll only find in films or dramas, never in real life. I acted in many dramas like that as a member of a county opera troupe. They were all much the same, and I fell asleep."

Qin Jiaying giggled. They were passing a row of street stalls where salted duck necks were sold. Customers were eating and drinking.

"Do you drink?"

"I like to drink with friends at home. I've been so busy here in Wuhan, I haven't even thought of it."

"Are you argumentative?"

"I used to have a temper. But during the three years my wife was sick, I mellowed out after seeking help for her," he lied.

"You were an actor. I've heard that actors are faithless. You're not the type to treat life like a play, are you? I'm pretty no-nonsense. Don't be offended if you don't like what I'm saying." Then she sighed. "I suffered a lot in my marriage."

"Some actors might be like that, but not me. Besides, I'm not an actor any more, I'm a stoker."

"You were an actor, so you must know how to spin yarns."

"Do you think I'm not being honest with you?"

She lowered her head and smiled. "I'm the only one who's asked any questions. How about you?"

He mulled that over. "I don't know what to ask," he admitted.

"My uncle was right," she said. "You're not a complicated man."

When Chen had a shift change, they went to Yellow Crane Tower and read the inscriptions on the columns:

People of the past flew off on the back of a yellow crane

Here there is an empty Yellow Crane Tower

"Do you know what these words mean?" Qin asked.

"It means when people are gone, the tower's empty, doesn't it?"

"That's you and me."

"I don't get it."

"The people who were here are gone, leaving only a single man and a single woman. Doesn't that describe us?"

With a nod, Chen said, "What a pleasant surprise that you made sense out of these and I didn't."

When Chen had a day off, they went to East Lake, and as they walked along the lakeshore, Qin Jiaying asked him, "What do you normally look for in a friend?"

"I'm an ordinary stoker. I have little choice in that." After a moment's thought, he added, "I like to be around people who don't talk much."

"People like that are better than the smooth talkers, I guess."

Again, he thought a moment before saying, "That's how I see it."

"What's your son like?"

"Like me. He doesn't say much." Once again, he thought before adding, "Like most boys, he can be a little mischievous."

"My daughter is six, and I hear her sigh sometimes. What do you think that means?"

"She loves her mother, a smart girl."

For lunch, they had rice balls and hot dry noodles. When

they finished, Qin asked, "How many times have we gone out?"

"Three," he said after thinking it over.

"We've gone places, we've taken walks, and we're not getting any younger. We both have a child, and can't date like youngsters. Let me ask a serious question. Would you like to marry me?"

"No."

"Why not?"

"No place to live."

Qin was holding a rice ball; her hand froze in mid-air. "My uncle was right. You're an uncomplicated man."

Chen Changjie and Qin Jiaying were married a month later. Because she was Chief Min's niece, the division found a two-bedroom apartment for them. They each had a child, and with four people sharing an apartment, space was limited. Chen and Qin slept in one room. Mingliang and the girl, Weiwei, slept in bunk beds in the other, Weiwei on the lower bunk, Mingliang on the upper. When Chen was out on a train, Weiwei slept with her mother, leaving Mingliang alone in the room. When he slept with his father in the workers' dormitory, he'd been afraid the whole time his father was away. After moving into the apartment from the dormitory, he looked forward to his father's absences, since he could have the room to himself. When it was just him and Qin Jiaying, she never said a thing to him, keeping busy with her own chores, acting as if he didn't exist. That suited him perfectly. He could treat her as if *she* didn't exist.

TWO

Mingliang had started attending Zhima Hutong Primary School in Hankou at the age of six. One day he returned home for lunch and was greeted by a guest. "Say hello to Uncle Li. He's from our hometown," his father said.

Mingliang had left Yanjin three years earlier at the age of three and had pretty much forgotten everyone he'd known there. Li Yansheng was one of those forgotten faces, but a shock ran through him, as if sensing his mother nearby. He recalled that both his parents had worked in the Yanjin Cotton Mill, and that they'd returned home each day covered with cotton fluff. They'd argued constantly when they returned home. He was too young to understand what their arguments were about, but he kept hearing the words "sick and tired" during their fights. Ultimately, his mother hanged herself over a bunch of chives. At the time, he did not know what it meant to be sick and tired, but many years later it became clear that it could make people hang themselves or jump off a building. Decades later, he read the news on his mobile phone, and learned that people were always hanging themselves or jumping off buildings. After it happened, people would ask, "How come?" "What could be that bad?" "Why'd they do it?" Mingliang would say, "Because they were sick and tired." "How do you know?" they'd respond. He wouldn't give an answer, but he had one: "Because of my Mama."

She hanged herself on a Sunday. They'd planned on making dumplings for lunch, so after breakfast, his father had gone to the market to buy chives. Maybe they weren't fresh, who knew? But they started an argument over them. They'd been fighting awhile when she said, "I'm sick and tired." His father reacted by kicking over the spittoon at the head of the bed – people used spittoons back then – and sputtered *he* was "sick and tired". He stormed out of the house, leaving Mingliang and his mother alone inside. She was crying so hard she lay on the bed and cried herself to sleep. He picked up the overturned spittoon, wiped up the spilled contents with a rag and sat on the edge of the bed, kicking his legs. His mother woke up before long. When she saw her son sitting on the bed, she took out two ten-cent coins and said to him, "Mingliang, you love soft drinks, don't you? Go out and get one."

He took the money, but instead of going out, he stayed put, kicking his legs until his mother fell asleep again. Then he jumped down and went outside with the money to buy a soft drink. He went to a beverage stall, bought a bottle that cost fifteen cents, received five cents in change and put it in his pocket before sitting down on a step and drinking his soft drink as he watched people come and go. When he finished, he returned the empty bottle and took the change to a sweet shop, where he bought two pieces of milk candy. When he came out, he put one piece in his pocket and sat down on the step, where he unwrapped the second piece, put it in his mouth and sucked on it while continuing to watch people come and go. When the piece of candy was gone, he took the second piece out of his pocket, unwrapped it and ate it. When he'd finished both pieces, he went to the crossroads to see his grandma, where she sold date cakes. Since his mother and her in-laws had argued, the two families had nothing to do with each other, so Mingliang had to visit them without telling his mother. He liked his grandmother, but not his grandfather. She would take him by the hand, talk to him and feed him whatever they had to eat. His goateed grandfather always had a sullen look and was universally stingy. If Mingliang came by when he was alone selling the date cake, he would not give him a piece. "These cakes are for sale, not to feed our own family," he'd say.

Mingliang's grandfather was alone at the stall when the boy walked up the street. He ignored his grandson, as usual. So the boy sat down to wait for his grandmother, hoping she'd give him a piece of cake. She still hadn't shown up at noon. Mingliang was getting hungry, so he got up and walked home. By then, his mother had already hanged herself.

From that day on, Mingliang believed that if he hadn't gone out for a soft drink and milk candy, and if he hadn't waited at the stall for a date cake, everything would have been all right. If he'd stayed home or gone back earlier, his mother wouldn't have hanged herself. He could have stopped her from doing that. He believed that he'd played a role in his mother's death; who knows, maybe he was responsible? After they cut her down from the rafters, they took her to the hospital and then brought her back home, where she was put in a coffin. Mingliang sat in front of the coffin without saying anything. The chives Chen Changjie had brought home had been trampled into pulp. That night, Mingliang found a photo amid a bunch of scrap paper by the coffin. It was his mother in the role of the White Snake. He kept it. They buried her in the potter's field, after which his father took him to Wuhan. The photo he'd kept with him for three years had faded quite a bit, and his mother felt further and further away. Surprisingly, a feeling that she was there beside him after all this time had come with the unexpected arrival of the guest from Yanjin.

THREE

Yingtao had come to Wuhan to get Chen Changjie to return with her to Yanjin to move her grave out of the potter's field and away from the spirit of the executed rapist-murderer. But when she got there, she found that Chen was a different man, no longer the one she'd come looking for. When she walked into his new home and saw the objects and furnishings throughout, there was no trace of her presence anywhere, no trace of their life together. He'd forgotten her completely. Nothing wrong with that. Even if they'd been a loving couple, as long as she was alive, they'd live happily together; but if she died, the man remarried. For the two of them, especially, two years after they were married, mutual love had been replaced with "sick and tired". There were no feelings of jealousy over his marriage to Qin Jiaying, and when she saw her son, Mingliang, she felt a connection with the place. She'd come to Wuhan looking for Chen Changjie, but once she got there, she knew her search had really been for her son. She'd come to get Chen to return to Yanjin with her, but now that she was here, she changed her mind. She no longer wanted to go back to Yanjin; now she wanted to be with Mingliang. Four people occupying the two-bedroom flat became five. She would take up no room, would eat nothing, would not cause them any trouble. She could ignore Chen, Qin and Weiwei, going to school with Mingliang in the daytime and sleeping with him at night.

By staying away from Yanjin, the vicious ghost in the potter's field could not follow her without attaching itself to a human. She was rid of him, and there was no need to move her grave. Her good feelings about this place stemmed not only from her son's presence, but also because he carried a photograph of her youthful self with him. Without that photo, there would be nothing for her to attach herself to; she could only attach herself to a relative or someone very close. If she attached herself to Mingliang or Chen, they would fall ill, not a workable solution. But since the photo was always with Mingliang, she could be with her son morning, noon and night.

Another reason Yingtao had come to Wuhan was to get Chen to teach her some jokes. Once she'd learned fifty funny one-liners, she'd return to Yanjin, repeat them to King Yama and earn the right to be reborn. But in Wuhan, she discovered that Chen had lost the ability to tell jokes. More than that, he had become a man of few words. Big Mouth Wu, who'd sold tripe soup in Beiguan, had become a smooth talker after he died, and Chen Changjie had swapped places with him. Now that Chen could no longer tell jokes, Yingtao had no means of acquiring fifty funny one-liners, and no way of getting King Yama to let her be reborn. Remaining on the wheel of Samsara, she would return to Yanjin still a spirit. Why not stay in Wuhan and be with her son all the time?

Yingtao went to school with Mingliang for two days. On the street, she discovered that Wuhan was a very sombre city; the people simply did not tell jokes. In that respect, it was quite different from Yanjin, where Hua Erniang waited in your dreams to hear you tell a joke. She was now also rid of Hua Erniang. Sombre was good, it suited her personality, she was thinking. Yet another reason to stay there. But at night, she was given to sighing. If your hometown is good, or your life in your hometown improved, who would willingly drift around in other places? Now that she had turned her back on her hometown, leaving Yanjin for Wuhan, she did not rely on King Yama, but on herself, and removed herself from the wheel of Samsara. But what would her life be about? A photograph? She sighed again.

FOUR

Mingliang discovered that since he felt the presence of his mother, the photo of her he'd kept with him had brightened up. Not only that, he could hear her speak to him.

"Mingliang."

"Ma."

"I came from our home in Yanjin to see you."

"I could feel you."

"Do you want me to leave you?"

"No."

"I don't want to leave you either, but you might be afraid having me with you."

"I'm not afraid."

"Mingliang, you can't tell anybody about this. I won't be able to stay with you if people know."

"I won't tell anybody."

When mother and son were talking, only Mingliang could hear her. Sometimes, when the family was eating, he would abruptly stop and start talking to himself. And sometimes he did that when he was out walking.

"What are you mumbling about, Mingliang?" his father would ask.

"Nothing." He'd hurriedly make excuses. "I'm memorising schoolwork in case the teacher calls on me today."

It took two weeks for Qin Jiaying to find out about Yingtao. And it was all Yingtao's fault. She'd planned to be the fifth, silent member of the family, concerned only about Mingliang, not the others. At first, here is how she went about it: she went to school with him during the day and slept with him at night. After he fell asleep, she'd remove herself from the photo and tidy up his school bag and his uniform, cleaning off food stains. Chen and his wife noticed that Mingliang was neater than before, assuming only that he was growing up. A week later, however, Yingtao did something that revealed her secret. After Mingliang fell asleep, she tidied up and cleaned his uniform and then went over to the doorway to clean his shoes. She heard sounds coming from one of the rooms that told her Chen and his wife were having sex. She froze, recalling that after two years of marriage, she and Chen had stopped having sex because Chen could no longer get it up. That was one of the problems leading to "sick and tired". Maybe if they'd been able to enjoy the marital bed, things wouldn't have fallen apart. He could do it with someone else, so why couldn't he do it with her? It must have been her fault. She kept listening, and as her anger mounted, knowing she couldn't make them stop, she went into the bathroom and tossed Qin Jiaying's underwear into the toilet.

Qin went into the bathroom the next morning, only to find her underwear floating in the toilet. Had she hung it on the rack carelessly the night before? She didn't let the fact that it had fallen into the toilet upset her. But then she discovered that every time she and Chen had sex, her underwear was floating in the toilet the next morning. Something was fishy. At first, she thought Mingliang was doing it to vent over what she assumed was jealousy and malcontent with his stepmother. But then, his uniform had been spotless recently, and he was always talking to himself, as if having a conversation with someone, so there had to be another answer. She didn't tell Chen about her doubts, in case she was wrong. When he went out on a train, Weiwei came in to sleep with her mother.

"Weiwei," she asked her daughter, "you share a room with Mingliang. Have you noticed anything different than before?"

"He's always talking to himself."

"I know that. Anything else?"

"He used to go to sleep right after he took off his clothes, but now, before he does that, he stares at a little photograph."

Late that night, Jiaying sneaked into Mingliang's room. Seeing he was asleep, she went through his clothes at the foot of the bed and found the photo in his pocket. She no sooner had it in her hand than a red glow emanated from it, so shocking her it fell from her fingers. When she bent down to pick it up, the red glow stunned her. She tingled all over and knew there was something very strange about it. Rushing back into her room, she put on the rubber gloves she used to wash the dishes and returned to Mingliang's room, where she picked up the photograph. This time it had no effect on her, so she took a close look at the image. It was Yingtao. She'd seen a picture of Chen's first wife the night before they were married. They were putting their new flat in order at the time.

"Let me see what your first wife looked like," she'd said to him.

"What for?"

"Just curious."

He took a picture out of his wallet and handed it to her. It had been taken a month after Mingliang was born. They'd taken him to a Yanjin photo studio to have it made. Yingtao was seated on a stool, holding Mingliang in her arms, Chen standing beside her. The backdrop was a painting of a vase with a spray of winter jasmine on top of a stool.

"She's pretty," Jiaying said.

"She put on make-up before we went to the studio. Actors are make-up experts. It makes them look good."

"How did she die?"

"Emphysema," he lied.

"Now that I've seen your ex," Jiaying said, "would you like to see a picture of mine?"

Chen shook his head.

"Why not?"

"Don't see any value in it."

She nodded her agreement. "There is no value in it."

Now Jiaying was looking at the photo of Yingtao that Mingliang had kept in his pocket, and she understood why she kept finding her underwear floating in the toilet. There was value in the photo.

"It's you," she said. "So, you've come to Wuhan. A good thing I'd seen your picture. Are you planning on breaking up our marriage? You're here to get revenge, aren't you?"

She went into the other room, where she wrapped the photo in a sheet of thin plastic so it could no longer emit a charge. Keeping the photo on her, she whispered to Weiwei, "Don't say anything about tonight to Mingliang's daddy."

The girl nodded.

In the morning, Mingliang discovered that his mother's photo was missing. Although he shared a room with Weiwei, they did not call one another brother or sister. They chatted and never argued, though they were not close. He figured she'd taken the photo, even though she'd slept with her mother during the night since his father was away on a train. All her things were in the room they shared, so before she went to bed, she'd have to come in for her sleepwear and return in the morning to get her school books.

When she came in, he asked her, "A photo of mine must have fallen out of my pocket last night. Did you see it?"

"No."

At breakfast, Mingliang said to his stepmother, "A photo of mine must have fallen out of my pocket last night. Did you see it when you were sweeping?"

"A photo? I don't know anything about it."

After the children had left for school, Jiaying took the photo to see the one-time Daoist nun Ma Dao Po in Hankou's western suburb. She'd been a nun at the Baique Nunnery before returning to secular life and opening a Daoist temple, where she told fortunes. She was also adept at the art of dispelling demons and spirits, human and ghost. Like everyone who came to see Ma Dao Po, Qin Jiaying had encountered an evil spirit, so she went to the western suburb and found the Daoist's house, where she told her everything.

"This won't be hard to manage if we know who created the problem. Let me see the photo."

Jiaying handed her the plastic-wrapped photo.

"Go up front to pay and leave everything to me. And don't worry, this spirit won't be going anywhere."

Mingliang's mother came to him in a dream that night. She appeared to be writhing in a briar patch.

"Mingliang, you have to come save me, this is killing me. I don't want to stay in Wuhan, I want to go home to Yanjin."

Mingliang woke up sweat-soaked. He'd thought that losing the photo had him thinking crazy thoughts, so he went back to sleep. But then she entered his dream the next night, still writhing in a briar patch, pleading with him to save her. This time he knew his mother was in serious trouble.

"You want me to save you, Ma, but where are you?"

"I don't know Wuhan and I can't tell you where I am."

"How can I find you if I don't know where you are?"

Yingtao burst into tears. "I guess I'm going to be like the White Snake, held under a pagoda forever."

At that moment, another voice spoke to Mingliang: "I know where your mother is."

"Can you take me to find her?"

"Yes," the voice said. "But if I help you today, when you return to Wuhan decades from now, you'll have to help me."

"Who are you?"

"You'll know when the time comes."

Mingliang stealthily dressed and followed the voice out the door and onto the street. At that hour, the street was deserted. He did not know which way to go as he listened for the voice.

"Come with me," he heard it say.

That is when Mingliang discovered that the voice was coming from a firefly. He followed it as it flew along. One intersection after another, one lane followed by another, on and on until they were in Hankou's western suburb. The firefly led Mingliang up to a small compound, where it passed through a bamboo fence. Mingliang climbed over it. The firefly flew up to a thatched hut. Mingliang came up and pushed open the door. A small glow emanated from a lantern in the centre of the room. The image of a person hung on the opposite wall. Years later, when he was an adult, Mingliang would know that the image was of Yama, King of Hell. A green-faced, fanged person standing beside the image was chewing on a little demon. As an adult, Mingliang would know it was Zhongkui, the demon chaser. Images – photos and drawings – were nailed onto a board standing atop a table in front of the image on the wall. The photo of Mingliang's mother was one of them. It was covered with needles. He unhesitatingly pried the needles out of the photo and took it off the board. She was crying.

"You came, Mingliang," she said to her son. "There are burns all over my body."

"What can I do?"

"Find some water and put me in it. The water will take care of it."

"This is a suburb I've never been to. I don't know where to find water."

"Follow me," the firefly said.

Holding the photo close to his chest, Mingliang followed the firefly out of the compound. They passed one intersection after another, one lane followed by another, on and on until a great opening appeared. They had reached the Yangtze. The moon over the choppy water made the river look as bright as it would in daytime.

"Ma, I'll toss you into the Yangtze, all right?"

"Go ahead. I used to be afraid of water, but no longer."

Mingliang tossed the photo of his mother in her youth into the Yangtze. In a split second, she emerged from the photo dressed like the character Bai Niangzi in *Legend of the White Snake*. At this moment, she was no longer his mother but had become the White Snake. She swished her long sleeves and, hovering above the river, began to sing the aria in which she denounces both Fahai and Xu Xian. The mournful notes penetrated the cloud cover. The firefly flew into the sky and exploded, sending fireworks raining down and filling the air with brilliant colours. Only Mingliang could see it and only he could hear the melody. He understood that though his mother had said she was afraid of water, the needles all over her body had created scars that did not fear water. He recalled what she'd said in his dream, that she wanted to return to Yanjin.

"Ma, you can stop singing. Return to Yanjin if you want to. That way, no one will be able to nail you to a board again."

A huge wave billowed up. His mother shouted "Forty-five..." as the wave caught her up and, in front of her son, swept her down the river and out of sight. What had she meant by "forty-five"? Mingliang assumed she was returning to Yanjin. He'd learned in his third-grade geography class that Yanjin was up north, while the Yangtze flowed east. She'd never get back to Yanjin if the Yangtze kept carrying her along.

So, where did she go?

APPENDIX

A CONVERSATION IN THE WOODSHED

As she was being nailed to the board, neither able to live nor die, she said to King Yama, "I know I was wrong, King. I said I was going to return to Yanjin, but I should not have gone back on what I said and stayed in Wuhan."

Before Yama said anything, Zhongkui, who was standing next to him, swung his iron staff. "There is no spot under Heaven that does not belong to the King. You thought that by going to Wuhan you could escape the grasp of the King, didn't you? You thought you could remove yourself from the cycle of Samsara."

"I never intended to remove myself from the cycle, King," she lied. "Didn't you yourself once say that those who are flattened by jokes could be reborn by telling fifty funny one-liners? In the days since I came to Wuhan, in addition to seeing my son, I came up with five one-liners on my own. If you will release me, I'll tell you those five, how's that?"

Again, before Yama said anything, Zhongkui commanded, "He said fifty, not five. This is the underworld, not your land of the living. The King stresses impartiality and incorruptibility. Otherwise, there would be ghosts of the wronged everywhere. You've thought up five, you need forty-five more. Keep thinking."

Mingliang came to fetch his mother's photograph late at night. Zhongkui made as if to hit him with his iron staff

"Forty-five to go."

Mingliang did not understand what he said, of course. Yama stayed Zhongkui's hand. "Did you not say there is no spot under Heaven that does not belong to the King? Let her go, and we'll see what she encounters over those forty-five jokes. Maybe something strange and fantastic will come from those encounters, which will be like another joke to us."

Zhongkui understood. He put down his iron staff.

FIVE

Mingliang's seventy-year-old grandmother came to Wuhan. When he was born, his mother named him Hanlin. When he started to talk, he said, "Everything is dark." His granny changed his name to Mingliang – Bright.

Granny's home was on Yanjin's North Avenue, in a compound with a date tree so big it took two people to gird it. Granny said the tree was two hundred years old, having been planted by Mingliang's great-great-grandfather, a camel trader. The date seedling had been transported from Ruojiang County in Xinjiang. After two centuries, it still boasted lush foliage and produced three full burlap sacks of dates each autumn. Mingliang's grandparents mixed the dates with millet to produce date cakes, which they sold from a handcart on the street. At night, they added a salt lamp to the cart. At the time, both of Mingliang's parents worked at the county cotton mill, which operated three shifts. Neither of them had time to look after their son, so before he turned three, he stayed with Granny. At bedtime, he loved to hear Granny's stories. The term they used was "chats".

They'd lie in bed, and Mingliang would say, "Let's have another chat, Granny."

"All right, if you say so."

Decades later, Mingliang recalled his three favourite "chats". One was about weasels. When she was a girl, Granny would say, they had a weasel problem in their back garden, and late at night, the mother would gambol with her brood of kittens. Granny's father would say, "Hey, weasel, knock it off and let us sleep." "Don't want to," the weasel would respond. Her kittens would rise up on their hind legs and line up with their paws on each other's shoulders, mother in the lead, and pass in front of the back window, wiggling their rear ends. One stormy night, there was a knock at the door. When Granny's father opened it, there stood the adult weasel. She bowed with her paws clasped. "Thunder God is coming for us. Will you hide me and my many kittens, sir?" "You're acting like a coward," he said. "I'm not acting." "Then are you trying to make trouble?" "No."

Granny's father went into the garden, opened the door of a thatch hut and let the family of weasels inside. The sky cleared the next morning, so Granny's father went out to the hut, only to find it empty – no weasels, except for one with a limp cowering in a corner. The mother had left this one behind. Granny's father heaved a sigh. "You're a clever one, old weasel, leaving this lame one for me." He put it into the pig pen to raise as a pig. Granny said she used to play with the little weasel when she was a girl, but even after more than a decade, the little weasel hadn't grown bigger. "How come you aren't growing up, little weasel?" "Because I'm a pig, and I'll be slaughtered if I get bigger." The day Granny left home to get married, the little weasel cried.

Another chat involved an ox. Granny told him she and the ox were born in the same year. "There are two kinds of oxen," Granny said, "lazy ones and tenacious ones. When lazy ones are yoked, they dawdle over their work, but tenacious oxen are happy to work." This particular ox was more tenacious than other tenacious oxen. Put in front of a plough, it worked tirelessly from morning to night, driving the ploughman to exhaustion. One day, Granny's third uncle went out to plough the field. A lazy man, he grasped the reins and said, "Slow down, will you? What's your hurry?" After an hour, Third Uncle crouched down to smoke his pipe. The ox pleaded with him, "Can you speed it up a little? It'll take forever to plough this field if you don't." "You'll kill me at this rate," Uncle said. "Whose land is this, anyway, your family's or mine? Keep it up, and I'll send you to the slaughterhouse." This made the ox mad as hell. It shook off the yoke and reins and kicked Third Uncle to the ground, then ran off to the mountains. Third Uncle formed a posse to go after it, but they knew they'd never find it among all the trees and shrubs. They rounded a bend in the mountain path and spotted an old woman with a bundle thrown over her shoulders as she took a rest. "Have you seen an ox running around her, Madam?" "An ox? No. There's a cat sleeping at my feet, does it look anything like your ox?" They looked down at a tabby cat sound asleep at her feet.

"Know who the old woman was?" Granny asked.

"No, who?"

"The Mountain Goddess, and the ox was really her cat. She'd turned it into an ox after it ate her cake with moulded designs and sent it down to plough fields. It could return after it had ploughed five hundred hectares. That's why it was so tenacious."

The third chat was about Granny's father. Her mother had died young, leaving all the work inside and outside the house to her father. The day she was married, her father said to her, "I was a father, my daughter, but could not be a mother. It's been hard on you all these seventeen years. Now that you're getting married, I didn't know what to do for you. I can't sew clothes or make mattress covers, so I cut down an elm tree and made you a chest of drawers as your dowry." "Father," she said, "all these years you've done everything around the house, inside and out, and done it well. I can't imagine a better present than this chest of drawers. Every time I look at it, I'll think of you. But now I'm getting married, I worry about you here all alone." "You don't have to worry, I can look after myself."

Her father died the year after she was married. That spring, she went into her room one night to open her elm chest of drawers to take out some wool she'd spun in the winter, planning to put it on her loom the next day. Seeing the chest reminded her of her father. "I miss you, Father," she said without thinking. "Don't worry," came a voice outside the window, "you can still see me." When she ran out into the yard, there was no one there. But then she sensed that it was the voice of the weasel, though it had been dead for at least six years. She searched and searched, but there was no trace of a weasel, and she soon forgot all about what had happened.

"Believe it or not," she said to Mingliang, "I took your father to the market one day when he was nine. Among the throng of people, I saw a man walking along eating out of a bowl. From the back it looked like my father, so I ran after him, but he disappeared into a crowd of people.

"I saw my father's back that day," she continued with a sigh.

Mingliang listened to his granny talk till he fell asleep.

A heavy rain fell when Mingliang was three. It rained for two days and two nights. There was water everywhere. Mingliang went to the water hole with a bunch of kids to throw dirt clods at frogs. Carelessly, he fell in. When Granny heard the other kids running around yelling, she ran to the water hole, where Mingliang was floating on top, apparently drowned. With the help of others, hand holding hand, they fished the boy out. Granny laid him out over a stone roller, where, with a "wa" he coughed up all the water he'd taken in and he came back to life. She cried, and so did he.

"Don't ever tell your mother or father."

He nodded, but Yingtao found out about it anyway. How? Mingliang told her. Still a little boy, he always told his mother what she wanted to know. He'd forgotten what Granny had said to him. He told his mother about all of Granny's chats, which made her very angry.

"We can forget about our son almost drowning, but she fills his mind with a bunch of nonsense."

"I'll talk to her," Chen promised. "No more chats."

"That's not all. We're not going to leave him with her from now on."

The very next morning, Yingtao enrolled Mingliang in the mill kindergarten. "Let him learn something real." She also had Chen tell his mother not to come and see Mingliang any time she wanted. But Granny sneaked over to the kindergarten when Yingtao was at work. She'd bring him slices of his favourite cake and his favourite soft drink. While he was eating and drinking, she'd say, "Don't tell your mother this time."

Mingliang had started school because he'd told his mother the truth. He was not happy there, especially with what the teacher said. He wished he could be back with Granny, listening to her chats again. That would not happen, but he'd learned his lesson, and wouldn't tell Yingtao that Granny came to see him. When she didn't come, there would be no cake or soft drink. But three months later, it didn't make a difference, because his mother had hanged herself. Granny could come to see him any time she wanted, but then Chen Changjie took the boy with him to Wuhan. He did not see his granny for three years, and when she came to Wuhan, she exclaimed, "My, how you've grown!"

Then she said, "When you were very little, you said everything was dark. Is that still true?"

Granny was sort of a stranger to Mingliang, and when she asked him that, he just shook his head. She took some date cake out of her bag for everyone, and as he ate, the unfamiliarity faded away.

"I haven't had a soft drink in a long time," he said, suddenly reminded.

"We'll get you some tomorrow."

With Granny's arrival, the two-bedroom flat was too small to accommodate them all, so after dinner, Qin Jiaying took her daughter with her to her parents' home. Granny moved in with Mingliang, Chen Changjie had the other room to himself.

"Granny," Mingliang said when they were in bed, "I'd like to hear more chats. I haven't heard one in a long time."

"I haven't given a thought to those for a long time and can't think of one right now."

"You can tell me one of the older ones again."

So she repeated the ones about the weasel and her father and the ox. Back in Yanjin, Mingliang would fall asleep after one of her chats. But in Wuhan, the more he listened to her, the less drowsy he felt.

"Mingliang," she said when she saw he was not sleeping, "you haven't seen your grandmother for three years. Would you like to tell me a story now?"

The boy thought about telling her how Yingtao had come to Wuhan, but then she had been nailed to a board and was covered with scars before being flung into the Yangtze, where she'd been tossed by the waves and disappeared. So frightened by what had happened, he chose not to tell Granny.

"I don't have anything to tell, Granny."

Decades later, after not "chatting" with his grandmother that time, there was no one he could chat with and no opportunity to do so. The tale stayed buried deep inside him, where it stayed forever. Mingliang could only sigh.

The next day was a Sunday, and Chen Changjie took them both for a walk. Granny bought a soft drink for Mingliang in a corner shop. They had hot dry noodles for lunch before leaving for Yellow Crane Tower. Wuchang fish for dinner. Chen was off on the train Monday morning, leaving Mingliang and his grandmother alone at home. She took him to school first thing in the morning and picked him up at noon for lunch, then took him back to school. She picked him up again when school was out in the afternoon. They talked in bed that night.

"Why did you come to Wuhan, Granny?"

"To visit my grandson."

"Why?"

"Because of a dream."

"What did you dream?"

"Someone said to me, 'You should go see Mingliang.'"

"Who was it?"

"I didn't get a good look at the face, but it sounded like your grandfather."

"Didn't he die?"

"Two years already."

"Granny, were there any dates on our tree this year?"

"More than ever. I think we'll need four burlap bags this year for them. Do you like it here in Wuhan, Mingliang?"

He shook his head.

"Why not? Does your stepmother treat you badly?"

It wasn't wrong to say she treated him badly, because she ignored him. What really scared him wasn't his stepmother, but what had happened to his real mother in Wuhan. Someone had stuck needles all over her, but he couldn't tell his grandmother.

"Can you and I go back to Yanjin, Granny?"

"We can't do that, you've got school here. Wuhan is a big city."

"Then you stay here and don't go back to Yanjin, all right?"

"If I did, Weiwei and her mother would have no room here. Besides," she continued, "I have to be back in the autumn to harvest dates."

She was ready to return to Yanjin in two weeks. Chen Changjie, Qin Jiaying and the two children went to the train station with Granny. Mingliang took her hand as she was boarding.

"Granny, when will you come here again?"

"After I've harvested the dates."

"You're not lying to me are you, Granny?"

"No, I'm not."

The train pulled out of the station.

A month later, Chen Changjie received a telegram telling him that Granny had died. Years later, Mingliang recalled that she had come to Wuhan a month before she died to see him one last time. He also remembered that she'd come to see him after his grandfather had told her to in a dream. Maybe he did that because he knew she'd be gone soon. He also missed his grandson, thinking how, when he was alive, he refused to give the boy any date cake.

"She was just fine a month ago," Chen Changjie said. "And she even visited Wuhan. It's a good thing she came, so we could see each other one last time."

Chen planned to return to Yanjin for the funeral. Mingliang wanted to go with him.

"You're still in school," his father said. "You'll fall behind if you're away. And there's nothing you could do if you were there."

Mingliang went to school the day his father left for Yanjin. The lesson that day was arithmetic, but Mingliang was so restless, he didn't hear a word the teacher said. When class was over, he threw his school bag over his shoulder and left the playground during the break. Instead of going home, he went to the railway station. He had more than thirty yuan in his bag, twenty from Uncle Li Yansheng when he came to Wuhan; the other ten was saved-up New Year's money. He bought a child's ticket to Xinxiang in Henan. Two trains were waiting at separate platforms, one on its way to Beijing from Guangzhou, the other heading to Guangzhou from Beijing. Since Henan was north of Wuhan, he should have boarded the train to Beijing. But he got on the one heading south to Guangzhou. The train was so crowded, he had to stand in the space between two carriages. The swaying of the train put him to sleep almost immediately; he didn't wake up till the following morning when the train pulled into a station called Zhuzhou.

The conductor checking tickets told him he'd taken a train heading in the wrong direction, so he got off. He now had only three yuan, not enough to buy another ticket, so he asked for directions and started walking, begging for food along the way. He reached Yanjin two months later and went straight to Granny's house on North Avenue. Leaves covered the ground in front of the empty house. The two-hundred-year-old date tree was gone. At noon, Mr Pei, who lived next door, went out back to fetch firewood and spotted a crying boy he'd never seen before trying to get into the neighbouring house. He walked over.

"Who are you?"

Mingliang was crying so hard he couldn't talk. Mr Pei noticed that the boy was wearing only one shoe and a thin jacket that was in tatters. Then it came to him.

"You're Mingliang, aren't you? It's been two months. We thought you were lost."

He still could not speak, but his crying had drawn a crowd.

Li Yansheng, who was working in the market, heard the commotion and ran up. "Do you recognise me, Mingliang? I'm Uncle Yansheng. I saw you in Wuhan some six months ago."

Still, Mingliang was crying too hard to speak. Li tried to pull his hands away from his face. Mingliang wouldn't let go.

"I'll take you to see your granny," Li said to the boy.

Mingliang took down his hands as Mr Pei ran inside to get one of his children's winter coats and a pair of warm shoes. He put them on and followed Li Yansheng to the family plot outside of town, where Li pointed out the grave site of his grandparents.

Mingliang ran up to it and bawled, "Granny, you said after you picked dates you'd come back to Wuhan, didn't you? You lied to me. Who's going to tell me stories now that you're gone? I've got a story I want to tell you."

He cried nonstop for three hours.

Li Yansheng took Mingliang's hand and headed back.

"Where's the date tree that was in Granny's garden, Uncle?"

"The tree died not even a month after your granny, before the harvest. Strange, don't you think?"

Li took Mingliang home and placed a call to Chen

Changjie in Wuhan. He explained how the boy had reached Yanjin. Chen arrived three mornings later.

"You frightened me to death," he said to his son. "I thought you were gone for good. Your stepmother was as scared as I was. She also thought you were gone. She said she never hit you. Come home with me now. Your granny's gone."

Mingliang shook his head vigorously.

"When we get home, you have to go back to school."

"I'm not going back to Wuhan, not even if you beat me to death."

"Why not? Is it because of your stepmother?"

It wasn't wrong to say it was her, because she ignored him. What really scared him wasn't his stepmother, but what had happened to his real mother in Wuhan. Someone had stuck needles all over her, but he couldn't tell his father; he knew he wouldn't believe him. Seen from one angle, Granny's death had given Mingliang an excuse to not go back to Wuhan, but to stay in Yanjin.

"It's not because of her. She treated me fine. Wuhan doesn't feel right to me. Only Yanjin feels right. If you force me to go back, I'll jump into the Yangtze River."

SIX

So Li Yansheng and Chen Changjie were meeting again. Li did not mention Yingtao or ask what happened with her in Wuhan. Some six months earlier, he had carried her to Wuhan. During those six months, many things had occurred in Chen's life: his mother had died, his son had travelled alone to Yanjin. Li knew this was not the time to bring up Yingtao's name, for recent events had overshadowed those of the past. On this night, Li invited Chen to a meal of pigs' feet at Marshal Tianpeng's Cafe.

"As soon as I arrived," Chen said, "I couldn't help recalling our time in the drama troupe and the factory."

"I know what you mean. The cafe hasn't changed, but we have."

"This business about Mingliang, I've got an idea. I don't know if it sounds all right."

"What is it?"

"The way he is now, I don't think I can take him back to Wuhan. He and his stepmother don't seem to get along. On the surface, everything seems fine, but they're wary of each other. If I force him to go back with me, he could run away again, and I'd have to try to find him. This time in Yanjin, finding him was easy, but what if he goes somewhere else? How do I find him then?"

"He's headstrong. I could see that when I went to Wuhan."

"So why not let him stay in Yanjin, here with you? I've been watching how he is with you these past few days, and I like what I see. Now that his grandmother is dead, there's no one in Yanjin for either of us."

"That shows a lot of trust in me, Changjie. Before we were both married, we could easily resolve any issue between the two of us. Keeping the boy with me for a few months wouldn't be a problem. But if he's here to stay, he becomes another mouth to feed. I'll need to talk it over at home."

"Discuss it with your wife, tell her I don't expect you to spend your own money on Mingliang. I can send you thirty yuan each month. That'd make it easy to win her over, wouldn't it?"

"That sounds easy, but how will you get by in Wuhan if you send us that money? What would *your* wife say?"

"I make good wages on the trains, and there's a travel allowance. I can take on a few more shifts for overtime. It would be on top of my regular pay, and my wife wouldn't know the difference."

Li Yansheng went home, and when it was time to go to bed, he told his wife about taking in the boy for an additional thirty yuan a month. She could not agree fast enough. He only earned a bit more than sixty a month selling all that soy sauce, vinegar and pickled vegetables, as well as peppercorns, anise and fermented tofu; she earned a little over fifty wrapping sweets in the factory. Taking in the boy was like adding a part-time worker to the family.

Early the next morning, Li Yansheng took Chen Changjie out for some spicy soup, where he told him what he and his wife had decided. Later that morning, Chen took his son out to buy him a soft drink and told him that if he didn't want to return to Wuhan, he could stay with Li Yansheng and his wife. What did he think of that?

"I don't care who I stay with as long as I don't have to go back with you."

So the next week, Mingliang was enrolled in Yanjin West Avenue Primary School as a year two transfer student. Old Dong's son, Dong Guangsheng, and Guo Baochen's son, Guo Zikai, were in the same class. From year two to year five, Mingliang and Guangsheng shared a desk.

Twenty Years Later

ONE

Nearly all of Mingliang's secondary school friends showed up at his wedding. The master of ceremonies was Dong Guangsheng. Guo Zikai, who was a graduate student in Beijing, decided to travel to Yanjin for the ceremony. Another schoolmate, Feng Mingchao, a purchasing agent for a department store in Zhengzhou, also took a leave of absence to attend. They were Mingliang's best men.

The twenty-six-year-old groom was a cook at Marshal Tianpeng's Cafe. Ten years earlier, in his first year of secondary school, Mingliang had decided to quit school, not because he didn't like it, but because of a letter he'd received from his father in Wuhan. In it, Chen had explained how he'd left Mingliang in Yanjin in the care of Li Yansheng, with the condition that he would give Yansheng thirty yuan a month. But over the years, as prices and costs spiralled upwards, by the time his son was sixteen, the monthly payment had risen to fifteen hundred yuan. The whole time, the boy's stepmother was unaware that her husband was sending Li money he earned by working more shifts. None of his fellow workers was willing to work overtime, but he'd had to beg for it and then conceal it from Qin Jiaying, a secret she'd discovered the previous month in spite of him.

Chen had sent a cash remittance from the post office every month before leaving on one of the trains. He'd pocketed the receipts. His wife had found one when she was doing the laundry. Immediately upon his return, she'd demanded answers. He'd lied by saying it was a loan to Li. Unconvinced, she'd gone to the finance department, where she learned that he'd earned overtime pay he hadn't brought home. Once again, she'd demanded answers, and this time he had to come clean, telling her it was an allowance for raising Mingliang. She'd wept when he told her. "I don't mind that you're paying your son's living expenses, but that you kept it from me. How could you not believe I'd have been understanding? We've been together ten years," she'd said, "and you haven't been honest with me. It's not about the money. But every month he gets money from you, which is a monthly reminder to hate me."

In the letter to his son, Chen had written that the real reason he'd chosen not to tell his stepmother ten years earlier was that he'd figured the less trouble the better; he told her only that the boy had become Li's adopted son, with no mention of money. When it was uncovered after ten years, it was too late to do anything about it. The Chen of ten years before had tripped up the Chen of ten years later. What made it awkward was that Mingliang knew nothing about the money his father had sent Li Yansheng all those months. In the letter, Chen had written that Qin Jiaying had cried when she found out, but more than that, she'd gone to the finance department and had all his subsequent wages, bonuses and overtime deposited into her bank account. Telling him what she'd done, she said there'd be no more monthly payments for his son, who would have no reason to keep hating her. "If he needs living expenses, he can come to Wuhan and confess that you and he hid this from me, and that he'd hated me for it for ten years. Then we can talk about living expenses." Chen wrote that she'd said this in anger, to punish him for what he'd done. She told him to sever relations with Mingliang, as if he'd formally adopted him out to Li Yansheng ten years before. She was settling the score for all those years.

"I'm stuck now," he wrote. "I tripped myself up, and have no money to send for your living expenses. What will you do now? I can't come up with a solution. I can only hope that Li and his wife will raise you as their own son.

"My heart is broken when I think that as a father I can't even provide for my own son. In the final analysis, you should write your father off as a failure." He'd concluded the letter by writing, "You know I'm a fifty-year-old man who's had health issues in recent years, and since your stepmother won't let me support you financially, I'll stop working overtime."

Mingliang read the letter but did not reply. He didn't know how. He'd not known about the living expenses his father had sent, and now that there would be no more, he could not force him to continue. Maybe Chen Changjie was the architect of the whole mess. Paying for a son's expenses is a time-honoured tradition. He shouldn't have kept that a secret from his wife and even lied to her in the process. Naturally, he lacked the confidence to raise the issue because he was afraid she would object. He feared her objection not solely over this incident, but over all sorts of issues. He was afraid of what might happen even before he brought it up, so he'd lied to avoid unnecessary trouble. Better to keep it secret.

For his living expenses, Mingliang could go to Wuhan to apologise to his stepmother, but when he considered her anger over a matter that spanned ten years, even if both he and Chen Changjie apologised, she would find something else to settle accounts. Even ten years is not too long to exact revenge. Maybe this situation perfectly fitted the definition. Besides, since Mingliang knew nothing about his father sending the money, what did *he* have to apologise for? No, a trip to Wuhan was out. It would probably be a waste of time anyway. He'd have to keep pretending to Li Yansheng that he knew nothing about it. And there would be no more money coming from Chen Changjie, that was a fact. As for his relationship with his father, they'd had no direct contact, so this would be no different. After reading the letter, Mingliang went to a river in the Yanjin suburbs and burned it.

Having nothing more to do with his father made no difference to Mingliang; it did, however, make a difference to Li Yansheng. When the next month rolled around, the money did not roll in, which meant that Mingliang's living expenses, including those at school, would have to be borne by Li and his wife. They let it go the first month; the next month, Li let it go, but his wife looked unhappy. During the third month, Hu Xiaofeng made veiled accusations over trivial matters. Li Yansheng could only sigh. Mingliang quit school after the third month and left their house, taking an apprenticeship at Marshal Tianpeng's Cafe, a job his geography teacher had found for him. The owner, a Mr Zhu, loved to sing opera, which he did whenever he had a free moment. Mingliang's teacher, Mr Jiao, shared Zhu's passion for opera, and when the two of them got together, they sang operas like *A Fisherman's Struggle* and *The Butterfly Lovers*. Cafe owner Zhu sang the lead roles, while geography teacher Jiao sang the woman's part. When Mr Jiao saw that Mingliang had come to a dead end, the next time he sang opera with Mr Zhu, he described his student's situation in operatic form: "Dear husband, see this child, orphaned with no country to call his own, be merciful and take him in. The principle is that no good deed is too small to perform."

Mr Zhu laughed heartily and responded in daily speech: "Old Jiao, pigs' feet are hard to cook. Is the boy lazy?"

"No, not a lazy lad. I would never bring a lazy lad to you."

"A lazy lad would never last here."

Mingliang began his apprenticeship the very next day. He received room and board, but no wages. His first job was to debristle pigs' feet that were sent over from the Yanjin slaughterhouse in buckets, picking them clean of bristles one at a time. In the past, they were scraped with a knife and looked clean, though customers found that there were still bristles in the meat. Now they were covered by a paste made of boiling natural bitumen, and the remaining bristles could be removed with a tweezer. The cleaned feet were placed in fresh water and then in a salt-and-pepper-infused brine to be pickled. Mingliang could finish three hundred pigs' feet a day.

The cafe opened at eleven each morning. By three o'clock in the afternoon, all the lunch diners had left, so they shut the door until six in the evening and then stayed open till nearly midnight. The staff rested between the hours of three and six, all but the apprentice, who kept debristling feet out back. Sometimes, at five in the afternoon, once the debristling was finished, Mingliang had an hour to catch his breath. Most of the workers went home to rest during break periods, but since he had no home to go to, and did not want to go to Li Yansheng's place, he stayed in the cafe. Of course, he could go out onto the street or stroll to the ferry landing, where people tended to congregate. But as an unsalaried apprentice, he had no money to spend, not even enough to buy a soft drink. Going there would be a waste of time. So he stayed in, partly to avoid running into former schoolmates, who would wonder why a student had stopped coming to school. Explaining it to them would take more time than it was worth, so why bother? When he was free, he went out back to be alone by the river. Every summer evening, owner Zhu installed electric lamps by riverside tables. It became a favourite spot for diners to enjoy a drink and pigs' feet. Cool breezes were refreshing, but summers meant mosquitoes, so he placed mosquito-repellent incense under each table. A field where wheat grew in the spring and corn in the autumn lay just across the bridge. Early each morning, Mr Zhu would come to the riverbank and sing opera to the field on the other side. The field and riverbank were deserted at five o'clock, when Mingliang came out, crossed the bridge and went into the field to take out a flute and play it, a skill he'd learned from his school friend Feng Mingchao. The boy's uncle was a flautist in the county wedding and funeral band. Mingchao had been raised in an aunt's house, where he'd picked up the flute by watching and listening to his uncle play. He told Mingliang he'd learned from his uncle that the key to playing the flute is to use the proper breathing technique in order to play high notes and hold them. Only by playing high notes and holding them with the right modulation can a flautist produce a melodious sound. Stopping to take a breath while playing is bad practice. Real flautists breathe without interrupting the playing. In addition to the breathing technique, there is tone manipulation.

Mingchao taught Mingliang how to play the arias from several operas. But when Mingchao developed an interest in trapping birds with bird lime, he gave up the flute. Mingliang, however, kept at it. At first, he played standard compositions, but as he got more skilful, he began improvising tunes to fit situations. It seemed random, but wasn't. He'd play in accordance with his mood or to fit his thoughts or about things that kept surfacing in his mind. Situations such as: when he was six years old, he rescued his mother's opera troupe photograph from a board in a Hankou woodshed, and then flung it into the Yangtze, where she rose up out of the image, and sang and danced above the water; he took a train heading in the wrong direction and walked for two months from Hunan to Yanjin, only to find his granny's house empty and leaves all over the ground, fallen from the two-hundred-year-old date tree that died along with Granny; where the tree had gone was a mystery... He created tunes for all these occurrences, and the longer he played them, the further he strayed from the beginning, playing hard-to-describe feelings about the world and his state of mind. Tunes about situations, but not just about those situations. The mood contained in these tunes could not be described in words. If it could, he thought, using plain language, then why play the flute? Feng Mingchao had taught him how to play the instrument, but only Mingliang realised all the things that could be played on it.

On this day, he was playing to the open field when he spotted Mr Zhu watching him on the opposite bank. He put down his flute. Mr Zhu waved to him.

"That's good music, boy, keep playing."

So Mingliang started again, but he'd barely begun when Mr Zhu gestured for him to stop.

"I can sing opera, boy. Do you think you can accompany me on that?"

Mingliang shook his head. "I'm sorry, sir, I can only play a few tunes. I never learned how to accompany."

"Don't worry about it," Mr Zhu said. "Just play what you want."

And so he did.

Later that day, while Mingliang was debristling pigs' feet in the rear of the cafe, a man came up and stood in front of him. It was Li Yansheng. He laid a large bundle on the table.

"Mingliang, winter is on its way. You need to change into warmer clothes. I've brought you your lined coat, trousers and shoes."

"Thank you, Uncle."

"Your father entrusted you to me, but I did a terrible job."

"You cared for me for ten years, Uncle."

"I want you to come to me if there's anything I can do for you."

"I will, Uncle."

"But, remember, come to the market, not the house."

"I will, Uncle."

"I'm friends with Mr Zhu here, and I asked him to look after you. He said he would."

"Thank you, Uncle."

Snow began to fall as they were talking and was soon falling heavily. The weather turned water-freezing cold.

One day soon after, Mingliang was in the yard debristling pigs' feet when Mr Zhu came out in a fur overcoat.

"You haven't played your flute for a while, boy," he said when he spotted Mingliang. "How come?"

"The weather, sir, it's too cold to play."

"You dope. If you can't play by the river, why not come inside to play?"

Mingliang had no answer.

"I asked you a question."

Mingliang took his hands out of the bucket. "My hands are swollen from being in ice water all day. I can pick up the flute, but I can't finger the holes."

Mr Zhu slapped his own head. "It's all my fault, boy."

The next day, Mingliang was transferred to the kitchen, where he was taught how to prepare pig's feet by a cook named Huang. The kitchen where they cooked was, obviously, warm, and he was now about to learn a skill, no longer assigned to hard, exhausting labour. To top it off, he would receive a monthly wage of two hundred yuan. Going from debristling to cooking was like a leap into Heaven. He did not know if it all came about because of his flute or if Mr Zhu was carrying out his promise to Li Yansheng to look after him. Maybe both. Asking was not an option, so why worry about it? At the end of the month, Mingliang received his pay and, during his first break on a very cold day, ran out to buy three soft drinks.

Three years passed, during which Mingliang stewed pigs' feet with Huang, getting so good at it he left his mark on his work, just as he'd done with the flute. He struggled for the first two years, producing either undercooked or overcooked, mushy pigs' feet. Or, a pot of pigs' feet would be unevenly cooked. Huang had to pitch in to correct his mistakes. Of course, nothing could be done with the mushy trotters except to sell them to toothless old men. But practice makes perfect, and after the third year, Mingliang could cook a whole pot of pigs' feet just right, not too hard and not too soft, and all pots were cooked evenly and ready at the same time. Both the flavour and texture were never quite as good as Huang's, who said, "What do you expect? I've been at this for thirty years, you've been here three. If yours tasted as good as mine, I should pack it in, wouldn't you say?" Mingliang had to agree.

The college entrance exams were to take place for secondary school students in June. The results were made public in August. Guo Zikai gained admittance into a Beijing college, and Feng Mingchao would attend a polytechnic school in Jiaozuo. Dong Guangsheng failed to win a place at any college or polytechnic school, however, so he stayed with his father, learning how to tell fortunes. Mingliang wondered if he would have made it to a college or polytechnic school if he hadn't dropped out of school. And if so, where would it have been? When he was born, his mother had given him the name Hanlin, hoping that, like the Hanlin in *Legend of the White Snake*, he would be a noted scholar. Now here he was, someone who stewed pigs' feet. After leaving school in year eleven, he would likely never have a chance to take the entrance exam, and would be stewing pigs' feet for the rest of his life. He heaved a sigh. What good does that do? he asked himself, and did not sigh again. He went out again during his work break, bought soft drinks, and watched people come and go as he drank. Yanjin, a place he'd once known so well, now seemed unfamiliar. He did not go out into the street the next day; instead, he went out back to play his flute by the river. Just playing what he felt like, the tune expressed his unfamiliarity with Yanjin, and as he played, tears fell from his eyes.

A new waitress was hired on at the restaurant a couple of months later. Ma Xiaomeng, a tall, slender, fair-skinned young woman, had come to work at Marshal Tianpeng's after failing the college entrance exam. Mingliang had no recollection of meeting her at Yanjin Middle School three years before; with a dozen sections in each year, no one could know every other student. Maybe he'd met her, but then forgot. He heard that the reason she'd failed the exam was a school romance. The boyfriend passed the exam, went to Guangzhou for college and broke up with her. Heartbroken, she tried to hang herself at home, but her mother discovered her in time. Just hearing about that reminded Mingliang of his mother, though the circumstances differed. One died, the other was saved. That his mother was not saved was not unrelated to Mingliang. He sighed. It was awfully late to be thinking about what had happened with his mother, and thoughts of Ma Xiaomeng could be nothing but groundless concern. Thinking about either was a waste of time, so he stopped.

Mingliang later learned that Xiaomeng's home was near the Yanjin ferry landing, where her family ran a convenience shop, which he recalled seeing when he strolled in the area. The sign above the door read "Ma Family Shop". What Mingliang found strange was why Xiaomeng did not go home during her breaks, staying in the restaurant to listen to the radio instead. On one of his breaks, he was playing his flute in the field when he noticed that Xiaomeng was watching him from across the river. He put down his flute.

"Mingliang," she said, "what's that you're playing? It's lovely."

"Just notes."

"Can anyone just play notes? I've sung your praises, but don't let it go to your head."

He wanted to say to her that he was just playing notes that reflected thoughts of his mother on the Yangtze, the vanished date tree in Granny's yard, the unfamiliarity of Yanjin... wasn't that how he felt? But trying to explain all that would be wasting his breath, and even if he tried, it wouldn't be clear enough, so why bother?

"It's the truth. Believe it or not, I don't care."

"Mingliang, I can tell you're antisocial."

"Where'd you get that impression?"

"I've been here a month, and you haven't even said hello. You obviously don't talk when you don't need to, you just play your flute. How come?"

He had to admit she was right. He wasn't someone who liked to talk. How come? He couldn't say even if he wanted to, so why waste the time? Ha-ha. A little laugh, that would have to stand for an explanation.

"There is something I want to ask you," he said.

"Go ahead."

"Your family has a shop, and you want a job. Why don't you work at the shop instead of working here?"

"Why is that your business?"

Again, she was right. That was none of his business, so he dropped it.

Within a month, Xiaomeng had changed jobs, leaving the diner to take a position in far-off Beijing. She hadn't breathed a word to anyone before leaving. That included Mingliang. Word had it that she'd found work in a Beijing restaurant, which, he assumed, had to be bigger than Marshal Tianpeng's.

Ma Xiaomeng did not return to Yanjin for five years. On her arrival, she opened a dress shop with the money she'd earned in Beijing. Mingliang learned of her return by accident. He happened to be out for a stroll when he noticed a new dress shop at the northwest corner of an intersection. And there, busy at work, was Ma Xiaomeng. She spotted him at the same time. He walked to the doorway, where they chatted. He asked when she'd returned and why she'd decided to open a dress shop. From there, they began to reminisce about their days as co-workers at the cafe.

"Mingliang, do you still play the flute?"

He scratched his head. Ah, he recalled, that was five years ago; he hadn't played in a long time. "I'd have forgotten all about that if you hadn't reminded me. By forgetting I don't mean forgetting I'd ever played the flute, but that it had been a long time since I stopped."

Xiaomeng laughed. They talked about how the city had changed. Pleasure boats with restaurants had begun docking at the ferry landing, from which they took passengers out onto the Yellow River to view the sights over a meal. A dancehall had opened on South Avenue, North Avenue boasted a new coffee bar, and there was a new cinema on West Avenue.

At that point, he said, "To welcome you back, how about a film tonight, my treat?"

She laughed. "Mingliang, you've become bold since I last saw you." She paused. "Since we worked together all those years ago, I'll take you up on it. But before we go, remember, we're just taking in a film, don't get any ideas."

"That's not me."

They went to the cinema that night. Mingliang bought two buckets of popcorn.

"Want something to drink?"

"How about you?"

"I've loved soft drinks since I was a kid."

"I did too, when I was in Yanjin. In Beijing I drank only cola."

"Then let's get colas."

After the movie, they went across the street to share a mutton hot pot.

"Mingliang, do you drink alcohol?"

"Not very often."

"I do. Not in Yanjin, but I picked it up in Beijing."

"I'll join you."

Once they started drinking, Mingliang discovered he could easily outdrink Xiaomeng. His mind was still sharp after half a bottle of *Baijiu*, while Xiaomeng was slurring her words. They kept talking, however, the conversation livelier than when they were both still sober.

"I want to ask you something, Xiaomeng."

"Go ahead."

"Why did you return from Beijing after being away five years?"

"You want the truth or will a lie do?"

"Up to you, the truth or a lie, they're both fine with me. I just thought I'd ask."

"I'll tell you the truth."

"Go ahead."

"I won't tell you why I came back, but why I left."

"All right either way."

"I have to start from when I was ten."

"Go ahead."

She began in fits and starts, slurred speech and all, telling him that her mother divorced her father when Xiaomeng was ten and married the owner of the Ma Family Shop by the ferry landing. They had a son the next year, her little brother. When she was fifteen, her stepfather molested her when her mother and brother were off visiting her parents. When she got into high school, she went to stay in the dormitory to get away from her stepfather. As a result of spending all her time at school, she got involved in a romance with a fellow student. When she failed the college exam, she had to return home, where her stepfather started molesting her again, telling her how nice it was that she wouldn't be going off to college and could stay home with him. Her feckless boyfriend broke up with her when he passed the exam; together with her stepfather's frequent molesting, she decided to end it all. Saved by her mother, she quit working in the family shop and took the job at the cafe. But that wasn't far enough, so she left for Beijing.

Xiaomeng told Mingliang that her stepfather was a beast, but he was good to her mother, so she never told her what he'd done. If she had, there would have been no more family. And there was her stepbrother to consider, she said. "Now I'm back from Beijing, and I've opened a dress shop here in Yanjin. I'll never go back to that shop by the landing. By all appearances, I have a home in Yanjin, but I really don't."

Mingliang was speechless, shocked by what had happened to her. He was also surprised that she would open herself up to him like that. She said she'd tell him the truth, and that is what she'd done. The cold, hard truth.

"I'm sorry I asked."

She pointed at him. "You're the first person I've told. Don't tell anyone. I know you're tight-lipped, that you don't talk much. That's why I told you. I don't think I would have if we weren't drinking. Am I drunk?"

She began to cry.

"You needn't worry, it's as if I never heard it. I can tell how hard it's been on you."

She dried her eyes and wiped her nose. "I have a question for you too."

"Go ahead."

"You were such a good student. Everything was fine at school. Why did you leave?"

"You told me the truth, so I'll do the same."

"Go ahead."

He took a drink. "I won't tell you why I left school, but why I started."

"Fine with me."

"I have to go back to when I was three."

"Go ahead."

Mingliang told her how her mother had hanged herself when he was three. After she died, his father, Chen Changjie, had taken him to Wuhan. There he'd remarried, giving Mingliang a stepmother. Then, after his granny died, he'd taken a train heading in the wrong direction and walked all the way from Hunan to Yanjin. It had taken two months. In Yanjin, his father had left him with a man named Li Yansheng and his wife, but after several years, his father could send no more money for his expenses, so he had no choice but to leave school and start working at Marshal Tianpeng's. Without stopping, he'd revealed to Ma Xiaomeng what had happened to him over a decade and more.

"That sounds terrible. But why did your mother do that?"

A tough question that no brief comment could answer. "It's complicated." He gestured to her. "I've never told this to anyone, so keep it between you and me."

"Why did you leave Wuhan and return to Yanjin?"

"I missed my grandmother."

That was true, but he chose not to divulge the more significant reason for his return. That, of course, was what had happened to his mother in Wuhan, how her body was covered with scars from being nailed to a board.

And so they talked, and they talked, until midnight.

On the very next afternoon, Mingliang went to the ferry landing on his break, heading to the Ma Family Shop. Before he got there, he saw Xiaomeng's stepfather standing in the doorway, hands behind his back, watching the flow of pedestrians on the street in front. Not particularly tall, he was somewhat overweight and had a red nose. He greeted each customer who walked into the shop with a smile. "What would you like?" he'd say. He didn't look like a beast to Mingliang. You can't tell what someone's like just by looking at them, he reflected emotionally.

Mingliang and Xiaomeng took in another film the next night, but instead of sharing a mutton hot pot when they left the cinema, they walked to the city wall, which, people said, was more than two thousand years old. The view from the top of the wall, surrounded by darkness, was one of bright lights. Mingliang put his arm around Xiaomeng in the darkness, and when he went to kiss her, she didn't object. When the kiss was over, he had the sense that she had a very long tongue. She pushed him away a moment later.

"Mingliang, will you play your flute for me?"

"I could, but I don't have it with me."

"I'll go with you to get it."

"It's been so long, it probably won't sound very good."

"So what?"

They got down off the wall and walked hand-in-hand to the cafe, where Mingliang retrieved his flute from the dormitory. They went out back to the river, where he began playing in the dark night. The sound wasn't crisp at first, but as he played, he forgot all about the notes and was submerged in the situations he was playing.

When he stopped, Xiaomeng asked him, "What were you playing?"

"Just playing."

"Just playing what?"

"You are the only person in the world I feel close to."

"Come on, you got that from TV."

"Yes, but there's a difference."

"And what's that?"

"On TV, it's not for real. But when I said it, it came from the heart."

"Are you being sentimental?"

"Sentimental, no. It's a sad commentary."

"What does that mean?"

"It just proves that there isn't a single person in the whole wide world I feel close to. Most people have family and friends. I have to search for them. Don't you think that's pathetic?"

Xiaomeng wrapped her arms around him and gave him a deep kiss with her long tongue. Once her tongue was out, she said, "I think you are the only person in the world I feel close to. Play it again for me."

So he played it again, and it was midnight.

Days before the Mid-Autumn Festival, Xiaomeng and Mingliang were married. Afterwards, Mingliang mused that other people came together after recognising one another's virtues; with him and Xiaomeng, it had been a result of each other's faults or things they'd kept hidden inside. Those sorts of things are not good. Mingliang had not told Xiaomeng the worst thing he'd kept hidden, of course. Attendees at their wedding included Mingliang's friends from school, his geography teacher, Mr Jiao, the owner of Marshal Tianpeng's Cafe, Huang, who had taught him how to prepare pigs' feet, and a few friendly co-workers. Ma Xiaomeng's mother and stepfather came. By rights, Mingliang ought to have notified his father in Wuhan, but he did not want to cause another rift between him and his wife. On top of that, in Chen's letter ten years earlier, he'd said that his wife was forcing him to break off all relations with his son, and they'd had no contact since. So, to avoid unpleasantness, he did not invite him. He did, however, invite Li Yansheng and Hu Xiaofeng. He had left their home ten years before, but he'd lived in their house from the age of six to sixteen. As emcee, Mingliang's classmate Dong Guangsheng treated the guests to many jokes; Guo Zikai and Feng Mingchao, his best men, were the first to get drunk. Teacher Jiao and Mr Zhu, the cafe owner, dragged Li Yansheng up to the stage, where they sang the parts from *A Fisherman's Struggle*. As the party heated up, Mingliang and Xiaomeng went from table to table to toast their guests. At the table where Xiaomeng's mother and stepfather sat, the two parents laughed happily, with no sign of what had happened in their house. At Li Yansheng and Hu Xiaofeng's table, Yansheng laughed happily, his wife cried.

"I'm happy," Xiaofeng said.

TWO

Mingliang and Xiaomeng had been married a year, and no signs of pregnancy. They hadn't been concerned after the first couple of months, not even after six months. But after a year, they were definitely troubled. The basic fact that no child was on the way was the primary cause for concern, but there was also the issue of who might have a problem. They each went to see an appropriate doctor, and both received a clean bill of health. That was more concerning than ever.

Ten years earlier, a fellow named Wei had followed Mingliang in the job of cleaning pigs' feet at Marshal Tianpeng's Cafe. After a year on the job, Mingliang had been promoted to the kitchen to prepare pigs' feet. Wei was still cleaning pigs' feet after ten years, and the owner complained that the feet were still poorly cleaned. He was told that he'd be promoted to the kitchen when his pigs' feet were clean, and not before. In Mingliang's view, Wei was sort of stupid. Not only was he incapable of debristling the pigs' feet to the owner's satisfaction, he actually damaged three out of every ten he worked on, products that could not be sold as perfect when stewed. But he was an honest young man, and so he was still there. Meat from the damaged feet was fished out of the huge pot with a colander to let the oil drain, and was sold as is. The other workers could sneak a bite or two when they were hungry; Wei never did.

Back when Mingliang was doing such a good job debristling the feet, the flute had also played a role in his promotion; Wei did not play the flute. Any time Mingliang saw the owner reprimanding Wei, he spoke up for the young worker, and would tell other workers to stop picking on him. Wei was one of the invitees to Mingliang's wedding. He cried during the ceremony, one of two weepers amid a sea of joyful laughter. The other was Hu Xiaofeng. They really shouldn't have cried, but they did. Wei was the silent type, just like Mingliang when he first came to work. For Mingliang, that changed when he met Ma Xiaomeng, but not for Wei. Every time he did something wrong and was told off by the owner, the other workers giggled with their hands over their mouths. All but Mingliang, who consoled Wei: "Don't let it get to you, give it time."

"How much time, Elder Brother?" he'd say with a sigh. Altogether, there were twenty workers at the cafe; he scorned them, all but "elder brother" Mingliang.

Wei rushed over to the kitchen one day and gestured to Mingliang, who was stewing pigs' feet.

"What's up, Wei?"

Wei kept gesturing, but said nothing. So Mingliang laid down his stewing fork and walked out. Wei led him out back to the riverside.

"This is really bad, Elder Brother."

"What have you done?"

"Not me, you."

Mingliang was speechless. "What'd I do?"

"Not you, your wife."

He handed Mingliang an advertisement the size of a business card. There was a picture of Ma Xiaomeng lying on a bed in revealing underwear, resting her head on her hand. The text next to it read: "Long legs, long tongue, ecstasy you'll not forget." On the bottom were an address and phone number. Obviously, an ad for call girls.

"Who the hell did this? That's disgusting. She's with me every day, how could she be doing something like that?"

"Look at the address," Wei said. "It's Beijing, not Yanjin."

Mingliang took a closer look. It was indeed Beijing, not Yanjin. He reread the text and broke out in a sweat.

"Don't believe it, Elder Brother."

Mingliang said nothing, but he did believe what he read. Because the card mentioned that Ma Xiaomeng had a long tongue. That was something only someone who'd dated her could know. And someone who'd had sex with her would know the delight of a long tongue. Only a prostitute would advertise having a long tongue. He realised that the card was about something in the past, as the address was Beijing, not Yanjin. Xiaomeng had told him she'd worked as a waitress in the capital for five years, but in reality, she'd been a prostitute there. He thought back to when they were dating and he'd asked her why she'd left Beijing for Yanjin. She'd told him only why she'd gone, not why she'd returned. To cover up what she'd done there, surely. They'd come together because they knew each other's personal flaws; he hadn't expected her to hide something so significant. She'd revealed minor flaws, not the big one, in the same way he hadn't revealed what had happened with his mother in Wuhan. But the essence of what they concealed was different.

"Where did you get this, Wei?"

"They're all over town. They weren't there yesterday, but now they're everywhere."

Mingliang knew someone was out to get Xiaomeng. Then something occurred to him. He left Wei and the pot of stewing pigs' feet and ran out of the cafe, hell-bent on getting home. Xiaomeng was already hanging from a rafter when he burst inside. He lifted her up, brought her down and checked to see if she was still breathing. Then he carried her to the hospital. Following emergency treatment, the doctor told him it was a good thing he'd moved fast, lifting her down from the rafter. If he'd been a minute later, it would have been too late. The year his mother had hanged herself, he'd gone out to buy a soft drink. She'd died. This time he got there a minute earlier, in time to save her.

"Mingliang," she said when she came to, "you shouldn't have saved me. What's on those cards is true."

"Let's not worry about that yet. Do you know who did this?"

"Yes."

"Who?"

"Xiangxiu, who lives on West Avenue. We were doing the same thing in Beijing. She came back a few days ago and wanted to borrow a hundred thousand. She got angry when I said I didn't have it, calling me a liar. This is how she got even."

Mingliang left the hospital and went straight to West Avenue to find Xiangxiu. He'd never met her but he did know her parents. When he got to their house, her mother told him she'd left early that morning to find work away from Yanjin.

"Where'd she go?"

"We don't know."

He spotted a framed photo of the family, with Xiangxiu's parents seated in front of a girl in her twenties and a teenage boy. The girl was Xiangxiu, the boy probably her kid brother. She had a moon face, big eyes and was smiling, showing a pair of dimples. How could a young woman in the flower of youth be so malicious?

THREE

Mingliang and Master Dong's son, Dong Guangsheng, were classmates in primary school and shared a desk from years two to five. After school, Mingliang often shouldered his school bag and went with Guangsheng to play at his house on East Avenue's Grasshopper Lane.

"Whose child are you?" Guangsheng's father asked Mingliang the first time.

"Chen Changjie."

"His father works on trains in Wuhan," Guangsheng said.

Master Dong nodded. "Ah, him. I saw him sing opera here in Yanjin," he said to Mingliang. "I'm a few years older than your father, so you need to call me Uncle."

"Uncle," Mingliang said.

"I'll give you a piece of sesame candy in a little while."

Guangsheng's mother's name was Kuai. Partially blind, she invariably asked Mingliang, "How is Guangsheng doing in school? Does he get into fights?"

"No, no fighting."

"How about his schoolwork?"

"He's always among the top in the class."

Years later, Mingliang apprenticed at Marshal Tianpeng's. One day Master Dong came to the cafe for pigs' feet. Mingliang walked up to him. "Uncle Dong."

"Mingliang, who'd you come here to eat with?"

"I'm not here to eat, Uncle, I work here."

"Really. Why's that?"

He explained to Master Dong that his father could not afford his tuition and living expenses, so he could not keep going to school or stay in Li Yansheng's house. And so he apprenticed at the cafe. Master Dong stomped his foot when he heard what Mingliang told him.

"I'm too late!"

"Why is that, Uncle?"

"If I had known all this before you left school, I would have become involved. I may be blind, but I'm fully capable of supporting a boy and keeping him in school. But you've already left Li Yansheng's house and come to work here. If I were to do anything now, that would make Yansheng look bad, wouldn't it?"

Mingliang held his tongue.

"Do you know the year, date and time you were born?"

"I do."

He told the old man, who began calculating on his fingers. After a long moment, he sighed and said, "Nothing I can say, it's your fate, that's all. But fate or no, it's just nonsense, nothing to take seriously."

"Even if what you said is nonsense, Uncle, you're the only person who has given me any thought at all. No one pays me any attention, no one talks to me about anything.

"Uncle," he went on, "I'll tell you the truth, now that I know my fate, cleaning pigs' feet doesn't seem so bad any more."

"Mingliang," a surprised Master Dong replied, "anyone who can see nonsense as the truth is endowed with wisdom."

Ten years passed. Master Dong was now in his seventies. His wife had died two years before, his daughter had married eight years before, and Guangsheng, who had passed neither the college nor the polytechnic exams, stayed home to help his fortune-telling father. When his mother was still alive, the two of them had taken care of the business; now that she was gone, the responsibility fell squarely on the son's shoulders. Mingliang was puzzled that his classmate had failed the examinations when his father could tell fortunes and seek help from the Celestial Master. Maybe that's what his birth dates dictated, the same way that Mingliang's dictated he would be apprenticed to the cafe. Those were their fates.

At first, Mingliang did not know how to deal with the situation. When his wife was asleep, he left the hospital and went to the Dong house on Grasshopper Lane, hoping to see what his fate held this time. He sat down in front of Master Dong, who waved him off when he had barely started to relate the business with Ma Xiaomeng.

"You don't need to tell me, I've heard, it's all over town."

"I just need to know what I should do about it, Uncle."

"Tell me the birth details of you and your wife."

Dates in hand, he calculated on his fingers. After a long moment, he asked Mingliang, "What do you want to do about it?"

"At this point, I'll have to divorce her. This is humiliating."

Dong shook his head.

"Why not?"

"You two were a couple in your last life. You are deeply in her debt, and this is what it has cost you."

Mingliang was stunned.

"Your marriage is not fated to end yet. If you insist on divorce, in your next life you will have even more debts to settle."

"What did I do in my last life?"

Dong again turned to his fingers. "You owe her half a life."

Mingliang could hardly believe his ears. He couldn't

blame Ma Xiaomeng for what happened to her, he had to blame himself for owing her half a life.

"Forget about your previous life, Young Nephew, but concentrate on the here and now. Your wife tried to hang herself. Divorce her and she'll do it again. I ask you, wouldn't you be owing her another life?

"There are some karmic transgressions that cannot be cast off," he continued, "even after several lifetimes. In fact, there are abundant examples."

He wasn't finished. "Fortune-telling is nonsense, plain and simple, so you don't have to take it to heart."

Mingliang was having none of that. "How can I not take something this important to heart, Uncle? How else can I find a way out of this? If I don't divorce her, what should I do?"

"If you don't divorce her, you'll have to divorce Yanjin."

"What does *that* mean?"

"Leave this place."

He understood. He'd had to leave Wuhan years before, and had only come back because of what had happened to his mother. Now he'd have to leave Yanjin and go somewhere else. In the end, Yanjin was just another Wuhan.

"Uncle," he said with a sigh, "leaving Yanjin is simple. But where do I go?"

"That's easy. We'll take a look."

He told his son to light incense to the Celestial Master. Then he stood up, walked to the image and bowed three times. He muttered something and shut his eyes.

When he next opened his eyes, he said, "Go west."

"Where in the west?"

"That I can't tell you. The signs aren't there."

"I don't know anyone out west."

"By now, Nephew, all of Yanjin knows what your wife was engaged in and that she tried to kill herself. It matters not what fate has in store for you or where you go, so long as you leave Yanjin."

FOUR

For Mingliang, leaving Yanjin and deciding where to go next were thorny issues. This was nothing like seeking employment in a different city. In that case, he could work for a spell, long or short, and return to Yanjin if he felt like it. As long as the money was right, where he went was unimportant. But, as a couple, he and Xiaomeng would never be able to return to Yanjin, so before they left, they'd have to plan carefully. Best to go to a place where they knew someone who could fill them in on the local peculiarities, also a resource in case they ran into a problem. Yanjin spoked out in four directions. Master Dong calculated that they should go west. That eliminated most of their options. Other than Yanjin, Mingliang had lived in only one other place – Wuhan, and it lay to the south. That was out. Besides, Wuhan held sad memories. Chen Changjie and Qin Jiaying still lived there, so that was definitely out. Xiaomeng had been to Beijing, which lay to the north, but it was where the profession she'd taken up was now common knowledge. It too was out. There were many places to the west, none of which were familiar to Mingliang, and none of its people.

Mingliang had learned the skill of stewing pigs' feet in

the cafe from a cook named Huang. He was a good guy, but had a sharp tongue. When Mingliang first went to work in the kitchen and turned out a pot of half-cooked pigs' feet, Huang said, "What you can't do is hard, what you can do is easy. Ice three-feet thick cannot form in a single winter." Mingliang knew these were barbs aimed at him, but as an apprentice, he had to take it and let it go. It he didn't, it could have turned ugly. Master teachers were always belittling their apprentices. They'd say something, and you'd just listen. Respond in a way that pleased him, you were fine; making him happy was all you needed. If you spoke up and angered your teacher, you were finished. "You're right, Chef," Mingliang said.

Mingliang became competent in pigs' feet in three years, even though they never tasted as good as Huang's. "I've been doing this for thirty years, you've done it for three. If yours tasted as good as mine, I should pack it in, wouldn't you say?"

"You're right, Chef," Mingliang said.

Ten years later, Mingliang's pigs' feet tasted about the same as Huang's. "A teacher starves when his apprentice has learned all his skills. This is like digging my own grave," Huang said.

"Not true. You'll always be my teacher. I'd be an ingrate if what you said was true."

Huang was somehow offended. "I was joking, you little dick. Couldn't you tell?"

"I'm afraid I couldn't. I thought you meant it, and it really affected me."

That got a laugh out of Huang. But there was no joking around where the matter of Ma Xiaomeng was concerned.

He was as angry as Mingliang. "Stabbing someone in the back is like sentencing them to death," he said, referring to Xiangxiu. "You're not the only one shamed by that. As the teacher, I lost face too," referring to his relationship with Mingliang.

When Huang was told that Mingliang and Xiaomeng would have to leave Yanjin and go west, as he continued stewing pigs' feet, he joined Mingliang in thinking about where to go. Suddenly, with a clap of his hands, he thought about a granduncle of his. A famine in 1942 that had taken countless Yanjin lives had driven many survivors to Shaanxi. Huang's granduncle, who was six at the time, had fled with his family. His parents both died on the road, but he and the other Yanjin refugees who hadn't starved boarded a train to Xi'an. Sixty years later, survivors in their twenties or older had all passed from the scene. Their children and grandchildren were now residents of Xi'an and had gradually cut all ties with Yanjin. His granduncle had been a child when he left Yanjin and was still alive and kicking sixty years later. He and Huang were still in touch.

"Is Xi'an west of Yanjin?" asked Mingliang.

"Yes, and it's where my granduncle lives. Why not go there? I'll contact him, and see if he can help you get settled."

He now knew exactly what it meant to be a mentor. Sarcastic in normal times, when the chips are down, he was supportive.

"Xi'an sounds good," Mingliang said. "It's a big city. Please see what you can do. But don't say why we're leaving Yanjin."

"Don't worry about that," Huang said as he stirred the

pigs' feet in the pot, "I'm not a fool. I'll phone him as soon as I'm finished with this pot."

When the pigs' feet were out of the pot, he went to the postal/telephone office to place a call. On returning, he said he'd made the call, but because his granduncle was nearly deaf – and telephones only made it worse – he didn't understand a word Huang had said. He did, however, have a grandson, who he was staying with at the time, so Huang told him that his apprentice was planning to move to Xi'an. The grandson, Fan Youzhi, was a bus driver in Xi'an's Daobei District. Huang told him that his apprentice, Chen Mingliang, had got into a fight with his brother over the inheritance of a house in Yanjin, and they'd become bitter enemies. Mingliang and his wife had soured on Yanjin and planned to start again somewhere else. Xi'an sounded ideal. But they'd never been there, and he hoped his cousin could help them find a place to live and a couple of jobs. Huang's cousin said he didn't normally do things like that, but he'd check around and get back to him within three days. "This is sort of urgent. Any chance you could let me know by tomorrow?" Fan said yes.

Mingliang thanked his teacher. The next afternoon, they went together to the telephone office to phone Xi'an. Huang's cousin reported that he'd made some enquiries regarding what they'd talked about the day before, but as a bus driver, there was only so much he could do. Finding Mingliang and his wife an inexpensive apartment to rent would be no trouble. As for jobs, he gave that plenty of thought, and the only person he knew who might help was a man named Sun, who was in charge of the city's Daobei Market. He'd spoken to him that morning and found the usually grumpy Sun surprisingly agreeable, saying he could make a stall available for them to sell vegetables. Why was he so helpful this time? Because he was a descendant of Yanjin people. He'd be happy to accommodate someone who'd moved here from there. Fan wanted to know if Huang's apprentice thought that selling vegetables was beneath him.

Huang turned to Mingliang. "No, absolutely not. Please ask Uncle Youzhi to rent an apartment for us."

When he hung up, Huang turned to him. "This is what's meant by Heaven doesn't seal all exits. It's good news. You'll have jobs in Xi'an, so you won't have to exhaust your savings. The man who runs the market is one of us, from Yanjin. And don't forget, when you get there, be sure to call Fan Youzhi Elder Brother, not Uncle."

"But he's your younger cousin, and you're my teacher, won't calling him Elder Brother disrespect the generational order?"

"Uncle is too formal, Elder Brother is friendlier, closer. You'll be in a new place, so keep things simple. Just take them as they come."

Mingliang could see that Huang was thinking for him, and once again, he understood what it meant to be and have a mentor. "You've thought this all out so carefully, I'd be foolish not to do as you say."

Mingliang went home to tell Xiaomeng what had happened and asked if she was willing to go to Xi'an and sell vegetables when they got there. She hadn't left the house since being discharged from hospital, and the rope bruise around her neck hadn't completely disappeared.

"I don't care where we go, just as long as we leave Yanjin.

Selling vegetables won't bother me. I've been selling dresses here, haven't I?"

"Then we'll just pretend we're fleeing a famine, going back to 1942."

They got on the road the next day. Mingliang watched Henan fields pass by the train window and one village after another fade into the distance. He thought back to how he'd travelled by himself from Wuhan to Yanjin at the age of six. That time, he was running by the tracks alone. Now, twenty years later, he was leaving Yanjin for a new place.

Seeing how he was lost in thought, Xiaomeng said, "Mingliang, there's something I want to ask you before we get to Xi'an."

"What is it?"

"Do you really not care about what I did?"

"How could I not care?" he said emotionally. "I think about it every day. My own wife, five years of sleeping with strange men. Most of all, I think about the long tongue."

"Tell you what – I'll get off at the next stop, and we can each go our own way."

He hadn't told her about seeing the fortune-teller and finding out that they were connected in this and in a previous life. He also thought about his feelings. He wasn't disgusted with her even after the immoral thing she'd done. To him, she was a loved one who'd made a mistake.

"But there is something on my mind, something I'd like to know."

"What?"

"You didn't use your real name when you were a prostitute in Beijing, did you?"

"I called myself Ma Li."

"That solves the problem. I married Ma Xiaomeng, not Ma Li."

She laughed at that, but then she cried.

"Mingliang, please don't let it get to you. With those men it was all like a game, not real. The only real one is you."

"One thing I can't stop thinking about."

"What is it?"

"In Beijing, how many men did you go to bed with?"

"I couldn't tell you," she said, "but half of them were duds."

"How come?" Mingliang was puzzled.

"They were impotent."

This surprised him. "I guess I have an edge over all of them."

"Mingliang, I know you've suffered because of me. But I want you to know that for as long as I live, I'll be devoted to you. I'll do whatever I have to in order to make it up to you."

"We won't talk about this ever again," he said. "It would only open old wounds."

Ma Xiaomeng nodded her agreement.

FIVE

Mingliang and Xiaomeng reached Xi'an the next day and by noon were at the Daobei home of Fan Youzhi. Mingliang wrapped a scarf around her neck and knocked on the door. No one was home. An old woman poked her head out from across the way.

"I'm sorry to bother you, madam, but is this the home of Fan Youzhi?"

She nodded.

"They don't seem to be home."

"They're at work at this hour."

"How about the old man? We know he's partially deaf, so maybe he didn't hear us knocking."

"You mean Old Man Fan? He went to live with his daughter yesterday."

So, there was no one home. Mingliang knew, however, that Fan Youzhi was a bus driver.

"Do you know which bus line Fan Youzhi drives for?"

"Number Seven."

"We're related to the Fans, madam. We've come from Henan and brought something for Youzhi. May we leave it with you for now?"

"Sure, that won't be any trouble."

Before setting out, Mingliang and Xiaomeng had prepared a gift of ten pigs' feet, two jugs of sesame oil and a bag of raw peanuts. Mingliang took them inside the old woman's house and thanked her. Then they picked up their bags and went out onto the street.

"Let's find the Number Seven bus stop. That's how we'll find Youzhi."

After asking directions, they walked several blocks to reach the Number 7 stop. They'd never met Youzhi and had no idea what he looked like. So whenever a bus drove up to the stop, letting passengers on and off, Mingliang went up to the driver.

"Elder Brother," he said, "are you Fan Youzhi?"

The drivers said, "The one before me" or "The one

behind me". After several buses had passed, though none was the one they were looking for, at least they knew he'd be along eventually. Finally, he asked a red-faced driver with a mole by his nose.

"I'm Fan Youzhi," he said. "What can I do for you?"

Mingliang recalled that his teacher had told him to call Fan "Elder Brother", not "Uncle". "Elder Brother Youzhi, we're from Yanjin. I was apprenticed to Old Huang, who stewed pigs' feet at Marshal Tianpeng's Cafe."

Fan smiled. "Ah, you're here. Hop on, I have to keep on schedule."

They boarded the bus and were told to take seats on the engine cover. Fan kept driving as he asked when they'd arrived in Xi'an. Mingliang told him they'd arrived early that morning and had gone straight to his house, and had left some gifts with a woman across the way.

"I'm just glad you're here, no need for gifts."

"Some local products from home, nothing of value. Some pigs' feet my teacher stewed, and not much else."

"Do this many people ride your bus every day?" Mingliang asked Youzhi when he noticed all the passengers fighting their way on and off the bus at each stop.

As he shifted gears, Youzhi said, "Fewer today than usual. The best part of driving a bus is all the people I see each day."

The bus looped around the city, giving Mingliang and Xiaomeng a free guided tour of half of Xi'an. At the end of the line, Fan stopped and went with his guests to another bus that would take them to Daobei District.

"Let's go first to the apartment I rented for you."

He gestured to the crowd of people.

"Daobei is filled with people from Henan. Grandparents and parents, they were famine refugees. This is a good place for you. They speak the same dialect, so no one will know you're strangers."

Mingliang nodded. "As soon as we arrived, hearing how people sounded gave us a good feeling. If you're new to a place, you can be targets of the locals."

Fan led them off the main street and along some back alleys, then past a number of lanes up to a train crossing. He turned west down a lane all the way to the end, where he unlocked the door of an apartment and let them in. One room, less than a hundred square feet, dank, with little sunlight.

"This is it. Don't know if it's what you had in mind since it hasn't much to offer. But I figured that when you've just arrived in a new place, economising is very important."

Having a place to stay as soon as they arrived was good enough for them, and it wouldn't cost much. They both agreed it suited them fine.

"One attraction is how close you are to the Daobei Market."

"Elder Brother, you've put in a lot of effort for us."

Leaving Xiaomeng in the apartment to get it ready, Mingliang went with Youzhi to meet Mr Sun at the market. As they passed a shop, Mingliang went in and bought two bottles of spirits and four cartons of cigarettes, and carried them out in a plastic bag.

"Sun Erhuo is the market manager. As I said over the phone, he calls Yanjin his hometown. Call him Elder Brother Sun. He'll like that."

This was the same instruction his teacher had given him

back in Yanjin. He nodded. After crossing the railway tracks and passing a couple of lanes, they reached the market, which was situated in a large tent. They entered and saw row upon row of stalls, dozens and dozens of them.

"It's the biggest market in Daobei," Youzhi told him.

"It *is* big."

They went to the market office, where Youzhi introduced Mingliang to a bearded man. "This is Manager Sun," he said. He turned to Sun. "This is the man I spoke to you about two days ago. He's from back home, and would like to run a vegetable stall."

"Elder Brother Sun," said Mingliang, as he went up and laid the plastic bag on a small table.

"Youzhi tells me you've come from Yanjin. Do you know someone named Li Quanshun, who lives on South Avenue?"

Mingliang shook his head. "I don't know all the residents of Yanjin."

"He's my uncle."

A man walked in just then. "Elder Brother Sun," he said, "I took care of the sugar cane pedlar Wu, the one who argued with you yesterday. He's outside now, wanting to come in and apologise."

"Kick his arse out and turn his stall over to this countryman of mine. This is a better stall than the one I was originally planning to give you." Then he pointed to the man who entered. "This is Sihai, he's head of security. See him if you have any problems."

"Thank you," Mingliang said to Manager Sun. "And you, Elder Brother Sihai, are you also from Yanjin?"

"No, I'm local."

Mingliang started selling vegetables the next day. At

three in the morning, he pedalled his new three-wheeler to the vegetable wholesale market in the northern suburb, where onions, leeks, pak choi, spinach, peppers, bamboo shoots, tomatoes and eggs were distributed. He checked with an old-timer, who advised him to buy products that were fresh, and buy a variety. The sun was up by the time he returned to the market. He opened for business, Xiaomeng brought breakfast. She noticed that one of the other stalls sold fibre-woven drinking glass sleeves. "I can do that," she said, and went to buy a dozen coloured plastic spools from a sundries stall. When she finished her household chores, she'd weave sleeves, with the idea of selling them at their stall one day.

She then went home to make lunch, which she delivered to the market. After finishing their lunch, he went back to selling vegetables, she returned home to her housework and to weave sleeves until it was time to make dinner. When he knocked off for the day, he brought the unsold vegetables home. They finished dinner. Then he took out a small box to see how he'd done that day. After deducting the wholesale cost, he'd earned more than a hundred and seventy-five yuan.

"Look," he said excitedly, "this much in only one day."

She too was excited. "Who knew you had such a head for business?"

"I'm glad it's such a big place. It's packed with shoppers. One of the benefits of selling food is that we can eat what isn't sold and won't have to pay for it."

As she wove the sleeves, Xiaomeng said, "Coming to Xi'an was a good idea."

That night, Mingliang embraced his wife and said, "Ever

since you know what happened, we haven't done you know what."

"Didn't you lose desire after all that?"

They folded into one another. "You have a very long tongue, dear wife."

"It's there for you alone."

Mingliang worked harder than ever.

"My God, you're amazing," she declared from underneath. "It feels so good."

Three months passed, when late one afternoon, Sihai came up to Mingliang's stall.

"Get your arse out of here starting tomorrow," he said. "Your spot's going to somebody else."

Taken aback, Mingliang could only sputter, "Why, Elder Brother Sihai?"

"There's no why, just a realignment. You replaced the sugar cane pedlar, didn't you?"

Mingliang knew he'd done nothing to offend Sihai, who was always yelling at one pedlar or another, telling someone to get his arse out of there, but he'd never thought anything about it. He dragged himself back home and told Xiaomeng what had happened over dinner.

"I wasn't going to say anything, but it's because of me again."

"Why?"

Xiaomeng had been home weaving sleeves that afternoon when Sun Erhuo showed up. He'd just returned from a short home visit to Yanjin, where he learned that she'd been a prostitute in Beijing. He brought one of the ad cards back with him and waited till Mingliang was at work to come to their apartment and demand sex with Xiaomeng. She cursed him. But he took out the card and said he wasn't unfamiliar with prostitutes, but had never come across one with a very long tongue. He was willing to pay. When he tried to get her down on the bed, she slapped him and threatened him with scissors. He hitched up his trousers and ran off.

"You can't tell what a person's really like by how they look. We're from the same town, and I never expected him to be so evil."

"I'll settle with him tomorrow."

"We're better off just forgetting it," she said. "Like they say, you have to bend down when you're under an eave. We're OK if he doesn't force us to leave. And he never touched me. We can still make a living selling vegetables."

After thinking things through all night, Mingliang had to agree with his wife. Early the next morning, he pedalled his three-wheeler to the wholesale distributor and went from there to the Daobei Market, where he discovered a dried-fruit seller doing business in his spot. Chestnuts, peanuts, melon seeds, hazelnuts, cashews, walnuts, pistachios and so on were spread across the counter.

"This is my spot," he said.

"It's mine, starting today," the man replied in a North-east accent. "I've already paid rent."

"Who said you could do it?"

"Manager Sun."

He's gone too far, Mingliang fumed. After trying to take advantage of my wife, he comes after me. We came all the way to Xi'an only for someone like him to try to ruin us. Sun was from the same place, a man from Yanjin. If he hadn't been from Yanjin or if he hadn't gone home, he would not have seen the card with Xiaomeng's photo, and none of this would have happened. Mingliang had been to see the fortune-teller before leaving Yanjin. He'd been advised to leave and head west. See how that turned out? Nursing a bellyful of anger, he headed to the office to see Sun Erhuo. Sihai was there with him.

"You've gone too far, Old Sun."

Sun looked askance at him. "What's the problem?"

"Don't put on an act with me. Give me back my spot in the market and I'll forget everything else. If you don't, I'll tell everyone why you went to my apartment yesterday."

"Since you brought that up, I'll be straight with you. Getting your spot back is easy. You only have to do one thing."

"What is it?"

"Let me borrow your wife's tongue one time."

Mingliang knew Sun was a bad man, but this bad? Say what you want about my wife, he fumed silently, but not her tongue. Mingliang's anger erupted. He picked up a teacup and flung it at Sun's head. With a yelp, Sun fell to the floor, his forehead bloodied. A panicked Mingliang thought he might have killed the man. But Sun struggled to his feet and, not worrying about his injured head, said to Sihai, "Grab him, Sihai."

The security chief pushed Mingliang to the floor as Sun Erhuo unbuttoned his trousers, whipped out his tool and pissed in Mingliang's face. "Your old lady didn't get to see this, so I'm letting you have a look first."

Mingliang tried to fight his way out of Sihai's grip. "Just

you wait," he sputtered. "I'm going to let the whole market know what a bastard you are."

"No need to shout that out. Sihai, go print copies of his wife's card and give one to every customer who shops at the market."

"Will do."

Xiaomeng was out when Mingliang got home. After washing his face, he started sharpening the kitchen knife and thinking about Sun. The man wasn't just bad, he was evil. Pissing in his face was one thing, passing out copies of Xiaomeng's card was something else. He was going to put an end to Sun's ugly existence. And not just Sun, but Sihai too, while he was at it. Xi'an was to be their refuge, and it wound up being worse than Yanjin, worse than Wuhan, so bad it was driving him to murder. Normally a cautious man, Mingliang had been humiliated, and it wasn't over – they planned to humiliate both of them by handing out Xiaomeng's cards. He had to kill them. At that instant, he'd be a different person. If he was willing to kill, what could he be afraid of? He hadn't done it yet, and he already thought of himself as a different man. Where he went after the murders was his next thought, as he kept working with the stone. Xiaomeng opened the door and was walking in. He hid the knife under a cupboard. She was leaning against the doorframe and was shaking.

"What's the matter, Xiaomeng? Has Sun tried something again?"

She just shook her head.

"Then what is it?"

"I just came back from the hospital."

"What's wrong?"

"I've been sick for two weeks and thought there was something seriously wrong with me. It turns out I'm pregnant."

Mingliang was at a loss for words.

She went over to their cupboard, took out a bag in which their winter clothes were packed and removed a bank card from the pocket of a padded jacket.

"I've got a hundred thousand on this card. Go to the bank tomorrow and withdraw it all. We'll leave the market and look for jobs elsewhere. This is money I earned in Beijing. I haven't touched it. I never told you, figuring I might need it if I got sick. But I'm pregnant, which shows I didn't pick up a disease in Beijing, doesn't it?

"Xiangxiu wanted to borrow money in Yanjin, and I said no. If I'd known what would happen, I'd have done it. We'll leave Daobei and go somewhere else in Xi'an, where no one knows us. This city is bigger than Yanjin, and size can work to our advantage. We won't leave here because we were treated badly, but because there's a new life inside me, and he must never know what her mother once did."

After hearing this, Mingliang chose not to mention the fight with Sun or what Sun had done to humiliate him or that Sun threatened to pass out copies of the Beijing card, and definitely not that he planned to kill Sun and Sihai. When he thought about it later, he realised that the baby had saved him from becoming a murderer. Without a word, he opened the door and ran to the local post office to phone his classmate, Dong Guangsheng. When the connection was made, he wanted Guangsheng to tell his father that Xiaomeng was pregnant and ask him to name the child, one that would give him or her a chance for a good life.

Guangsheng was happy for him. "That's great news. If you were here, we'd expect you to throw a party."

Mingliang laughed. "Next time you're in Xi'an, I'll treat you to a meal of stewed mutton."

"Tell me the child's birth dates."

"How can I do that? He's not even born."

"Right," Guangsheng admitted. "I'll ask my father to think about it."

Mingliang was reminded of Sun Erhou.

"I'd like you to do some calculations for someone else. I want to see if there's some way to get back at him. His name is Sun Erhou, originally from Yanjin."

"What did he do to you?"

"He did something really nasty to the two of us."

"Do you know his birth dates?"

"No. I can't ask that of a bitter enemy. But he's got an uncle in Yanjin, on South Avenue. Name's Li Quanshun. You can probably find it out from him. Give it a try, why don't you?"

"I'll do that."

Dong Guangsheng returned Mingliang's call the next day, saying both matters had been taken care of. "If Ma Xiaomeng has a boy, name him Hongzhi. If it's a girl, name her Hongyan. Both of them refer to lofty ambitions. As for Sun Erhuo, my father discovered he'd been a cat demon in his last life."

"Those are great names. But how do I deal with a cat demon?"

"My dad said to raise a snake at home and place a sheet of paper with Sun's name and birth date into its cage."

Mingliang understood. It would be like raising a dragon to fight a tiger. "What kind of snake?"

"A cobra, a really venomous cobra would be best."

Guangsheng told Mingliang Sun's birth dates so he could write them on the paper to put it in a cage with a snake. The plan sounded good to him, but it wouldn't work at his house. He wasn't afraid of snakes, but Xiaomeng completely lost it if she spotted even a gecko. If they kept a cobra in the house, before anything happened to Sun, Xiaomeng would be frightened to death, especially now that she was pregnant. So that was out. Years later, Mingliang realised that Old Dong's suggestion to raise a snake wasn't limited to raising a dragon to fight a tiger, but that Mingliang's mother, Yingtao, who had performed the snake in *Legend of the White Snake*, might have been able to lend him a hand.

SIX

Mingliang and Xiaomeng left Daobei and took a house with a storefront, where they opened a cafe in Xi'an's southern suburb. The landlord, a local, wanted fifty thousand a year, with a three-year lease, a hundred fifty thousand up-front. Since they did not have that much, they talked the landlord into two years' rent for a hundred thousand. Since Mingliang had stewed pigs' feet in Yanjin, the plan was for him to do the same in Xi'an. He would not be new to the work.

"When I was working at Marshal Tianpeng's in Yanjin,"

he said to Xiaomeng, "I considered stewing pigs' feet to be a dead-end job. In fact, it's come to our aid here."

"The future is always hard to predict," she said with a smile.

They gave their cafe the same name as the one back home, hoping they'd enjoy the same thriving business in Xi'an. They had a view of the Giant Wild Goose Pavilion through their front window. Since the site had previously housed a restaurant, everything, from the tables, chairs and benches to pots, pans, bowls and ladles, was there waiting to be used. That was one of the reasons they rented the place. Once they purchased oil, salt, soy sauce and vinegar, plus peppercorns, anise, spring onions, ginger, leeks and hot peppers, they stocked up on pigs' feet and greens, and were ready to open for business. On their first day, they cleaned the place thoroughly, inside and out. Mingliang spotted a Pekinese sniffing around the front while he was cleaning the store window. Looking for a handout, probably.

"You'd better go somewhere else," Mingliang said to the dog. "We haven't opened yet."

After they'd got the place in tip-top shape, Mingliang rode his three-wheeler to the local market to buy what they'd need to start welcoming customers. He was intrigued to see the little dog pattering along behind him.

"What are you doing?" He stopped. "Don't follow me, you won't be able to find your way home."

The dog stopped to consider. Mingliang set out again, and the dog pattered its way behind him.

"Are you a homeless mutt?" Mingliang said. "Want to come live with us?"

The dog nodded its head up and down.

"I'll let you stay with us," Mingliang said, suddenly inspired. "With one condition."

The dog stared at him.

"We'll call you Sun Erhuo."

Again, the dog nodded.

Mingliang got off the three-wheeler and kicked the dog into the air. "Fuck you, Sun Erhuo!"

Sun Erhuo landed and bounded off yelping. Mingliang stared at it.

"I can't keep a snake in the house, but I can beat up a dog."

On his way back from the market with all his provisions, Mingliang saw the dog, following behind him again.

"Sun Erhuo, stop following me. I'd keep you around only to beat up on you."

Sun Erhuo sat on his haunches, thinking it over. This time when Mingliang headed home, the dog stayed where it was.

SEVEN

They opened for business with eight tables. Mingliang stewed more than a hundred pigs' feet that first day, but not a single customer came through the door. Nor on the second day. On the third day, the little dog was at the front door barking. A man was standing there looking at the signboard. A closer look told Mingliang it was the street sweeper Guo Baochen's son, his classmate Guo Zikai, now a graduate student in Beijing. Zikai had made a special trip back to

Yanjin for Mingliang and Xiaomeng's wedding to serve as best man. Since moving to Xi'an, the couple hadn't been visited by anyone from home, and they avoided looking folk up in the wake of Xiaomeng's affair. Guo Zikai was their first visitor.

Mingliang went up and slapped his friend on the back.

"What are you doing here? This is quite a surprise."

With a little laugh, Zikai said he'd come from visiting a teacher of his in the nearby city of Baoji, and decided to look him up as he passed through Xi'an. "Finding you wasn't easy. I started with your co-worker Huang at the cafe in Yanjin, who told me about Fan Youzhi, who told me you came here to open your own place. He said when you first arrived, you sold vegetables in Daobei. Why'd you stop doing that and go back to your old line of work?"

"It's a long story."

"How's the restaurant business?"

"We've been open three days, and you're our first customer."

Ma Xiaomeng, who also was excited to see Zikai, went into the kitchen to make him something to eat. She brought out a bowl of steaming pigs' feet.

"Seeing you two together is a rare treat. Here's a bottle to help you celebrate."

"Everyone's gone their separate ways," Mingliang said. "A drink is definitely called for."

Guo Zikai rubbed his hands and agreed. He told Mingliang that he'd received his graduate degree and would be leaving to study in England. The teacher he'd gone to see in Baoji was his thesis advisor and the one who'd secured his place at the school in the UK. Originally from Shaanxi, he'd moved from Beijing to Baoji, wanting to spend his retirement years in his ancestral home. Hearing the good news about Zikai's pending move to England, Mingliang offered a toast.

"Drink up. We were classmates from primary school through to secondary school. You've done better than any of us, and now it's off to England."

Zikai shook his head. "Schoolmates don't talk like that. How a person makes out might have less to do with him than with external conditions."

"What does that mean?"

"You were a better student than I was, especially in physics. But in your first year of high school, you dropped out." He took a book from his satchel, in such bad shape its cover was missing. "This is your physics exercise book. Look at what you wrote in it."

Mingliang took the book and read. In a somewhat careless hand, he'd written, "I stand in Yanjin, I gaze out at the world". In another spot, he'd written, "The road runs from Yanjin High straight to Oxford and Harvard." He'd forgotten ever writing these lines, but there they were.

"You see, you had high aspirations. But then you quit school and left your exercise books with me. Remember your nickname in school? We called you Newton. If you'd stayed in school, we might both be heading overseas now, you to study physics, me to study mathematics."

"Let's not talk about that. I'm someone who stews pigs' feet. I'll die in front of a steaming cauldron and be buried behind one."

"Don't talk like that. Every trade has a leading light. Do you recall why we became friends?"

"No, why?"

"My father was a street sweeper who loved to gamble. Lots of kids looked down on me. No matter how bad your dad is, you said, you're better off than me. I don't have a dad in Yanjin."

Mingliang didn't remember saying that either. Zikai did, and that's what makes a friend a friend. He'd even brought Mingliang's exercise book with him. All the time they were talking, Zikai never asked Mingliang why he and Xiaomeng had left Yanjin. Her affair was known all over town, and Zikai could not have been in the dark before he came to Shaanxi. He still came to visit them, and never brought the subject up. That's what's called a friend. They talked on and on, drinking the whole time, while outside a dog was barking, which annoyed Mingliang. He went out to see – it was Sun Erhuo, again. He picked up a stick and chased away the dog, which scurried away with a yelp. He looked up – the moon was out.

Mingliang and Zikai got drunk in an all-but-vacant dining room. Mingliang did not know what time his friend left to return to his hotel.

When he opened the door the next morning, there was Sun Erhuo. He went over to the sleeping dog and kicked him. With a yelp, he hobbled off. He was back at noon, barking, but before Mingliang could kick him, he saw some people looking up at his signboard.

"A long-established name, come in and give it a try. You won't pay a lot if you like it. You won't pay anything if you don't."

They entered, his first customers. More people walked past and, seeing seated guests inside, joined them.

At dinner time, Sun Erhuo was once again barking at the door. Mingliang went outside, where people were studying his signboard.

"An old, established name. Come in and give it a try. If you don't like it, it's free."

There were at least thirty per cent more customers than at lunchtime. When dinner was over, Mingliang went to close up and saw Sun Erhuo lying in the doorway. Finally, he understood.

"Sun Erhuo, it's you who's bringing in the customers." When he was young, he recalled, his granny had told him the story of the weasel and the ox, and his heart softened. "Sun Erhuo," he said, suddenly grasping something important, "you can stay if you want, I won't kick you any more."

Tears filled Sun Erhuo's eyes, and Mingliang suddenly felt like Xi'an was home, thanks to a dog.

After Another Twenty Years

ONE

Mingliang received a text message on his phone one day in March:

Dear Mr Chen Mingliang,

Greetings. As kids, we were stepbrother and stepsister. Then we grew up and went our separate ways. Time flies. Forty years have passed since then. Sorry to trouble you out of the blue. I'm writing to you about your father, my stepfather, Chen Changjie, who has been bedridden since late last year. He was hospitalised for a cardiopulmonary problem. He and my mother have been together all these years. They had no children together, so there is no one closer to them than you and me. Ever since last month, he has been muttering your name in his dreams, so after you read this, try to come to Wuhan for father and son to reunite while there's still time. Don't be concerned, I got your mobile number from Uncle Li Yansheng in Yanjin. I hope all is well. - **Qin Weiwei**

The message arrived when Mingliang was sampling pigs' feet at the latest Marshal Tianpeng's Cafe. He had opened five branches in Xi'an over the past twenty years, each a replica of the original cafe near Giant Wild Goose Pagoda, and each accommodating only a dozen tables. He'd been advised to expand the size because his pigs' feet were so popular. He disagreed.

"We need to recognise who we are," he said to his wife, "a couple of poorly educated shopowners who can handle a place this size. If it were any bigger, we'd have to be inside working."

"We're in our fifties and should go easy on ourselves," she agreed.

"Yes. We'll be content with what we've got, enough to live comfortably."

Mingliang sometimes reflected on the beginnings, when they were able to open the cafe with Xiaomeng's hundred thousand, money she'd earned in Beijing. The initial days of the first cafe were somewhat tainted, and subsequent ones that were opened from its profits were also tainted. He contemplated the process, but could not share his thoughts with anyone, not even his wife. He sometimes went out behind the kitchen to watch the workers clean baskets of pigs' feet. Brought over from the slaughterhouse, the feet were muddy and the bristles caked in mud. After being scrubbed and debristled, they were washed in fresh water, debristled and washed again; only then were they clean. That had been his job two decades earlier. It was what happened with pigs' feet, and probably with everything else as well. No changes. Dirty becomes clean may define the essence of life. He shook his head and sighed. Yet he could not reveal the source of that sigh, which would remain buried inside. After a long time, he gradually ignored it.

Cafe number five opened in Baqiao District and was managed by a man named Ma Pite, a nephew of Xiaomeng's. He had arrived from Henan two years before to be with Mingliang and Xiaomeng. His name was Ma Qi when he came, but he changed it to Pite a year later. Mingliang and Xiaomeng had long since severed relations with family and friends over her scandal. But she was now a woman in her fifties, her son was nineteen and relations had gradually warmed, as the past was forgotten. When young Ma arrived, he got a job as a waiter in cafe number two, slowly working his way up to head waiter. When cafe number five was planned, he pleaded to be given the manager's job.

"Since he's so determined," Xiaomeng said to her husband, "why not give him a shot at it?"

"I like the idea that he wants to work his way up, and it's worth a try. But a manager's position isn't like an official sinecure. If he's up to the task, he can take on the job permanently. If not, it's back to being head waiter."

At the opening of each branch, Mingliang personally sampled the first batch of pigs' feet. One bite would tell him if they were properly prepared and flavourful enough. When he showed up at cafe number five, he noted that the waiters all looked like flight attendants and the walls were decorated with printed slogans:

> *Cafe #5, home to a million pigs' feet.*
> *Marshal Tianpeng, our pigs' ancestor.*
> *You may not have eaten pigs' feet, but you've watched pigs run.*
> *Run how? Eat one and you'll know.*
> *Full of collagen, an enhancement to beauty and fine skin.*
> *Yang Guifei ate pigs' feet daily, it's said.*

Mingliang laughed when he saw the outfits and the wall declarations.

"Ma Qi," he said, "isn't that going overboard for a meal of pigs' feet?"

Ma Qi tolerated hearing his name spoken only by Mingliang. For everyone else, it was to be Manager Ma or Pite. And in public, Ma never called Mingliang Uncle, but insisted on calling him Manager Chen.

"Not at all, Manager Chen. It's what's called forging ahead."

"How in the world do you know that Yang Guifei ate pigs' feet daily?"

"A rumour. I added 'it's said'."

Mingliang sat at one of the tables for Ma Pite to bring out the first pig's foot. Before he bit into it, he poked it with his chopsticks to see if it was done. Then he pulled meat off the bone with his chopsticks, spreading it into eight sections. He turned them over and over and examined them carefully. He did not sample any.

"Now bring me another one."

"I don't understand, Manager Chen."

"Just bring me another one."

Pite went back into the kitchen and brought out another, as instructed. Once again, Mingliang spread the meat into eight sections, which he turned over and over and examined carefully.

"One more."

Full of misgivings, Pite nonetheless brought out a third one. Mingliang repeated the process and then tossed down his chopsticks. He looked up at Ma Pite.

"Is there a problem with the texture, Manager Chen?"

"The texture's fine."

"Is the colour wrong?"

"The colour's fine."

"Then why didn't you even take a taste?"

Mingliang picked up his chopsticks and moved the meat around.

"Look there," he said, pointing with his chopstick, "there are bristles on all of them. One could have been an accident, but three shows that none of them was picked clean. Good texture and excellent colour mean nothing if they haven't been picked clean."

Then he pointed to the outfitted waiters and wall posters. "What is accomplished by fancy outfits and witty posters if the food isn't done right? Throw away all of today's output. Do it right, we'll open tomorrow."

An embarrassed Ma Pite went into the kitchen area and screamed at the kitchen staff: "Who the fuck debristled today's pigs' feet? You're all fired!" Then he said to

Mingliang, "What a waste to throw out hundreds of finished pigs' feet. I invited some friends over to show support."

"You should be happy if they don't come," Mingliang said. "If they show up and eat mouthfuls of pigs' bristles, who suffers?" He pounded the table. "Not you, that's for sure. It's Marshal Tianpeng's Cafe that suffers. Do you think you're ready to be a manager?"

Red-faced Pite could only say, "I messed up, Manager Chen, but you can take my word that something like this will never happen again."

"Talk is cheap. Starting today, you'll go out back and debristle pigs' feet. When you've learned how to do it right, you can be the manager. Back when I worked at the cafe in Yanjin, I did that for a year."

Ma Pite looked unhappy, but Mingliang's attention was taken by an incoming text message. It was the message from Qin Weiwei in Wuhan. The language she used showed him how much better educated she was than he was.

The original Marshal Tianpeng's – the flagship cafe, to use Ma Pite's words – was located between the Giant Wild Goose Pagoda to the east and a ploughed field to the west, where wheat grew in the spring and corn in the autumn. Then came the development, with rows of tall apartment buildings. Chen Mingliang had bought a unit in the building next to the cafe. When he came home for dinner that night, he told Xiaomeng what had happened with Ma Pite.

"He already phoned to tell me," she said. "He was crying."

"I told him at the beginning he had to get things right

the first time. I won't tolerate carelessness. That went in one ear and out the other, so I've got him cleaning pigs' feet."

"It's what he needs," she agreed. "He didn't think it was fair. One little mistake, and you overreacted, he said."

"How big a mistake is permitted to us common folk? We sell pigs' feet. If there are bristles on them, is that a little mistake? This wasn't only about bristles. He's impetuous and needs to work on it. Don't tell him I said that. It will lose its effect and he won't take it seriously. He needs something like debristling pigs' feet."

"Don't worry, I understand."

Mingliang took out his phone and showed Xiaomeng Qin Weiwei's text.

"This is important," she said. "You've had no contact with your father for forty years. But he's still your father, and now that he's sick, you'll have to go."

"I think so too."

"I'll go with you."

"That would be perfect, having you with me. But there's so much to do here, and with the new opening, what if there's a problem while we're both away? I don't know if anyone else could deal with it."

"Then you go," she said after thinking it over. "But be careful on the road."

"You take care of things at the new branch for a few days. We'll figure out who to make manager when I get back from Wuhan."

"Sounds good."

TWO

Mingliang boarded a train to Wuhan. Qin Weiwei had said over the phone she'd meet him at the station since he didn't know his way around the city. After forty years, they might not recognise each other, so she held up a sign with his name on it. He spotted the sign in the crowd after passing through the inspection point, held by a somewhat portly middle-aged woman in dark-framed glasses. They greeted one another, she put away the sign, and they walked off together.

"Forty years, a long time," she said. "There's one thing we need to settle up front."

"What's that?"

"What should we call each other?"

"Whatever you say is fine with me."

"We never called each other brother and sister. After all this time, it would be awkward to start now, don't you think?"

"I agree, it would be awkward. 'Hey you' would be rude, so why not just use our names?"

"But you're older than me. You can call me by my name, but it wouldn't be appropriate for me to call you by yours."

"So what do we do?"

"What's your child's name?"

"I have a son, his name is Hongzhi."

"I have a daughter, her name is Zhao Chenxi. How's this? I'll call you Hongzhi's Dad and can call me Chenxi's Mum. What do you say?"

He laughed. "You've got a good head on your shoulders, Chenxi's Mum."

"But I'm just an ordinary worker, while you're a successful businessman. Uncle Li Yansheng filled me in on how you're doing."

"Your so-called successful businessman deals in pigs' feet."

"I've heard some dumpling companies have become publicly traded."

Mingliang asked what she did. She said she was an accountant in Wuhan's logistics division finance department, a job her granduncle had arranged just before he died twenty years earlier. That jogged Mingliang's memory. The old man must have been his stepmother's uncle, who ran the division all those years before. He'd been dead for more than two decades. Nothing had changed but the people. He did not pursue the matter. They hailed a taxi. Weiwei told the driver to take them to the railway workers' hospital. The Wuhan that passed by Mingliang's window, its streets and buildings, was unfamiliar, definitely not the Wuhan of his childhood. In fact, he didn't know what these places had looked like forty years before, or what had changed during those years. He hadn't been in this area as a child. He'd lived in the city from three to six years of age, but the stay was limited to the maintenance division dormitory and their house in Hankou. He had hardly been anywhere else. An auditorium stood in front of the dormitory, he recalled, a cafeteria behind it. Then his father had married Qin Jiaying, and they'd taken a place on Xinyi Lane, which opened onto Dazhi Gate. To the left of the gate was Sandeli Alley, to the right was Tiansheng Avenue. Yihe was the first lane after Tiansheng Avenue; everything beyond that was a mystery to him.

Some significant incidents from his days in Wuhan were still fresh in his mind. In year two, he recalled, the language teacher taught them how to write and use the word "snow". They read along with the teacher: "snow," "heavy snow" and "snowstorm". Snow seldom fell in Wuhan, and if it did snow, it merely sprinkled in the morning and would be done by noon. "Teacher," one of the students asked, "how much snow has to fall for it to be heavy snow?" "A lot," the teacher said. "We're just learning the word, so repeat it after me." As a student from snowy Yanjin, where heavy snow and snowstorms were fairly common in the winter, Mingliang could almost hear the snowflakes falling on Yanjin streets. One winter, when he was two years old, snow fell for three days and nights. It stopped on the fourth morning, which was clear and bright, so his granny had put him in a wheelbarrow with homemade date cakes and set out to sell them on the street. Before they got there, the wheelbarrow hit a wet spot, tipped over and spread the cakes all over the street. Mingliang went with it. Granny and Grandson burst out laughing, with no concern for the spilled cakes. He also recalled that the people called eating breakfast "getting through the morning".

Their taxi drove past the Yangtze River Bridge. This was not Mingliang's first view of the river or the bridge, but both had changed over forty years. "That's one of three Yangtze bridges," Weiwei said. She pointed to a pair of bridges in the distance. "The first one is Number Two Bridge, the other is Number One Bridge. Number One Bridge is the only one we had as children."

At the hospital, they went straight to the fifth floor, where Weiwei led him into one of the wards. All five beds were occupied. She walked him over to the far end, where an old man with a mottled face and a coat draped across his shoulders was sitting up drinking a glass of water. If he had seen him anywhere else, Mingliang would not have recognised his father. He was nothing like he remembered. The old man could not tell who Mingliang was either, and so said nothing. But when Weiwei told him who it was, his eyes opened wide.

"Mingliang, what are you doing here? Who told you to come?"

"I asked him to come," Weiwei said.

The elderly woman standing by the bed studied Mingliang, who knew who she was – his stepmother. She was as slim as ever.

"Ma," he said.

"It's been forty years," she said, her eyes moist.

"Yes, we're all getting on in years."

"Back then, you said you were leaving, and you did, nearly frightened me to death."

"I was just a dumb kid then."

"Let's not rehash the past, all right?" Weiwei spoke up.

"What's wrong with Pa?"

"I'm old."

"That's not it, he's filled with anger," said Qin Jiaying.

"Towards who?"

"He just got here, let's not talk about that," Chen Changjie said.

Qin Jiaying let it drop.

"Mealtime," came a shout from the corridor. "Come get your meals."

Mingliang's stepmother picked up the container at the

foot of the bed. "I'll get a bit more, and you can eat with us."

"All right."

"He's just arrived," Weiwei said. "I'll take him to a restaurant."

"Sure, that's a good idea," said Qin Jiaying. "Go have something decent to eat." She walked out to get the food.

A nurse walked in. "Bed Thirty-Five, you need to pay your fees. You can go downstairs to settle."

"She's talking about us," said Weiwei. "Wait here, I'll be right back."

She took her purse off the bed frame and went out to pay.

Mingliang followed the nurse to the nurses' station.

"How much has Bed Thirty-Five paid for his hospital stay so far?" he asked.

She checked. "A hundred eighty thousand."

Qin Jiaying came in with their lunch, and Weiwei returned from paying the fee. While Qin Jiaying helped Chen Changjie with his food, Weiwei took Mingliang outside to find a place to eat.

"What would you like, Hongzhi's Dad?"

He recalled something he'd eaten in Wuhan. "Some hot dry noodles. And some Wuchang fish."

Weiwei laughed. "You can't get both in the same place."

"Noodles, then."

They talked on the way to a noodle restaurant. A signboard over the door read, "Best in Three Counties". A pair of vertical scrolls adorned the doorframe. The first one read, "No business like the cooking business". The second one read, "All around the world, noodles are best".

"Any memory of this place?" Weiwei asked. "The four of

us ate here over the Mid-Autumn Festival one year."

He had no recollection of the restaurant, even though they'd eaten here once. The couplet, on the other hand, seemed familiar, because several of the characters were ones he hadn't yet learned at the time, and he recalled his father telling him what they were. But there were plenty of restaurants with couplets at the door, and he had no way of knowing if this was the one. With thoughts of food, he recalled an incident when his father had picked him up from school, still wearing his railway work clothes. His father was off on one of the trains and rarely came to his school to pick him up. On most days, Mingliang walked home alone, carrying his school bag. This time, instead of heading home to Xinyi Lane, they'd walked in the opposite direction.

"This isn't the way home, Pa."

His father did not respond. Hand-in-hand, they walked past lane after lane until they reached the Yangtze River. Chen Changjie took a cooked chicken out of his bag, tore it in two, and gave half to his son.

"Eat up. I bought this on the platform at the Fuli train stop. Don't say anything when you get home."

Mingliang nodded. Father and son then sat on the riverbank and ate their chicken without exchanging a word.

Mingliang and Weiwei walked into the noodle restaurant, which was packed with lunch customers. She took a plastic bag out of her trouser pocket and told Mingliang to grab a table. She went up to the counter to buy their food and returned with a tray with two cold dishes, a plate of beef stewed in soy sauce, some celery and peanuts, plus two bowls of hot dry noodles.

"Back at the hospital," Mingliang said as they were

eating, "Ma said Pa was filled with anger. What did she mean?"

"He filled himself with anger."

"I don't understand."

"Pa was always a simple, honest man, don't you think?"

"Yes."

"A simple, honest man who worked on trains. After retiring, he got ideas."

"What do you mean?"

"He wanted to get rich. He had a friend named Xing, who'd also started out as a stoker. Now that they were both retired, he urged Pa to go into business with him. Pa withdrew all his life savings, half a million yuan, and tried a little of everything with Xing. They opened a hot dry noodle restaurant, a carwash, a metal grille fabricator and a pedicure shop. They even sold aquatic products, one venture after another, all failed businesses. Then Xing took Pa's last fifty thousand and ran off."

"Where'd he go?"

"No idea. Losing all that investment money was bad enough, but coupled with having a friend run off with his last fifty thousand is what put him in hospital. You know as well as anyone that Pa isn't very broadminded."

Mingliang nodded his understanding. He noticed that while Weiwei ate with her right hand, she clutched her purse with her left.

"Chenxi's Mum, there's something I'd like to say."

"Sure, go ahead."

"It's about the medical costs."

"What do you mean?"

"From now on, all of Pa's hospital charges, for however

long he's there, not counting reimbursable amounts by the railway company, are on me."

"Hongzhi's Dad, that's not why I asked you to come."

"I own restaurants in Xi'an, and although it's a small business, it generates income every month, certainly enough for me to help here. If it weren't, I wouldn't have come."

With a sigh, Weiwei said, "Hongzhi's Dad, I guess that is why I asked you to come. I won't lie, that man of mine is a jobless layabout who spends all his time shooting the breeze with a grocery store friend in town. What do you get by spending all your time with someone who sells stuff? I'd be embarrassed for you to meet him. I'm a low-level office worker, Ma is a retired enamelware worker. Our father worked his whole life for the railway and can't claim reimbursement for much of his medical expenses. His hospital charges are more than we can handle, but I can't tell him. I won't let you take care of everything, so how about fifty-fifty?"

"Chenxi's Mum, I'm a plain speaker and I don't like to beat around the bush. If it would bother you for me to foot the whole bill, then fifty-fifty it is. Let's not fight over this, all right?"

She thought it over. "How's this – you pay two-thirds, I'll pay the rest. After all, his work on the railway paid for much of my upbringing."

"All right, that's how we'll do it."

"One more thing. Were you planning to stay at their place tonight? When Ma knew you were coming, she prepared a bed for you."

"The same place after all these years?"

She nodded. "Ma said you can sleep in the room you and

I shared as children."

"I think I'll get a hotel room near the hospital. I can spend more time looking after Pa that way, and it's more convenient."

"All right, we'll do it your way."

"You and your mother can go home and rest. I'll stay and do the night shift."

Qin Weiwei and her mother went home that evening. Mingliang stayed with his father. A nurse came in at night with meds for the five patients and changed IVs. When she left, family members helped the patients into the lavatory to wash and get them ready for bed. Mingliang took his turn with his father, whose weakened system made walking difficult.

Back in bed, he said to Mingliang falteringly, "I'm fine here, Son, go home and get some rest."

By home he obviously meant his and Qin Jiaying's place, not knowing that Mingliang had taken a room at a nearby hotel. He had no desire to stay at their home, not just because a hotel was so much more convenient, but also because his mother, Yingtao, had been there forty years before. Soon after that, he'd seen her nailed to a board in a woodshed, leaving scars all over her body. That was one place he did not want to visit. He couldn't explain that to his father, and hadn't said so to Weiwei at noon either.

"You get some sleep, Pa, don't worry about me. We don't get to see each other often. I'll stay awhile."

Chen Changjie let him have his way.

There was no more talk that night. The nurse came in to check the next morning. Mingliang took his father to the toilet and helped him wash himself. Then back to bed to catch his breath. At mealtime, Mingliang went into the corridor to get two portions from the meal trolley and brought them back to eat with his father. When they were finished, he washed the bowls and returned to the bed as the nurse came in with meds, just before the doctors made their rounds. The sun was out, so Mingliang asked if he could take his father downstairs for some sun and fresh air. "A good idea," the nurse said, "but don't let him catch cold."

Mingliang helped his father downstairs and into a small garden, where they sat on one of the benches. Taking in some sun and fresh air wasn't the only reason he'd brought his father out; he mainly wanted a secluded spot where they could talk in private. Yet now that they were alone, neither knew what to say, so they just sat there silently.

After a while, Chen Changjie said, "Have they told you how I lost a lot of money in business deals?"

Mingliang nodded, knowing who the "they" were.

"I knew they would. But that's all right, I'm not afraid of how I look to other people. At this point, I can't blame anyone but myself. I've lived a life that can be characterised by one word: poor. I've been a stoker, a train engineer, day and night, overtime, a life not much better than a donkey at a millstone. Now I'm an old man who should be content with his poverty, but I refused to accept my lot. So I went into business to get rich, and this is how I wound up. Your father's been a complete failure, a joke."

"Don't say that, Pa."

"I know they sent for you so you can pay my hospital bills. We haven't seen each other for forty years, and now here you are just so you can spend money."

"I attended school in Yanjin from the age of six to

sixteen, which you paid for without telling Mother, all those years. This is my chance to pay you back."

"That just makes me want to slap my own face for not giving you a chance to finish high school," he said with a sigh. "Sometimes I think I'd like to see Li Yansheng again."

Mingliang took out his mobile phone. "I'll call him and tell him to come to Wuhan, how's that?"

Chen Changjie stopped him. "What would we talk about? I handed you over to him, and as soon as I stopped sending him money for your tuition and expenses, you had to go out to stew pigs' feet."

"He had no choice."

"So you say, but meeting now would be embarrassing. No matter what, it's all because I'm a failure."

Chen then asked about Mingliang's wife and child. He filled his father in.

"Do you have to hide from your wife that you're paying my hospital bills?"

"No, I can do what I want at home."

"Then you did better than me."

The reason he did better than his father, and could afford his father's hospital bills, was a result of learning how to stew pigs' feet. He'd gone to Marshal Tianpeng's Cafe to learn the skill because his father could no longer afford to pay for his living expenses in Yanjin. That was the story of the forty years, a real head-scratcher of a tale.

Something else was on his mind, so he said, "It's just the two of us here. There's something I'd like to ask."

"What?"

"Why did my mother die all those years ago? Was it, like people say, over a bunch of chives?"

Chen Changjie had a coughing fit. Mingliang thumped his back. Chen was wheezing once the coughing stopped.

"Yes, and no."

"What does that mean?"

"We had an argument over chives that day, and when I was leaving the house, I could see that something was troubling her. I left anyway. She hanged herself.

"We were always arguing, and maybe deep down I was looking forward to her dying. Resentment between family members can be worse than between bitter enemies. She committed suicide, but in fact, I killed her."

Mingliang's heart nearly stopped. For four decades he'd blamed himself for his mother's death for going out to buy a soft drink. He was surprised to hear his father say he bore the responsibility. Maybe they shared it, that father and son both killed her.

Mingliang breathed an emotional sigh.

"I've taken the wrong road twice in my life," Chen said.

Mingliang just looked at him.

"First, when I was in the drama troupe and we were putting on *Legend of the White Snake*, I shouldn't have explained the play to your mother and Li Yansheng. I wouldn't have hooked up with your mother if I hadn't."

Mingliang said nothing.

"The second was when I came to Wuhan. The railway put on a show on International Workers' Day, May first. Do you remember that?"

Mingliang thought back. He nodded.

"The operations section could not perform, so I took their place and sang arias from the opera. If I hadn't, I wouldn't have hooked up with Qin Jiaying."

As he listened to his father, Mingliang was thinking that, if his father had not hooked up with Yingtao or Jiaying, who else was there during those years? Looked at differently, if he'd hooked up with someone else, what difference would it have made? He couldn't say that to his father, so he said nothing.

Mingliang spent a week in Wuhan. His father's condition was stable. Before leaving, he talked to the doctor, who told him that Chen's illness was unpredictable. He could be just fine one minute, and in crisis the next. If there were no drastic changes, that is probably how the next year or so would go. With that knowledge, and the reality that things were piling up back home in Xi'an, with the fifth Marshal Tianpeng's Cafe opening, he could not stay longer. He talked it over with Weiwei, who agreed he should return to Xi'an.

"Hongzhi's Dad, Pa's situation is what it is. You go on home. Mother and I can look after him. You've taken a load off my shoulders with what you're spending on his care."

"Don't say that, Chenxi's Mother. Taking care of the patient is harder than paying the bills."

In the hotel the night before Mingliang left for Xi'an, a woman spoke to him in his dream.

"Have you forgotten what you said?"

"What did I say?"

"You were six. I helped you save your mother, and then you threw her into the Yangtze."

He recalled how his mother had come to Chen Changjie

and Qin Jiaying's home in Wuhan, only to be nailed to a board in a woodshed. A firefly had led him to the shed, where he'd rescued his mother. The firefly told him that many decades from then, when he returned to Wuhan, he would have to do him a favour. The firefly had now come to him.

"I'd forgotten about that, but now it's all come back to me."

A woman's voice: "I took you to your mother to save her back then. Now it's your turn to save me."

"Who are you?"

"I'm Ma Dao Po."

"Who's Ma Dao Po?"

"The person who stuck needles into your mother."

That was a stunner. "If that was you, why change into a firefly to save her?"

"I did both, put in the needles and then saved her. You know the Buddhist adage: Lay down your butcher knife and become a Buddha."

With a look that suggested he might have grasped a principle, but not quite, he said, "How am I supposed to save you?"

"Take me away from Wuhan."

"Why?"

"I've spent a lifetime sticking needles into people, a sinful existence by any judgment. I may be dead, but I want to leave this troubled place."

"Why did you first come to me way back then?"

"You were six years old, but I figured you'd be big and strong in forty years. If I'd gone to an adult, how would he even be alive in forty years?"

"How do I take you away?"

"I've already done what your mother did, attached myself to a photograph. All you have to do is take that image with you."

"I'm returning to Xi'an."

"Just get me out of Wuhan, where to doesn't matter."

Mingliang figured that in the unseen world, this is what he'd come to Wuhan for. "My father's illness," he exclaimed, "did you cause it to happen so you could get me to come?"

"No, he caused it himself."

"Where's the photograph?"

"At Yellow Crane Tower. There's a small pavilion on the hill behind the tower. My photo is hidden beneath a column in the right-hand corner."

"When did you pass away?"

"Three years ago. I've been waiting for you since then."

Mingliang woke up, turned on the light and looked at his watch. Three a.m.

He got out of bed, dressed and left the hotel, hailing a night taxi to take him to Yellow Crane Tower. He recalled his primary school days in Hankou, how he and his schoolmates had been taken on an excursion to the tower. Then, when his granny came to Wuhan, his father had taken them there too. The taxi let him out at the foot of the hill on which the tower stood. He gazed up at it and could see it was nothing like it had been back then. There were no visitors at this late hour. The main gate was shut, but when he walked up, it opened on its own. He knew Ma Dao Po had done that, which he assumed proved that her photograph was indeed hidden there. He trudged up the hill until he reached the entrance to the tower, on which a pair of scrolls flanked the opening:

People of the past flew off on the back of a yellow crane

Here there is an empty Yellow Crane Tower

He went around to the rear of the tower, where there stood a little pavilion. He was told that the photograph was beneath a column in the right corner. How in the world was he to retrieve it from under an unmovable column? When he walked up and touched it, it moved aside on its own, like plucking a blade of grass. And then he saw the pavilion turn into a model he could hold in the palm of his hand. The tower in front had also changed into a model. He shifted the pavilion to one side and found the hidden photograph. It was of a five-year-old girl with a red ribbon in her hair.

"Is this you, Ma Dao Po?"

"Me when I was a little girl."

He held on to the photo and replaced the pavilion, which reverted to its original shape and size. And the Yellow Crane Tower? It was once again the lofty scenic tower by the Yangtze River.

"Where shall I leave your photo in Xi'an?"

"Just remember to place it in a high spot," the little girl with the red ribbon said.

The next morning, Mingliang went to the hospital to say his goodbyes to everyone.

"You came a long way," Qin Jiaying said. "Why not stay a few more days?"

"No, Hongzhi's Dad has to take care of business at

home," Weiwei said.

Mingliang's father nodded his agreement. "You'd better go home and open your newest cafe. I'll stay here to recuperate."

Mingliang took another look at the two women and discovered that in their eyes, his father's confidence had grown since his arrival in Wuhan. Why was that? Was it because he'd paid off most of the hospital bills? No matter how dreadful that sounded, it was undeniably the case. If he'd never opened a cafe and was as poor as ever, Weiwei might not have asked Li Yansheng to help her contact him and invite him to make a visit. Which meant he'd never have seen his father again after leaving Wuhan as a child.

"I'll be back after I've taken care of my business in Xi'an."

"When I get better," his father said, "I'll come see you in Xi'an."

"That'd be wonderful. You can all come and we can visit the Giant Wild Goose Pagoda and see the Terracotta Army together. And you can sample our famous mutton soup."

"We can also go to your place for stewed pigs' feet," Qin Jiaying added.

They laughed, which regrettably resulted in Chen Changjie experiencing a coughing fit. It went on for several minutes, until he was red in the face, and wouldn't stop. Weiwei ran out to call a nurse, who came in and put an oxygen mask on him.

"Maybe I ought to stay a couple more days," Mingliang said.

His father waved him off. "You go. This is just how I am. I'm not going to die any time soon."

So Mingliang left the hospital and hailed a taxi. As he rode along, he couldn't help thinking, He won't die anytime soon, but he won't get better anytime soon either. He can hang on in the hospital, but his health won't return. It's not likely he'll come to Xi'an, as he said.

Chen Changjie couldn't come to Xi'an, but with Ma Dao Po's photo in his pocket, she'd be going to Xi'an with him. A totally unanticipated development. Mingliang sighed.

When he walked out of Xi'an train station, rather than go straight home, Mingliang told his taxi driver to take him to the Qinling. There, he climbed until he could look out at one mountain peak after another and a layer of forests. He took the photo of the little girl with the red ribbon in her hair out of his pocket.

"I'll leave you here, Ma Dao Po, how's that?"

"Good," the little girl said. "It's high and it has a wonderful view."

"I'd like to ask you a question before I leave you here."

"Go ahead."

"Back when I flung the photo of my mother into the Yangtze, I wondered then and still wonder where the river took her."

"My powers are limited to Wuhan," she said. "I don't know where she went after she left the city."

"That's too bad. Now that I've brought you to Shaanxi Province, where do you intend to go?"

"Where I'm from."

"Didn't you come from Wuhan?"

"By that, I didn't mean where I came from."

"What did you mean?"

A gust of mountain wind rose up, bending all the trees noisily.

"No more questions," the girl said anxiously as the wind whistled through the trees. "You wouldn't understand if I told you. Put me down, and hurry, so I can catch the wind. I don't want to miss it. It could be the last."

"Take care, then," Mingliang said.

He let the photo go and watched the wind carry it into the sky, where it rolled in the air before disappearing among the whistling trees.

THREE

Counting back, Sun Erhuo had been dead five years. Three days before he died, he stopped eating. When he'd first arrived at Mingliang's house twenty years earlier, stewed pigs' feet were his favourite. He was not fed straight out of the pot, but Mingliang took the bones left on plates by diners after closing each day and put them in the dog's bowl. Then one day they were no longer his favourite. Marshal Tianpeng's served more than just stewed pigs' feet. There were cold dishes, stir-fries and alcohol. One of the cold dishes was chicken livers and spinach. After closing on some nights, Mingliang would put uneaten chicken livers from customers' plates into Sun Erhuo's bowl along with pigs' feet bones. He would push the bones aside to get at the livers.

Mingliang would come up and nudge him. "Sun Erhuo, you've become a decadent animal."

During those days, Mingliang would go to the wholesaler before sunrise each morning to buy pigs' feet, chicken, duck, fish, pork and an assortment of vegetables. Ma Xiaomeng would get things ready in the kitchen after sending Hongzhi off to kindergarten. Neither of them had time to walk the dog, so Mingliang made a dog door to a small garden in the rear. Sun Erhuo used the door in the mornings and nights to relieve himself outside. In the mornings, he would then rush off to Marshal Tianpeng's and return home after closing. One evening, as Mingliang and Xiaomeng were having dinner, Sun Erhuo came in through the dog door and tugged on the hem of Mingliang's trousers to get him to follow him outside. Mingliang pushed him away.

"We're eating dinner. Go out and play."

The dog continued to tug. Not knowing what he wanted, Mingliang got up and followed him outside. Sun Erhuo kept looking behind him to make sure Mingliang was coming. The dog led him to Marshal Tianpeng's, where water was spilling out under the door. He opened the door and saw that the place was flooded. He waded to the kitchen, where it was clear that the man cleaning pigs' feet had forgotten to turn off the tap. If it had stayed on all night, everything in the restaurant – the refrigerator, cupboards, hundreds of pigs' feet, provisions, meat, fish and vegetables, not to mention the electrical outlets – would have been ruined. Mingliang turned off the tap and patted the dog's head for getting him to come in time to save everything.

"Sun Erhuo, you're a great watchdog."

The dog looked up and seemed to smile. He ran off.

The next day, Mingliang read the riot act to the man who cleaned pigs' feet: "Even a dog has got more brains than you!"

On another occasion, Mingliang and a friend spent most of the night drinking, getting so drunk he couldn't get up the next morning. At eleven o'clock, the dog ran home from the restaurant, went in through the dog door and up to Mingliang's bedroom, where he barked and scratched at the door. Unable to work the doorknob, he ran frantically back to the restaurant, where he took Xiaomeng's trouser hem in his teeth to get her to follow him home. There she found her husband in bed, still dead to the world. She immediately phoned the restaurant to have the workers take Mingliang to the hospital, where the doctor ran tests and said his blood-alcohol level was 2.8. He ordered an immediate IV. Fortunately, he told them, he'd arrived in time. Otherwise, he would not have survived. After Mingliang was released from the hospital, Xiaomeng brought Sun Erhuo in and told him how the dog had saved his life.

"You were afraid I'd die, weren't you, Sun Erhuo?"

The dog nodded and ran off.

There was a jewellery store next door to Marshal Tianpeng's. The owner, named Jin, and two apprentices placed bars of silver on an anvil and hammered out silver jewellery every day, everything from bracelets and necklaces to chains, earrings and studs, and rings. They also made holes from which added pieces could be hung. On occasion, after the lunch crowd had left and the dinner patrons were yet to arrive, Mingliang would saunter next door to sit and watch the silversmiths at work. He saw them turn bars of silver into all sorts of jewellery. Mingliang: You're a fine artist. Jin: An insignificant craftsman. Practice makes perfect. Mingliang: Different trades are miles apart. I could never get the knack. Jin: You can't do this if you lack patience. It's not a trade for the restless. Mingliang: Much like stewing pigs' feet. Jin: The same principle applies to everything in this world, I guess.

The two men got on well. Sometimes, Sun Erhuo would come along with Mingliang and sit by him, tongue out and panting. Jin pointed at the dog one day while they were chatting. "Looks like a well-behaved dog," Jin said, "not one to run around all the time. I see him stationed at the cafe's door every day." Mingliang told him how the dog had saved his shop from being flooded and had also saved his life.

"Quite a loyal dog," Jin said as he hammered away on a piece of jewellery.

"That's not all. He's smart too. How else was he able to do what a human would do? Know why he's so smart?"

"No, why?"

"Because he's got an extra-large head, bigger than most dogs. He's a common pug, but his head isn't ordinary. Feel it and you'll agree that most dogs don't have such a big head. I worry his neck won't be strong enough to support it."

Jin stopped hammering to rub Sun Erhuo's head. "You're right, it's bigger than other dogs' heads."

The dog wagged his tail and seemed to smile.

Fifteen years passed in a hurry, and Sun Erhuo got old. Legs are the first to go when people get old. Same with dogs. He started slowing down and, before long, began to stagger just a bit when he walked. He'd take a few steps, stop to pant awhile, his energy slipping away. He'd move around at night, going nowhere, then sleep all day in the restaurant doorway. When he awoke, he'd gaze off into the distance. Mingliang took him to a veterinary hospital for an exam, including blood, heart, brain waves and a CT scan. The doctor reported that the dog was old. His arteries had hardened, his blood was too viscous and his blood pressure was high.

"Can something be done? Surgery?"

"How old is he?"

"Fifteen."

"That's the equivalent of nearly ninety for humans, an advanced age. At his time of life, surgery would be out of the question. Take him home and look after him."

That's what Mingliang did. Over the coming days and weeks, Sun Erhuo often went out to do his business and forgot to come back in. Mingliang would have to bring him home. He knew his memory was failing. One night, the dog did not come home, so Mingliang went looking for him. He did not find him. He was still not home the next day, which scared Mingliang and Xiaomeng. They searched, near and far. The restaurant staff joined the search. No luck. Mingliang printed a bunch of posters for a lost dog, giving Erhuo's appearance when he went missing and the promise of a reward. He appended a photograph and his mobile number, pasting them in streets and lanes all over the Wild Goose neighbourhood. There was no response.

"Sun Erhuo, you can't die away from home."

On the morning of the third day, Mingliang's mobile phone rang. Someone had spotted a dog that looked a lot like the one on the poster lying under a bridge in South Park.

Mingliang rushed to the park, and there was Sun Erhuo, huddled in a corner under the bridge, only half awake.

"Sun Erhuo, you scared the life out of me."

Seeing he was too weary to stand, Mingliang picked him up and carried him home. He stopped eating after a couple of weeks, so Mingliang mixed some chicken liver in a bowl. He sniffed it and lay back down. Mingliang carried him back to the veterinary hospital.

"He hasn't eaten in three days. Is he going to die?"

The doctor listened to the dog's chest with his stethoscope.

"It's his time. His organs are failing. For him, living is suffering."

"Then why doesn't he die?"

"Dogs fall into two types, some prefer to die at home, others do not. This is something I've learned over time after so many dogs in my life."

Mingliang understood why he'd gone to lie under the bridge in South Park.

"Where do they go, the dogs that don't want to die at home?"

"Somewhere away from human eyes. They want to die with dignity."

With a nod of understanding, Mingliang drove off with Sun Erhuo but did not go home. Instead, he headed for a remote area out of town.

"Sun Erhuo," he said to the dog as he drove, "since living is suffering for you, it's time to die."

Sun Erhuo nodded.

"Since you want to die far away, let's go as far as we can."

Sun Erhuo nodded.

"Since you want to die away from human eyes, we won't be anywhere around people."

Sun Erhuo moved from the passenger seat onto Mingliang's lap as he drove along. They left Xi'an and drove through the countryside up into the mountains. They did not meet another car on the mountain road, nor see a single human being. Just before the car began to climb, they came to a cornfield. Mingliang stopped the car and carried Sun Erhuo into the field. When they reached a spot deep in the field, where there was no one anywhere around, he laid the dog down and said, "How's this spot, Sun Erhuo?"

The dog nodded and walked unsteadily into the field without looking back.

Mingliang drove back home. He lay awake all night. The following day, he drove back to the cornfield, wanting to see what happened to Sun Erhuo. Had he died? If so, he hoped to find the body and give him a proper burial. He looked and he looked, but did not find Sun Erhuo, dead or alive. He broke down and cried.

"Sun Erhuo, where are you? I miss you, Sun Erhuo."

Five years passed. As Mingliang was having his back scrubbed in a public bath one day, the scrubber mentioned that the mind of the former manager of the Daobei Market, Sun Erhuo, was shot. The man had sold vegetables in the market before coming to work at the bathhouse. Twenty years. Mingliang had long forgotten the man. Now that his name had cropped up, he was reminded of a dog with the same name that had died five years before. He'd let him loose in a cornfield. Imperceptibly, the dog had faded away and

Mingliang had got older. He had named the dog after the market manager, making it an avatar for the man he hated. He still missed Sun Erhuo the dog, and decided to visit Sun Erhuo the man. He got the address from the bathhouse worker and went to the Daobei Market the next morning, taking with him two bottles of alcohol and four cartons of cigarettes, a repeat of his first meeting, when he'd carried the gifts in a plastic bag. He went to Sun's home and knocked on the door, which was opened by a young man who had dyed his hair blond.

"Who are you looking for?"

"Is this Manager Sun's home?"

"Who are you?"

Mingliang handed the young man his business card.

"Oh, you're the general manager of Marshal Tianpeng's. My friend and I have eaten there. Not half bad. How do you know my father?"

So this was Sun Erhuo's son.

"I once sold vegetables in the Daobei Market," Mingliang told him, "and your father looked after me. I heard he was ill, and have come to see him. We were both originally from Yanjin."

Sun's son accepted the gifts and invited Mingliang in. He was led into a room, where a white-haired old man was sitting in an armchair, looking around blankly, his head wobbling back and forth. The man who had pissed in Mingliang's face had not aged well over the twenty years since he'd last seen him. Aware that someone had come into the room, he turned his head.

"Who are you?"

"Mingliang."

"Did you say Sihai?"

"Sihai was one of my father's friends. He died last year. He thinks everyone he sees is Sihai."

"I'm Mingliang, not Sihai."

"Good to see you, Sihai," the old man insisted.

He didn't know how to react. He'd come on behalf of Sun Erhuo the dog to see Sun Erhuo the man, who thought he was Sihai. The difference between this Sun Erhuo and the one that died five years ago was obvious: Sun the dog's head was big, the size of a gourd; Sun the man's head was small, like a pear. His son assumed that the two men were old friends, while Mingliang's purpose in coming was to get an idea when the man would die.

His son said to Mingliang as he was leaving, "He doesn't know who you are, so you'll waste your time if you come again."

"He doesn't know me, but I know him."

From then on, every time he thought about his Sun Erhuo, he went to see the other one. He missed the loyal one, he gloated over the demented one. On one visit, Sun Erhuo's son went into another room to play video games, leaving them alone.

"Sun Erhuo, twenty years ago, when you were manager of the Daobei Market, you mistreated Mingliang and his wife, forcing them to leave. Remember?"

"Who's Mingliang?"

"That's not what we're talking about. Yes or no, you mistreated them."

That got a rise out of Sun. "What did they do wrong? I always have my reasons for dealing with people."

Mingliang knew he could never explain to the demented

Sun that he'd wanted get his own back. Repeating the reason would be pointless and revenge was out of the question. So, with a sigh, he got up and walked out.

Mingliang and Xiaomeng had begun sleeping in separate rooms two years earlier, since she was annoyed by his snoring and he found her frequent visits to the toilet irritating. But he knew that those weren't the real reasons for the night-time split. The main reason was that the part of Mingliang that ought to be hard had softened, and the parts of her that ought to be soft had hardened. The long tongue of her youth had shortened, he discovered. Though their days of intimacy were behind them, if there was something to deal with, it was comforting to have the other person beside you.

Mingliang once had an acute attack of gallstones, which led to an infected gallbladder that required surgery. As he was being wheeled into the operating room, Xiaomeng was in the toilet. He asked the doctor to wait while he said something to his wife. The doctor said there was no time, that there was a queue of people waiting to have their gallbladders removed. Then I won't do it, Mingliang said. So the doctor told a nurse to rush to the toilet and bring Mingliang's wife out. When she got there, the doctor said, "Whatever it is, say it fast." But he said nothing and had them wheel him in, where the anaesthetist put him under. When he came to, he complained to Xiaomeng, "What was the idea of going to the toilet while I'm about to be operated on?"

"I was so scared, I had to pee."

. . .

Mingliang was on the sofa watching TV one night and checking his phone until he got sleepy. He went to his bedroom, undressed and was about to hop into bed, when Xiaomeng walked in dressed in nightclothes.

"What's this about?"

"Don't worry, I just want to talk to you about something."

"What?"

She sat on the edge of the bed. "Remember the girl Xiangxiu on West Avenue in Yanjin?"

He did. She was the one who'd spread the word about what Xiaomeng had done in Beijing twenty years earlier. It was she who'd forced them to move to Xi'an.

"What about her?"

"She phoned me today."

That was a shocker. "How's that possible?"

"She got my number from my aunt back home."

"What does she want?"

"She says she wants to pay us a visit."

He didn't know whether to laugh or cry. "I thought you were bitter enemies."

"She says she regrets what she did and wants to apologise. She says we were forced to leave our home because of her, and she'll never be at peace until she apologises in person. If she didn't do that in this life, it would be terrible to be reborn as a farm animal. That shows how much it means to her."

The reason behind Xiangxiu's visit to their home was not what Mingliang expected. He thought this might be similar to the bad blood between him and Sun Erhuo. If Sun's mind had not deteriorated and he were to offer to atone for what he'd done, would Mingliang have accepted it? Maybe not, after all that time. Not if he'd been in worse shape than Sun, but maybe if he were in better shape than his enemy. That is to say, if one is in a superior position, one need not retaliate tit for tat. Still, he was uneasy.

"Could she have something up her sleeve?"

"After all this time, after we've gone our separate ways and become old, what sort of scheme could she come up with?"

That made sense to Mingliang.

"Where is she now?" he asked.

"She's a milker up in the Mongolian city of Ulanqab."

Learning of the woman's plight, Mingliang said, "What's past is past. We don't need to make a big deal out of it. Let her come."

"That's how I feel. But there's a problem. Over the phone, she said she'd bring someone with her."

"A man or a woman?"

"A woman."

"One more guest can't make any difference to us. They can come together if they want."

"But there's something you need to know about the woman."

"What is it?"

"Her face is disfigured."

This gave Mingliang pause. "Who is this woman?"

"A close friend, Xiangxiu said. They were in the sex business together. The woman contracted the dreaded disease and never had it taken care of. They're together now."

Mingliang leaned back, hands clasped behind his head and said nothing.

"You're not the only one who has doubts about a woman with a diseased face. Me too. Shall we just say no? It's not us that worries me, it's our son."

"You're right," Mingliang agreed.

"I'll phone her tomorrow and tell her she can come, but only if she comes alone."

"Sounds good."

Xiaomeng got up and went back to her room.

That same day, Fan Youzhi from the Daobei Bus Company phoned Mingliang to say his daughter, Furong, was getting married on the eighth and invited Mingliang to the wedding. He followed that with a text message telling him to meet him on the west lawn of Daobei Zhongshan Park before ten in the morning. We'll catch up.

Mingliang had often visited Youzhi during the holidays since he had been a big help when they arrived in the city. He was now partially paralysed, confined to a wheelchair. No longer able to drive, he survived at home on employee benefits.

At nine-thirty on the morning of 8 May, Mingliang arrived at Zhongshan Park in Daobei, Furong's wedding site. He'd discovered that the groom came from a family of Xi'an real estate developers named Jin. They had built the house Mingliang lived in. A stage had been set up on the grass, a flower-bedecked archway had been erected at the entrance, with a red carpet leading to the stage. At least a hundred tables had been set up on the grass, each with a white tablecloth. Red ribbons decorated the chairs. A crowd of attendees filled the area in front of the stage, where a brass band was playing. Mingliang stopped first at the reception table to leave his monetary gift and was given a boutonniere to pin on his lapel to thread his way through the crowd. Eventually, he found Youzhi at a table in the shade of a peach tree at the edge of the grass. Seated in his wheelchair, he was wearing a suit and a red tie. They shook hands.

"Quite an event, Youzhi. Good for Furong to marry into a prosperous family."

"Thanks for that." He drew Mingliang down into a chair beside him. "She is marrying into a prosperous family," he whispered, "and woe is me."

"What does *that* mean?"

"Since I'm disabled, they asked me to stay home and not attend the ceremony. I was outraged, so here I am."

"How dare they! They can't get away with that."

"It's not them, it's Furong. She says all the guests will be prestigious, and she's afraid I'll embarrass her."

Mingliang was speechless.

"When she saw I came anyway, she had them put me over here and won't let me sit at the head table during the banquet."

Mingliang saw that the peach tree table was more than a dozen tables away from the stage.

"It doesn't matter where you sit, Youzhi. The food will be the same."

Youzhi lowered his voice. "They're rich, all right, but you don't want to dig into their background."

"How's that?"

"His father was sort of a gangster in Daobei."

"No one asks where a hero comes from, Youzhi."

They were interrupted by the band's playing of *The Wedding March* to start the ceremony. Two flower girls walked through the archway and down the red carpet, sprinkling flower petals. The bride and groom came next, accompanied by two pairs of maids of honour and best men; then came two boys in suits holding the train of the bride's gown. When the new couple reached the stage, the master of ceremonies announced the start of proceedings. He began with the couple's romance, which drew laughter on and below the stage. Then he invited the wedding official to join him on the stage and say a few words. After that, he invited up the witnesses and asked them to say a few words. Finally, two distinguished guests were invited to make short speeches.

Mingliang recognised them all – wedding official, witnesses, distinguished guests – having seen them on television, the cream of Xi'an's moneyed class: developers, financiers, internet providers, mine owners and more. Up on the stage, they were talking, laughing, cracking jokes, drawing laughter and applause from below the stage. The master of ceremonies waited until they were finished before asking the new couple up to say their vows and exchange rings. He then pronounced them man and wife. "You may now kiss the bride," he said, bringing the hour-long ceremony to a close. The banquet could begin. Mingliang knew that at most weddings, the parents of the bride and groom were invited to say a few words, before the young couple offered tea to the parents of the bride and groom. Both were skipped at this wedding. It was not hard to know the reason why and that Youzhi had told the truth. Mingliang looked at Youzhi, who was sweating.

"Furong was right," he whispered. "It's a good thing we weren't asked up on stage. They're rich and influential, so when they speak, people listen. If it had been me up there, I'd have made a fool of myself."

One look at him, and Mingliang had to agree. He was just sitting here and already sweating. If he were up there, he'd have been shaking with fear. It would have been a terrible loss of face.

"You're one big family now, Youzhi, so don't let these things get to you."

As servers began carrying food to the tables, the master of ceremonies returned to the microphone.

"You have just witnessed a Western-style wedding ceremony, solemn and full of life. Now while you enjoy the food and drink, General Manager Jin has hired a Henan opera troupe to liven things up. Many of our guests are residents of Daobei whose ancestral homes are in Henan. They will enjoy the performance."

Gongs and drums preceded the opening bars of the opera by plucked string instruments. Then the actors took the stage to sing the aria *Broken Bridge* from the opera *Legend of the White Snake*, where Xu Xian and White Snake first meet at West Lake. Since it is raining, there is an umbrella, which they pass back and forth on the lake shore.

At first, Mingliang paid little attention, but as he began to watch the drama and listen to the music, he thought the woman who was playing White Snake looked very much like his mother, Yingtao, and not just in appearance, but the way she spoke and sang too. He had never discovered where his mother had been carried to when he flung her photograph into the Yangtze nearly half a century earlier. He'd later carried Ma Dao Po from Wuhan to Qinling, but when he asked her if she knew where his mother was, she said she did not. And when he asked her where she was going, she said back to where she came from. At the time, he did not know where that was. Now he had an inspiration, not about where Ma Dao Po had come from, but a realisation of where his mother had come from. In the human world, she'd been Yingtao, but on the stage, she was a snake. Now that she was no longer a person, she'd come back to life as a snake, so Mingliang could see her. He knew, however, that the opera and the snake were make-believe. An opera had brought her back to life. Ma Dao Po had said she did not know where Yingtao had gone, but now, thanks to Ma Dao Po's comment, he knew where she had gone. As he listened to the White Snake sing up on the stage, tears ran down his cheeks.

"What's wrong, my friend?" Youzhi asked him.

"This truly is a happy event, elder brother. I'm thrilled."

FOUR

Sun Erhuo's son showed up at Marshal Tianpeng's Cafe one day, looking for Mingliang.

"My father wants to see you, Uncle."

"What for?"

"Don't know."

Since it was the end of the month and accounts for the main cafe and the branches needed to be checked, Mingliang said, "How about in a couple of days? This is a busy time for me."

"That's not right."

"What does *that* mean?"

"You've visited my father a dozen times over the past couple of years. He was home waiting for you every time.

Now he wants to see you, and you say you're busy. Would you say that's right?"

Mingliang had to admit he made sense.

"You're right, it's not."

"Who told you to keep going to see him? He thinks you're Sihai. Wouldn't you say this is a situation you created?"

"I would."

"OK, then, come with me."

Mingliang put on a coat and went with Sun Erhuo's son to their house, where Sun slapped his head when he saw Mingliang.

"Sihai, I won't make it past the end of the year."

His son was there beside him. "He's been in this room so long his imagination is running wild. I usually ignore his wild talk. Today, there's something I have to do, so I'll leave you here with him. On your way out, don't forget to lock the door behind you. I don't want my dad getting lost. If he does, I'll come looking for you."

He turned and walked out, to Mingliang's befuddlement. "What did you want to see me about?" he asked Sun.

"I want you to do something for me."

"What?"

"There's a man named Dong back in my hometown of Yanjin, a fortune-teller who can see into the future. I want you to phone him, give him my birth details and ask him to tell me about my next life. I'd have done it myself, but I don't have a mobile. You do. My son ignored me when I asked him to do it. I'd go outside to phone Dong myself, but my son has me locked up here. It won't cost you much to make a call, and it won't waste a lot of your time."

Before leaving, Mingliang had considered a dozen or so reasons why Sun Erhuo had wanted to see him. This was not one of them.

"Why do you want to know?"

"I haven't lived much of a life this time around. Who'd have thought it'd end like this?"

"What are you hoping for in your next life?"

"Anything so long as it's not like this."

"You don't want to be Sun Erhuo again, is that it?"

Sun nodded and took out a heavily stained pocket-size notebook. "You'll find Dong's phone number in here. I got it ten years ago when I made a trip to Yanjin. At the time, I wanted to find out who stole my van, and forgot to ask about my next life."

Twenty years earlier, Mingliang had asked Dong to determine what Sun Erhuo was in his last life, and learned that he'd been a cat demon. He'd seen what Sun's current life was like and was curious to know what he'd be next. He and Old Dong's son had been classmates. So he knew Dong's phone number, but he pretended to look through the notebooks, took out his phone and dialled his classmate's number. He told Guangsheng what Sun wanted. After hearing him out, he said his father did not predict future lives. Mingliang recalled that Dong's policy was to look into past and current lives, but not future ones. That way, he said, in addition to the unknowability of Heaven's mysteries, the client was better off. If you know the facts of all three lives – past, present and future – what's the point in living?

Mingliang put his hand over his phone and said to Sun Erhuo, "The signal's weak in here. I'll go out onto the balcony to talk."

He shut the balcony door behind him and said to Guangsheng, "Tell your father that not predicting the next life of a good man is a good idea, but revealing aspects of a bad man's next life can't hurt anyone."

"Who is it you're talking about?"

"Your father told his fortune twenty years ago. He's the one who ruined things for us in Xi'an, the cat demon. Then ten years ago, he asked your father to find out who stole his van. I'll ask him for his dates and tell you."

"I know what you're saying, but even if my father agreed to predict what 'cat demon' would be like in his next life, he won't be able to do it, even with the dates."

"Why not?"

"He caught a cold last month. At first, his mouth twisted a little, but then he couldn't hold water in it, and now he can't talk."

Mingliang could only ask, "Can he still tell fortunes?"

"He can't talk, but we can do a living transmission."

"How can he do that if he can't talk?"

"Here, living transmission means to summon the Celestial Master. My father uses hand gestures I can understand."

Knowing how things were, Mingliang said, "Then can you ask your father to do that for the cat demon?"

"It's more complicated than fortune-telling. Birth dates alone won't do it. The person must be present. Just think, the Celestial Master would be present."

But owing to Sun's demented state, his son had him locked in his room and never let him leave, so how could he ever go to Yanjin?

"If he can't appear in person, what then?" Mingliang asked.

"The next best thing would be to have a tuft of his hair."

"Hair can be a stand-in for the person, is that what you're saying?"

"A person's physical information can be found in the hair. In ancient times, a man's hair could stand for his head."

Mingliang returned to the room from the balcony and told Sun Erhuo what he'd learned over the phone.

"Bring me scissors," Sun said without a second's hesitation.

"I don't see how these old bones could ever make it to Yanjin, Sihai, so take my hair as my substitute and let Dong work with it. That's the only way I can die with no regrets. I'll pay for everything, don't worry."

"Can we get somebody else to do this for you? It's the end of the month, my busy time."

"No."

"Why not?"

"You're the only one I trust. I've been cooped up in this room for at least four years. Who else but you, Sihai, has come to see me?"

Without waiting for Mingliang, he got up and took a pair of scissors out of a drawer. He walked up to a mirror, grabbed a handful of hair, and snipped it off. He handed it to Mingliang.

"Go now, Sihai, there's no time to waste."

Mingliang had no choice. He took the hair. "I'm going, I'm going."

FIVE

Despite agreeing to go to Yanjin for Sun Erhuo, Mingliang did not leave at once. Sun's mind was functioning badly, and he was sure he wouldn't make it past the end of the year, but daft people say daft things, so he did not take him at his word. If Sun had been a friend, he'd have gone to any extreme to carry out his request. But Sun was not his friend, he was his arch-enemy, and the only reason Mingliang had visited him was because of the dog that had died. He'd be doing his enemy a favour if he didn't do the opposite of what he asked. Not only that, Sun believed he was talking to Sihai, not Mingliang, so why should Mingliang give it more than a passing thought?

Mingliang had kept the other Sun Erhuo's dog bed on the balcony at home. After leaving Sun's house, he took the hair and tossed it in. He left it at that. At first, he was well aware of what he'd promised; slowly but surely, however, over the coming busy days, he put it out of his mind.

Qin Weiwei phoned Mingliang from Wuhan one day during the Mid-Autumn Festival to tell him that his father's cousin had called from Yanjin to tell them that a highway from Jiyuan, Henan to Heze, Shandong was planned that would go through Yanjin. One section would pass by the Chen family ancestral plot, where Mingliang's grandparents were buried. Affected families were told they must move their ancestral graves to a spot by the Yellow River that had been selected by the government for them. Chen Changjie was adamant about going personally to take care of the move, but he was still in the hospital and if something happened on the road, it would be a family tragedy. So Weiwei phoned Mingliang to see if he could take time out to go to Yanjin. The request fell on eager ears when he learned that he would be going for his grandparents. Forty years earlier, when he was six years old, his grandmother had come to Wuhan to see him. She'd died soon after returning home, and when Mingliang asked his father if he could go with him to attend the funeral, Chen Changjie had said no, that it would interfere with his schoolwork. He responded by leaving school and taking a train, the wrong train, to a city in Zhuzhou. He'd disembarked and walked all the way to Yanjin, a trip that took two months.

"I'll go, don't worry, and tell Papa to stay where he is."

When he told his wife that it was for his grandparents, she agreed that he should go to Yanjin to take his father's place. He got on the road the next day. He and Xiaomeng had moved to Xi'an twenty years before, after spending a day and a night on a local train. Now the trip on a high-speed train took him four hours.

In Yanjin, rather than stay with schoolmates or friends, he went to a hotel, where he could attend to personal matters without disturbing anyone. After checking in and having a wash, he was hungry and realised he'd missed lunch, so he strolled down West Avenue. He hadn't been in Yanjin for twenty years. It had changed. The buildings and shops were all new, the pedestrians were all strangers to him, and him to them. He belonged to the city's past, an out-of-towner.

He spotted a restaurant that advertised oven-baked wheat cakes and lamb tripe soup, food he'd enjoyed as a child. The place was crowded, but he found a table and ordered two wheat cakes and a bowl of soup. While waiting, he overheard someone at a nearby table say that Old Dong the fortune-teller had died.

"Friend," he asked the man, shocked by the news, "are you talking about the fortune-teller on Grasshopper Lane on East Avenue?"

The man nodded.

"When did he die?"

"They buried him yesterday."

The news triggered a memory from when he was sixteen. Since his father could no longer support him, he'd left Li Yansheng's home and apprenticed at Marshal Tianpeng's Cafe in town. One day he met Old Dong there. The blind fortune-teller stomped his foot. Had he known earlier, he could have taken care of the boy's studies, saying he might be blind, but it was within his ability to support a child in his schooling. Mingliang would have moved into Dong's house as a virtual member of the family. His food arrived, but the enjoyment he'd anticipated was dampened. He ate what he could, paid the bill and went straight to Dong's home on East Avenue.

When he arrived, he saw Dong Guangsheng outside sweeping the compound of ashes and firecracker debris from the funeral. Grey hair had crept into his sideburns; he wore a black armband.

"Guangsheng."

He looked up and, after a moment's hesitation, saw it was Mingliang. His eyes reddened. He tossed down his broom. "When did you get back?"

"Just got here."

"I wasn't going to cry, but just seeing you, I can't help it."

He took Mingliang's hand and began to weep. Mingliang's eyes also reddened. Once he stopped crying, Guangsheng asked what he'd come back for. Mingliang told him about the planned highway and the need to move family graves. He asked his friend what illness had caused his father to die so suddenly.

"No illness, his head rolled to the side and he was gone. He was wearing his ceremonial robe and was helping someone's living transmission."

Old Dong, a blind man, had told the fortunes of sighted people all his life. Had he anticipated his own precipitous death in the midst of telling a fortune?

"It's sad your father died so suddenly," he said, hoping to console his friend, "but it was quick and painless, good fortune for a well-lived life."

"That's how I look at it."

"Will you be taking over from your father, Guangsheng?"

"I'd like to, but I haven't got what it takes."

"Nonsense, not after all these years by his side."

"Fortune-telling skill is something you're born with. It has nothing to do with the duration of time. He couldn't see, but he had what it takes. I don't. I'd only be cheating people. Cheating people in other ways is one thing, in fortune-telling it's immoral."

Mingliang sighed when he realised that Old Dong's skill in fortune-telling would be a lost art in Yanjin. It was then he recalled that a month or so earlier, back in Wuhan, Sun Erhuo had asked him to bring a tuft of his hair to Yanjin for Old Dong to predict what he would become in his next life. Now he'll never know. Even had the old man not died, he wouldn't have been able to do what Sun wanted, since Mingliang had forgotten to bring the hair to Yanjin with him. He'd tossed it into the other Sun Erhuo's dog bed. Obviously, the whole affair had not meant much to him. But another thought came to him.

"Guangsheng, your father told fortunes all his life. Did you ever ask him what he'd be in his next life?"

"I did. He said he'd be a sighted person."

"Did you ask him what'd he'd do in his next life?"

"I did, but he said that celestial secrets should not be revealed, only that I'd see him again one day at a train station."

That reminded Mingliang of one of the tales his grandmother had told him as a child. It was about her father. Many years after he died, she'd spotted him from the rear at a market.

"It's predestined. Since you won't take over from your father, what will you do now?"

"That's what I keep asking myself. Do you remember our school classmate Feng Mingchao?"

"Sure. The one with small eyes. He taught me how to play the flute when we were still in school. He came all the way from Zhengzhou to be at my wedding."

"For a while, he was a buyer for a Zhenzhou department store, but then he moved to Shanghai to work in a Japanese restaurant. He came back a couple of days ago to pay his condolences, and when he took a look at our compound, he said it had good feng shui, that it would attract wealth, a sure-fire spot to open a Japanese-style pub he called an *izakaya*. The first of its kind in Yanjin, he said. The place can no longer serve my papa, and there's nothing else planned, and I said I'd think it over. You're a restaurant owner, what do you think?"

That a compound once reserved for fortune-telling would be converted into a pub made Mingliang wonder if the old man had seen it coming. Being the first of its kind had its appeal, but first to open can also lead to first to close. But since nothing had been settled, he chose not to comment.

"It's worth a try," he said to Guangsheng. "I just wonder if people in Yanjin would find raw fish to their liking."

More than two hundred people were buried in Mingliang's ancestral graveyard, those on the highest ground being the earliest, reputedly from the Qianlong period of the Qing dynasty. Generations followed, more than a dozen, all part of the Chen heritage; unlike the ones who stayed in Yanjin, those who left were total strangers to each other. Their shared family was the only thing connecting them. Mingliang said goodbye to Guangsheng and went to find his father's cousin, a distant uncle by the name of Chen Changyun, who took him to the gravesite, which faced the Yellow River and backed to mountains, quite decent scenery, and, all in all, good feng shui, according to his uncle. The people were glad to cooperate since the government was compensating them for the move, and, more importantly, the feng shui was good. In the afternoon, more than a hundred members of the current generations of the Chen family met in Chen Changyun's compound to discuss the planned move.

Chen said, "We are twenty-six branches of the Chen family over the generations, and to keep things from getting out of hand, each of us is responsible for our ancestors' graves. Only one problem. One of us, Chen Chuangui, is a depot guard at the Yumen oilfield in Gansu and could not get a leave of absence to return until four days from now. Should we wait?" The representatives talked among themselves.

"It's my view," he volunteered, "that we should wait. If the rest of us go ahead and leave holes all over the ground, all but one mound, people would laugh at us. We are, after all, members of the same clan. A month or two would be too long. But we're talking about four days. Do we wait or not?"

"Since Chen Changyun recommends waiting," someone said following the discussion, "I say we wait."

"Agree." Another voice.

For Mingliang, this presented a problem. If it were ten days or a couple of weeks, he could go home to Xi'an and return when it was time to make the move. But four days put him in limbo. If he went home, he'd have to come back two days later. Unable to make up his mind, he phoned home.

"It's only four days," Xiaomeng said. "Don't wear yourself out travelling back and forth. Everything's fine here, and you can get a couple of days' rest."

"But what about the Mid-Autumn Festival?"

"It comes around every year. Missing one year is no big deal."

That made sense to him. Might as well deal with this unexpected turn of events by spending the holiday in Yanjin.

After hanging up, he strolled over to the ferry landing, where a setting sun cast its light on the river, giving off golden sparkles as it flowed east. As he walked on a bit, he saw that the Ma Family Shop had given way to a nightclub, whose neon sign spelled out Paris Nightclub in English. It had once been Ma Xiaomeng's home. Her stepfather, a real bastard, had begun abusing her when she was fifteen. That had lain behind her decision to move to the school dormitory, where she'd had a boyfriend and failed the college entrance exam. She'd then gone to Beijing, where she'd earned her living as a prostitute. Old Man Ma was at the centre of all this. Now, twenty years later, he was gone, as was Xiaomeng's mother, reducing all that happened to smoke and dust.

Xiaomeng had a younger stepbrother, currently a man in charge of the scales at a Jiaozuo mine. His son, Ma Pite, Xiaomeng's nephew, worked at Mingliang's Marshal Tianpeng's Cafe. While these thoughts were running through his head, a couple walked out of the nightclub. He had a mohawk haircut, she was wearing a tank top with spaghetti straps. She said goodbye and headed into town, while he leaned against a stone lion by the entrance and lit up. Mingliang ignored him, but was surprised when the man stared and said, "Is that you, Mingliang?"

A close look revealed that it was Sima Xiaoniu, one of Mingliang's classmates, from a different section. His father, Sima Niu, had been Mingliang's chemistry teacher.

"It's you, Xiaoniu. I didn't recognise you with that haircut. It's been thirty years."

"When'd you get back?"

"Only this morning." He told Xiaoniu about the

planned highway and the need to move the ancestral graves. He assumed that Xiaoniu was enjoying a night out.

"It's still light, too early to be out for fun."

"I own the place," Xiaoniu said. "No customers yet, I came out for some fresh air."

From student to nightclub owner in the years between, Mingliang had to take another look at the club.

"Pretty classy. Business must be good."

"Not bad. I don't have the customer base of a big city."

"How's your father?"

"He left us last year."

What a shock that was. "Teacher Sima always looked to be in the best of health," he said.

He was reminded of something his teacher had wanted to do. There was a figure in Yanjin known as Hua Erniang, who came to people in their dreams looking for jokes. She had flattened many people. His teacher's lifelong goal had been to write a biography of Hua. In class, when he was lecturing on chemical reactions, he even managed to bring Hua Erniang into it. He said he wanted to write the book not only to describe her situation in Yanjin, but also to study the chemical reaction between her and Yanjin, on account of jokes. "I recall that your father was going to write a biography of Hua Erniang. I wonder if he finished it before he died."

"He accumulated so much material during his life that if you piled it up, it'd be as tall as a haystack, but he'd barely started writing. He was always saying there was more to get, and by the time he started writing, he was gone after only a few sentences."

With a sad shake of his head and a sigh, Mingliang said,

"What a pity." Then he asked, "Do you know where the material is now?"

"My mother burned it the day he died."

"A lifetime of work," he said, "how could she burn it all?"

"Nobody but my dad thought the stuff was worth anything. Besides, wouldn't leaving all Hua Erniang's material lying around the house be inviting disaster, just waiting for her to come in a dream looking for a joke?"

Mingliang found no fault in Xiaoniu's reasoning. "You said he started an opening to the book. Do you know what he wrote?"

"My mother burned the whole thing. How would I know?"

Sima's book, like the Ma Family Shop, had vanished in smoke and ashes. Nothing more needed to be said on that score, so the two friends exchanged a few pleasantries, and Mingliang took his leave. He strolled up to a street specialising in snacks by the ferry landing. Suddenly, he felt sort of hungry after a so-so lunch, and this was the place to take care of that. He checked his watch, it was already six o'clock, time for dinner. As he walked in, he saw a sign that advertised soup-filled buns from Kaifeng and spicy soup, two Henan items he hadn't enjoyed in a long time. The restaurant tables were arranged outside under a tall willow tree, where night breezes cooled the area. He stopped. A man and a woman were making buns by the door, placing them in a steamer basket, while a cauldron of spicy soup simmered on an open-air stove.

"Are you from Yanjin, my friend?" he asked the man.

The man took a steamer basket off the stovetop. "Yanjin,

you say? You're talking to someone who makes traditional Kaifeng food. I'm from Kaifeng."

With a laugh, Mingliang sat at one of the shaded tables and ordered a steamer of buns and a bowl of soup. While waiting, he spotted a sweaty man with a bedroll over his back, a whip in one hand, and, in the other, a tether hooked to a metal chain around a monkey's neck. To all appearances, he was a travelling performer with a trained monkey. He looked around before taking a seat by Mingliang, who ignored him. The man abruptly jumped to his feet and laid into the monkey with his whip. The animal yelped and jumped around, but couldn't get far with the metal collar and chain. The man was getting angrier by the minute, his whip landing on the monkey's head and body, drawing blood.

"What are you doing that for, friend?" Mingliang asked when he couldn't stand it any longer.

The man mopped his brow. "You don't know how crafty this thing is. At every performance, when I want him to spin around ten times, he does eight. When I want him to make twenty somersaults, he does fifteen. If he knows what he's doing, he's crafty. If he doesn't, the audience will think I'm cheating. If this isn't ruining my reputation, what is it? That's why I'm so mad."

"How old is he?"

"He's been with me fifteen years."

Mingliang thought about a monkey's lifespan and figured this one must be middle-aged.

"Maybe he's getting old, and that's taking a toll on his body. He can't run around like he used to."

"He can when I whip him. Crafty, that's what he is."

His anger resurfaced. The whip landed again on the monkey, which yelped and jumped around.

"People who travel a lot shouldn't think like a monkey. Otherwise, even a good meal can't make them happy."

With that, the man stopped the beating and pulled the monkey over under the tree. "I'll take care of you later."

The monkey shuddered in terror. Once it caught its breath, it began licking its bloody wounds. Mingliang studied the animal, whose callouses on its rear end and feet were deeply cracked. It was not a young specimen. Probably Mingliang's age in monkey years, a middle-aged animal that had to perform tricks for people and get whipped daily, which made him terribly sad. His ordered buns arrived.

"Would you like your soup at the same time?" the woman asked.

"No, after I've eaten the buns. I like my soup hot."

Mingliang took a bite from one of the buns – it was delicious. The soupy filling dripped onto his plate. Soup-filled buns were available in Xi'an but did not have the same authentic quality. He noticed that the monkey was staring at him and he felt sorry for it, so he took one of the buns from the steamer and handed it to the monkey. It didn't dare take it until it had sought permission from the man.

"He's offering it to you, so take it."

It accepted the offering and began to eat.

"Have you forgotten how to say thank you?"

It looked up, held out the bun and bowed.

"You don't have to thank me, it's just a bun."

It lowered its head and continued eating.

Having finished his meal, Mingliang got up and walked off. The monkey-man was still sitting there nursing a drink.

His monkey was leaning against the willow tree, fast asleep, arms folded around its midsection, the collar and chain still in place around its neck. Many of its wounds hadn't yet healed. It did not wake up when Mingliang left.

Mingliang went to Li Yansheng's house the next morning to visit him and Hu Xiaofeng. Even though they had let him leave school so he could apprentice himself to the pigs' feet cafe at the age of sixteen, they had provided for him for the ten years before that. If he hadn't gone to work, he would not now be the owner of six cafes. He also recalled how Li had given him twenty yuan in Wuhan, and when his granny died, that money and the gifts he had saved up had paid for his train ticket from Wuhan to Yanjin, though unfortunately, he had taken the wrong train.

Li and his wife still lived in the house they'd shared for more than forty years. It was looking its age and seemed squatter and smaller. They had opened a hole in the frontage wall, put in a windowed door and turned their house into a general store. Mingliang knew that years before, Li had sold grocery items of all types in the market on East Avenue. Prior to leaving for their house, Mingliang learned that Li was afflicted with osteomyelitis, a very painful infection. The pain was so bad one night that he'd got out of bed naked, gone outside and climbed the stairs along the side to the rooftop. He jumped. It was, of course, a suicide attempt, but he only broke a leg. Mingliang took with him four bottles of alcohol and four cartons of cigarettes. On entering the house, he saw a bed on one side of the shop. Li was lying on it. Hu Xiaofeng sat behind a counter doing cross-embroidery while tending the shop.

"Uncle. Auntie." They were surprised to hear Mingliang call to them. When Li saw who it was, he sat up in bed.

"Mingliang, when did you get here?"

"Yesterday."

"Just seeing you is enough," Hu said. "You didn't have to bring anything."

"Mingliang," Li Yansheng said as soon as his guest sat down, "have you heard that I jumped off the roof?"

"That's the first thing he says when he meets people," his wife said. "Had you heard? It's like some glorious achievement."

"You talk too much," he said with a glare.

"Me? You're the one who brought it up."

"I heard," Mingliang said. "You shouldn't have done that."

"Damned useless, couldn't even die when I wanted to. I've made my life a joke."

That line, it was the same thing Mingliang's father had uttered at the Wuhan railway hospital.

While the three of them were talking, Mingliang noticed something stuck up on the shop wall, a faded, insect-ravaged photograph of Li Yansheng, Chen Changjie and Yingtao in the opera *Legend of the White Snake,* taken fifty years before.

"The old Yanjin opera house was torn town last year to make room for a shopping centre and office building," Li said when he saw Mingliang looking at the poster. "There were some rolled-up posters in the warehouse. The demolition foreman was her nephew, so she went over and took one."

"You were all so young then."

"Never thought I'd wind up like this."

"Mingliang," Hu Xiaofeng said, "you used to like soft drinks. We sell them. Want one?"

"I've got stomach problems, Auntie, and cold drinks are no good for me."

"Your father's stepdaughter phoned me from Wuhan six months or so ago," Li Yansheng said. "She wanted your phone number, said your father wasn't well and hoped you'd make a trip to Wuhan. Did you go?"

"As soon as they called."

"Has your father recovered?"

Mingliang was not about to tell him the truth, in part because he assumed that Li had apprenticed him to a cafe at the age of sixteen, with which his father was not happy. And since both men were in poor health, neither able to do anything to help the other, any emotions would be pointless. Why waste his breath on meaningless talk?

"Just a bad case of the flu. A couple of days in the hospital with an IV, and he was fine."

"That's good to hear. That had me worried for a while."

"Papa said he planned to make a trip back to Yanjin in the spring."

"He should do that. When he does, I'll treat him to some pigs' feet. He can't wait too long to come back. There aren't many of us left."

That afternoon, Mingliang made a trip to the Yanjin Nursing Home to see the town's one-time street sweeper, Guo Baochen, whose son, Zikai, had been his classmate. A man who loved to gamble, he'd been told by the fortune-teller that in a previous life he'd been a high official in the early years of the Republic. His son had left for school in England twenty years earlier. Before leaving, he'd gone to

Shaanxi to see a former teacher and had stopped in Xi'an to visit Mingliang. They had got drunk at Mingliang's cafe. After Zikai left for England, they'd kept in touch by mail, so Mingliang knew he'd received his PhD, found a job, married an English woman and fathered two children. Then, with the advent of mobile phones, the two friends often exchanged texts. Mingliang received texted photos of Zikai and his family, including his attractive wife.

Now they were both in their fifties. At the rest home, Mingliang found Guo Baochen in a chair scratching his head. The nurse's aide said that his cerebral arteries had hardened, and he was suffering from dementia. He seldom spoke, and when he did, it was usually about gambling: "It's your turn, hurry up and play!"

Mingliang sat down. The old man did not know who his visitor was, and didn't understand Mingliang when he tried to explain. Hit with a sudden inspiration, Mingliang took out his mobile and checked the international time zones – morning in London. He phoned Zikai.

"I never expected a call from you at this hour," his friend said. "You usually call when it's night here."

"Guess where I am."

"How am I supposed to guess? Xi'an's a big city."

"I'm in Yanjin, sitting in the Yanjin Nursing Home. Came to visit your father."

"What a surprise. Since you're there, let's do a video chat. That way I can see my dad. His mind's shot, so he can't use a mobile phone. I never get to see him."

Mingliang turned the phone to face the old man.

"See, he looks good," Mingliang said, before turning to the old man. "Here, talk to your son."

"Pa," Zikai said to his father, "how're you doing?"

Guo Baochen waved him off. "Stop the bullshit and play!"

Seeing that wasn't working, Mingliang turned the phone to face himself.

"Physically, he's in good shape. It's just the dementia."

"He looks heavier. His jowls are sagging a little. Tell the staff from me not to let him eat all the time."

"Will do. What are you up to there now?"

"Just went to the laundry and am on my way home. See there, that's the Thames," he said as he sent images of the river and river traffic. "I'm sitting on the riverbank." He showed people walking past, mainly tourists. He turned the phone skyward. "Look, there's Big Ben."

"I see it. London looks like quite a place."

With a sigh, Zikai said, "I tell you the truth, Mingliang, seeing my father like that makes me think I should never have left."

"Are you kidding? You've done better than all of us."

"I screwed up. I've been in London all these years, and I never once got my father to visit. If I arranged it now, he wouldn't know what was going on. The tree prefers calm, but the wind does not stop. The child wants to support, but the parents can't wait."

"Loyalty and filial piety have always been at odds. You had your career."

"This has nothing to do with my career. It's about cultural differences."

"Meaning?"

"You know I married an English woman. When I told her I wanted to invite my father over, she asked 'Who will pay his travel expenses?' 'Me, of course,' I said. 'Why can't he pay his own way? And where would he stay?' 'He'd stay with us, of course.' 'If he can pay his way here, he should be able to afford a hotel,' she said. 'My dad bought a train ticket from Manchester to London and stayed in a hotel.' That led to an argument, and I had to put off a visit until my dad's mind failed him. I'm thinking of coming back to China to work. But what about England? I've got a wife and two children here. I don't know what to do. These are family issues, so I've kept them to myself. I never knew what cultural differences were all about, but now, they're part of my own family."

Mingliang was thinking about what his father had said outside the Wuhan hospital. "I've lived a life that can be characterised by one word – poor."

He then thought about what Fan Youzhi had said at his daughter's wedding. "Don't blame your wife for that," he said to Zikai, "and don't blame cultural differences."

"Who *do* I blame?"

"Bad timing."

"I don't get it."

"Fortune-Teller Dong said your father had been a prime minister in a previous life. If you could have gone back in time, and he was prime minister, he'd go to England on a state visit. You couldn't pay for his travel expenses even if you wanted to."

"You've got a point."

"A prime minister wouldn't bunk with you."

"Ditto."

"If he went to Ten Downing Street to meet the English Prime Minister, would your wife want to accompany him?"

"You bet she would."

"If, before he left, he wanted to give her twenty thousand pounds for spending money, would she take it?"

"In a minute."

"Would you call that a cultural difference?"

"Fuck!"

They both laughed.

"This has been the best day I've had this year, Mingliang."

"I've gained an insight."

"What is it?"

"Now that we've lived this long and think back to all the upsetting things in our lives, things that at the time seemed crippling, and worse, were really nothing."

"You got that right. Now that we're talking, there's something I want to say."

"Go ahead, say it."

"I may gave studied abroad and received a PhD, but you're wiser than me."

"I'm just an uneducated country bumpkin, Zikai, so please don't joke with me like that."

"I mean it."

"We're just a couple of old friends having a heart-to-heart, which makes for good times." Mingliang added, "Be sure to come to Xi'an when you return. We'll go out for pigs' feet."

"It's a deal. And we'll get good and drunk again."

When he hung up, Mingliang realised that Zikai hadn't returned the invitation when he invited him to come to Xi'an. Obviously, London didn't really suit him. Too bad. Mingliang sighed.

The next day was the Mid-Autumn Festival. When the owner of Yanjin's Marshal Tianpeng's Cafe learned that Mingliang was back, he invited him to dinner. Mingliang bought six bottles of the best spirits and six cartons of quality cigarettes at a local shop that afternoon and showed up at Marshal Tianpeng's in the evening. Owner Zhu, who once sported a full head of hair, now kept it cleanly shaved. He was waiting for Mingliang at the entrance. He laughed and rubbed his slick head when he saw him. Thirty years earlier, when Mingliang was Zhu's apprentice, he called Zhu "Sir" or "Boss". Now it was "Mentor".

When Zhu saw the gifts, he said only that he was happy to see Mingliang.

Instead of taking him into the cafe, he led him around back, where he had set up a table under the old willow tree. A light hung from a branch.

"We can talk better here," Zhu said. "If we were inside, you'd have to stop and chat with all the old friends you ran into."

"We can also enjoy gazing at the moon when it comes up."

"You've thought of everything."

They sat and sipped tea while Mingliang asked about the waiters Li, Zhao and Liu, two of whom were gone. Old Huang, who had taught Mingliang how to stew pigs' feet, had retired with a heart condition that had required four stints. After the Spring Festival, he'd gone to Qingdao, where his son was in the seafood trade. When Zhu asked about Mingliang's situation in Xi'an, he told him about the cafes he'd opened there. The first course of food arrived, brought to the table by a man Mingliang did not recognise at first.

But on a closer look, he saw it was Wei, who had taken his place cleaning pigs' feet. He was turning grey, evidence of the twenty years that had passed.

When he brought the next course, Mingliang said, "You're Xiao Wei, aren't you? Why didn't you say hello?"

With a laugh, Wei said, "You were having such a friendly chat, I didn't want to interrupt. You'll have to stop calling me Little Wei and make it Old Wei."

"He's one of the cafe's old-timers, and everyone calls him Old Wei," Zhu said. "Ten years ago, I promoted him from pigs' feet cleaner to pigs' feet stewer. He didn't have what it takes, kept burning the feet. I should have sent him back to clean the feet, but he wasn't a youngster any more, so I trained him to be a waiter."

Wei laughed. "The boss takes good care of me, really good care."

"Back when he was cleaning feet, I had to yell at him all the time. Same thing when he was stewing them."

"Bad memory. I kept forgetting things," Wei said with a laugh again, before picking up the tray and walking off.

"I mention the scolding," Zhu said, pointing at Wei, "and he runs off."

"I yelled at you when you were an apprentice, Mingliang. You don't hate me, do you?"

"When did you do that? I don't recall you yelling at me."

"Can't remember, huh? You once burned a whole bowl of pigs' feet with bitumen. I did more than yell, I gave you a couple of swift kicks."

"If I burned the feet, I deserved it. In Xi'an, when apprentices do something wrong, I yell at them too." He stood up, held out his glass and said, "It's time that I formally toast my mentor."

"What's that for?"

"I often tell myself that what I have today I owe to my mentor here. If you hadn't taught me a skill back then, I'd be starving in Xi'an."

Zhu waved him off. "I won't accept that. I've had plenty of apprentices, and you're the only one who's become such a success. As the saying goes, a teacher can get you through the door, but you're on your own from there."

As they talked and drank, the moon climbed in the sky, looking like an icy disk on a willow tree, whose shadow quivered on the ground and was reflected on the shimmering river behind the restaurant. Twenty years earlier, when Mingliang and Xiaomeng had worked there, he'd strolled to the bank to play his flute during breaks. The opposite bank was now an endless field of corn. As the stalks sang in the wind, Mingliang felt cold enough to drape Zhu's coat over his shoulders and put his on.

"I seem to recall that you used to sing opera. Do you still do it?"

"No longer, lost my voice. Or maybe I just lost interest. You used to play the flute. How about now?"

It had been a decade or more since he'd played. "Not for years. Like you, I guess I lost interest."

Wei walked up with a platter of moon cakes.

"This time you got it right," Zhu said. "Fifteenth day of the eighth lunar month, mooncake day."

"Old Wei, you're one of us," Mingliang said. "Take one for yourself and join us for a drink or two."

The man smiled and looked over at Zhu.

"Mingliang doesn't get back very often, so join us, like he said," Zhu urged.

Another laugh as he sat down. The three men ate mooncakes and drank. Zhu asked about the grave relocation. Mingliang filled him in on the details.

"Your granny was a good woman," Zhu said. "When I was young, your family sold dried bean curd on the street, not date cakes. Your grandfather had poor eyesight. We rowdy kids often stole and ate pieces of bean curd. He caught me once and was going to whip me until your granny stopped him. Boys will be boys, she said. I got away without a whipping that time."

"You have a good memory."

"After that, they made and sold delicious date cakes. She said the dates all came from your tree."

"Granny told me the tree was two hundred years old, and she filled several burlap bags with its dates each year, too many to eat. Not wanting them to rot on the ground, she had the idea to make them into cakes. She died some time ago, and so did the tree. Is that weird, or what?"

"It sure is. There are reasons for everything."

"I don't know what happened to the tree after it died."

"I know," Wei spoke up.

"Where did it go?" That got Mingliang's attention.

"After the tree died," Wei volunteered, "someone from your Chen clan cut it down and sold the wood to Old Fan, who took it home to Tapu to make furniture. My grandmother lives in Tapu. When I went to visit her one year, people were talking about the old days, and I heard Fan say so."

"Who's Old Fan?"

"A Tapu carpenter."

That night in the hotel, Mingliang dreamed that his granny was sitting beneath the date tree making date cakes and telling him stories. The tree slowly changed into tables and chairs and benches; then the two of them were seated at a bench, eating flatbread and fried eggs and spring onions at one of the tables.

SIX

Early the next morning, Mingliang hired a taxi to take him to Tapu, a township in Yanjin. He got directions to the home of Fan the carpenter. Sorghum stalks were stacked by the door. An old man was leaning against them enjoying the sun's warmth.

"That's the man you're looking for," someone on the street said.

Mingliang walked up and greeted him.

"Don't think I've seen you before. Who might you be?"

"You wouldn't know even if I told you. But I'll tell you who my father was. Chen Changjie, who used to sing opera in Yanjin."

Fan nodded. "Ah, he was well known, sang in *Legend of the White Snake*."

"The reason I've come today," Mingliang said, now that the connection had been made, "was to ask you something."

"What might that be?"

"Forty years ago, after my grandmother passed away, I believe you bought a date tree that had stood in her garden."

"Yes," Fan said with a nod. "It wasn't cheap. I offered fifty yuan, they wanted seventy. We settled on sixty."

"I hear you chopped it up and made furniture with the wood."

"That's right. Wood from a two-hundred-year-old tree is top quality."

"Is any of that furniture still around?"

"Who wants to know?"

"If some of it is, I'd like to buy it. Name your price."

"What a shame," Fan said, clapping his hands. "It's all gone."

"Where is it now?"

"Nowhere. It's gone."

"What does that mean?"

"I have five sons. I divided up the family property three years ago, including the furniture. Those bastard kids of mine didn't want any old furniture, so they chopped it up for firewood."

Mingliang was sickened by the news.

"Why did you want it anyway?"

"She was such a good grandmother to me, I wanted to keep something of hers. Just looking at it would remind me of her."

"I see. You're a good man, and I'm sorry you came too late."

Mingliang said his goodbyes and started walking off, just as Fan was reminded of something.

"Hold on."

Mingliang stopped. "What is it?"

"All the wood is gone, but I did keep something."

"What did you keep?"

"The centre of the trunk. Hard as iron. In the past, people used those for ploughs. It was too good for furniture, so I kept it back. Ten years ago, I sold it to a man named Jing in Tangyin County for two hundred yuan. He used it to carve a gate placard."

"Do you remember what he carved?"

"I never knew."

APPENDIX

INSCRIPTION ON A PLACARD

Jing lived in Tangyin, a city in Anyang, near Yinxu, a World Heritage archaeological site where antiques were sold. From the age of twenty, Jing worked for a dealer in antiques. After twenty profitable years selling antiques, he bought a piece of land beside the old yamen in the county town and built a manor. The area around the yamen was the bustling centre of town. The manor had several compounds within the main gate, over which Jing wanted to hang a placard. He knew that stately homes in the Qing dynasty and early Republican eras hung placards over their main gates, on which they engraved phrases such as "Glory Splendour Wealth and Rank" and "Good Luck Cheerful Tidings". Since the placards were exposed to the elements, they needed to be made of high-quality wood, such as Chinese cedar, sandalwood or date wood. One of Jing's aunts was a resident of Yanjin's Tapu Township. The year after building his estate, Jing visited his aunt. During a meal, he learned that a local carpenter had bought a two-hundred-year-old felled date tree, from which he'd made fine furniture. He'd kept the centre of the trunk at home. Jing paid Carpenter Fan a visit, saw it was a rare item, old and hard as steel, and bought it for two hundred yuan. A city in Anyang called Linzhou was home to carpenters who specialised in wood carving; they charged triple the fee of other carpenters. A man called Jin was the finest carver among them. Jing invited him to his house to see the trunk centre of the tree that had belonged to Mingliang's grandmother.

After rapping it with his knuckles and turning it over and over, the man said, "Good, a fine piece of wood."

"Good enough to hang over a gate?"

"Yes, but the question is, what would you like carved on it?"

"'Glory Splendour Wealth and Rank' or 'Good Luck Cheerful Tidings'."

"Which one do you want?"

"Whatever hangs over a gate has about the same meaning. I'll leave it to you."

Carving the placard would take a week or longer, so Jin would have to work at the estate. He was the first resident, with space to use as a workshop. They put a bed in a side room up front in the empty house. On the first morning, he transferred from a calligraphy sampler the words "Glory Splendour Wealth and Rank" and "Good Luck Cheerful Tidings" onto sheets of paper and spread them out on the ground to choose the one he'd carve. He simply could not make up his mind, not because of any difference in meaning between the two, but owing to questions regarding the strokes in each of the characters. Those with many strokes were difficult to carve, for the wood in spaces between dense strokes was thin, requiring care in the carving process; there was more unused space, with solid wood between characters that had fewer strokes, requiring less effort and time in carving.

Both had four characters, some denser than others, and about equal in terms of total stroke numbers, and, as a result, the same amount of work. He was trying to decide when a man walked into the yard, hands clasped behind his back. He took a look around, from front to back, first one side then the other. Assuming it was a member of the family, Old Jin ignored him. But when he did take notice, the man's expression told him he was a stranger.

"You'd better leave once you've had a look. This isn't my house, I'm just a hired worker. If you stick around and the owner hears about it, he may wonder about you."

"Was this compound modelled after the Anyang Ma Manor?" the stranger asked after taking another look.

"I'm just a carpenter, not a builder. I know nothing about that."

"It looks similar on the outside, but the construction is nothing like the Ma Manor and isn't worthy of the work put into it, the material or location. Everything about it is different, which shows how ignorant the owner is."

"You sound like an educated man," Old Jin said.

"Not so much," the man replied, "just someone who enjoys taking in the sights. I visited the old yamen and saw there was a new estate here. The gate was open, so I walked in. Sorry to bother you."

As he turned to leave, he spotted the calligraphy samples on the ground.

"What are those for?"

"I specialise in carving gate placards. I'm trying to choose which one to use."

The stranger laughed. "Excuse me for being impertinent, but these are both as tasteless as the estate itself."

"That's one of the reasons I've had trouble choosing. I'm sick of carving these same phrases, done it all my life. You're an educated man, any suggestions?"

"Even if I had, you work for the owner and can't decide for him."

"Actually, when he hired me he said it was up to me to carve what I wanted."

"I repeat, an ignorant man," the stranger said with a laugh. "But his ignorance works to his advantage. Let me give it some thought."

He looked down, mulled it over before looking up and saying, "I was reading a book on the train this morning and came across something quite familiar, but which seemed extraordinary for that book. It was 'one day three autumns', which meant not seeing someone for a day felt like the passage of three autumns, a single phrase worth ten thousand sentences when dealing with sentiments between people."

"Yes, but is it appropriate for a gate placard?"

"When it goes up over a gate, it has a different meaning, since it's no longer about sentiments between people. It's now about people and place. Living here for one day is like living elsewhere for three autumns. Appropriate?"

"That's so meaningful," said the carpenter, "and not tasteless. I like it. It's what I'm going to carve."

After the stranger left, Old Jin began carving the four characters into the wood. Truth to tell, he preferred the suggested phrase not for its meaning or for its good taste. A total of seventeen strokes in all was less than half the number of either of the other two phrases, making it an easier job. Since the owner had told him he could carve whatever he wanted, he discarded the two that Jing had suggested and chose "One Day Three Autumns". But when, after the work was finished, he invited Jing to see his work, the owner could hardly believe his eyes.

"What's this? I told you to carve 'Glory Splendour Wealth and Rank' or 'Good Luck Cheerful Tidings', didn't I?"

"Both those are tasteless, vulgar. This one has good taste, class."

Old Jin then told Jing how the stranger had explained the meaning to him.

"It is in good taste, but I'll have to explain it to people. The other two are tasteless, but the meaning is obvious to everyone. You've turned something simple into something complicated. Why didn't you check with me first?"

"You told me it was up to me."

Jing had to laugh, but he felt like crying. "What I meant was, choose what you thought was better – 'Glory Splendour Wealth and Rank' or 'Good Luck Cheerful Tidings'. How could you have misunderstood?"

"Well, then, get me a new piece of wood and I'll carve it for you."

"Forget it, it's only a placard, something to hang up there. Let's not make it even more complicated. 'One Day Three Autumns' isn't all that bad."

Old Jin heaved a sigh of relief. "No, it isn't."

SEVEN

Mingliang learned from Fan that the heart of the old date tree had been made into a carved gate placard for the Tangyin estate of a man named Jing. After thanking him, he called for a taxi and went straight to Tangyin. The ride took more than three hours. He asked around and found Jing's house, which, regardless of what Fan had told him, was not a grant estate, but a Western-style house with an old gatekeeper. When he approached the gatehouse, the old man came out to ask what he wanted. Mingliang said he wanted to speak to the owner. "You'd have had to come the year before last to do that. He and his family emigrated to Canada and sold the house to a local named Zhou."

"I was told Jing had built a grand manor. Where did this building come from?"

"I'll tell you what happened," the old man said. "Mr Jing built a manor with three compounds within the main gate. Mr Zhou, who was doing business in Zhengzhou, had his eye on this property but did not like what he built, so he bought it, razed it and built what you see, a four-storey Western house. The Zhou family is in Hainan on vacation. I'm watching the place for them."

Mingliang asked if he remembered the placard over Jing's gate.

"I was here when they turned the property over, and there was a placard."

"What was on it, do you recall?"

"I think it was 'One Day Three Autumns', carved, I was told, by a carpenter named Jin from Linzhou, which is known for woodcarvers who charge three times the fee of other carpenters. Among the carvers, Jin is the most accomplished–"

"Forget about Jin. What happened to the placard?"

"Mr Zhou got rid of it somewhere."

"It was a fine piece. Didn't he want to keep it?"

"He has no interest in antiques or old stuff. He knocked down a whole traditional manor, so what could a placard mean to him? Just look at this building. See anything that makes you think of China? It's Western from top to bottom."

Mingliang took a close look. It was, all right, and it reminded him of what he'd seen in Zikai's video chat.

"So where would Mr Zhou have disposed of the placard?"

"I'd say it must have been among the construction debris."

"Where'd they take it?"

"Villagers scavenge for used lumber and masonry."

Disappointment overwhelmed Mingliang. He turned and left what had been Jing's house, but had been replaced by the new owner Zhou. After a few steps, he went back to the gate and said to the old man, "Mr Zhou did not want the placard, but it's very important to me. Would you ask around and see what you can find out? I'll give a hundred thousand yuan to anyone who can find it for me."

He asked the old man for a piece of paper and wrote down his address in Xi'an and his mobile number.

The trip from Tangyin back to Yanjin was a weary one, so after dinner, he went to the bathhouse on North Avenue. A bath there cost only ten yuan, much less than one in Xi'an, where the price was forty or fifty for a scrub bath. Taken as a whole, life in Yanjin was easier on the wallet. He returned to the hotel after his bath, brushed his teeth, and had no sooner stretched out on the bed when there was a knock at the door. A girl in a tank top, wearing heavy lipstick, was leaning against the frame.

"Care for some service, sir?"

Mingliang knew she was a prostitute and what kind of service she provided. He wasn't opposed to what she was offering, for Xiaomeng had been in the same line of work as the girl, and he could only imagine how many men she had slept with. That alone would stop him from taking her up on it.

"No."

"Why not?"

"Too tired."

"Then this is just what you need to be refreshed."

"Then I can only say I'm not one of those men."

With a pout, the girl said, "Such lofty morals."

She walked off with a swish of her hips. "Not lofty morals," Mingliang said to himself with a sigh, "but a shadow over my heart. Because of that, there's no way I'm up to bedroom activity." He went back to bed and quickly fell asleep. Later that night, he was awakened by a nudge. His eyes snapped open and he was treated to the sight of a girl standing at the head of his bed. Thinking it was the same girl, he said, "Why are you back?"

"Have I been here before?" she asked, puzzled.

Mingliang took a closer look. It wasn't the girl who'd come earlier. This one was better looking and had a nice figure. Then he noticed that she was carrying a basket over one arm, filled with lantern-like persimmons. She smiled.

"You can sleep anytime, tell me a joke."

Now he knew. This was Hua Erniang, and he was dreaming. Yanjin residents' dreams were Erniang's playground. When she entered your dream, you had to tell her a joke. If it was good enough to make her laugh, she rewarded you with a persimmon. If not, you must carry her on your back for a bowl of spicy soup, and end up flattened beneath a mountain. Mingliang had run into Sima Xiaoniu at Yanjin's ferry landing a few days earlier, and when they were talking about Sima's father, Sima Niu, Hua Erniang's name came up. Mingliang was deeply moved by the father's death, never expecting Hua Erniang to come into his dream one night. He'd been so busy for days that Hua Erniang's visit took him by surprise. Concentrating on worldly affairs in his waking hours, he'd neglected to prepare a joke for her. With the thought that Yanjin was a city of half a million residents, and this was his first time back in twenty years, it did not seem possible that she would visit him. Not once in the twenty or more years he'd actually lived in Yanjin had she come into one of his dreams, so he'd carelessly neglected to prepare a joke. Trying to come up with one on the fly was out of the question. He broke out in a sweat, which produced an inspiration.

"Erniang," he said, "I'm OK with your looking for jokes in people's dreams, but you've come to the wrong person this time."

"How so?"

"I came to Yanjin on business. I'm not a resident."

She laughed. "I checked you out before I entered your

dream. Your name is Chen Mingliang, isn't it? You were born in Yanjin and you're here now, aren't you? I don't tolerate people who get slick with me."

"I'll show you my ID card."

He took it out and showed it to her. "Erniang, be an impartial judge."

Mingliang's ID card was clear: he was a resident of Xi'an.

"All right, so you're a Xi'an resident. But you were once a resident of Yanjin. Since you must be considered half a Yanjin-er, I'll give you a fifty per cent discount on jokes."

"What does that mean?"

"You need to tell your joke, but I don't have to laugh. Lightening my mood is sufficient. I'm willing to make do, but I can't let this trip be a total waste of time."

Discount or not, Mingliang could not come up with a joke. Once again, on the verge of disaster, he had an inspiration. The girl who'd come to offer services before he went to bed was a prostitute. Xiaomeng had once been a prostitute. There was something that had happened to her often when she was a working girl.

"Erniang, the joke I want to tell you is a little off-colour. Are you OK with that?"

"The colour of a joke is unimportant," she replied. "What matters is if you can lighten my mood."

"There was a girl who worked as a prostitute for five years and had slept with thousands of men, but didn't do anything with at least half of them. Know why that was?"

"I don't believe it," she replied. "People don't just throw money away."

"It was because half the men she entertained couldn't get it up."

Hua Erniang digested that for a moment, then burst out laughing. "That's something I never thought of. And you said you couldn't tell jokes. That was a good one."

She reached into her basket and took out a persimmon. "I'm giving you one of these. Enjoy it."

She vanished. A sweat-drenched Mingliang held the persimmon in his hand. Although saved from certain death in Yanjin by a moment of inspiration, he was embarrassed by having made reference to his wife's former profession, even ashamed. But he'd had no choice. Given that this latest incident had occurred in Yanjin, the city frightened him yet again. They'd been driven out twenty years before, and now he was back, only to be shamed by a joke. What, after all, was a joke? That question itself was a joke. What was a hometown? This was. With an emotional sigh, he said to himself, "In the future, I'm staying away from Yanjin."

He looked out the window. Dawn was breaking.

EIGHT

Two days later, Chen Chuankui returned to Yanjin from the Yumen Oilfield in Gansu to join the rest of the Chen family in moving more than two hundred graves of twenty-six branches of the family to a new spot by the Yellow River. Mingliang planted cypress trees all around his grandparents' site and watered them, then fell to his knees to pay obeisance. He'd carried out his duty. After arriving in Yanjin, he'd wanted to pay his respects at his mother's grave or find a good place to move it. But as a suicide, she could not be buried in the family plot and had wound up in a potter's field. Once located in the south of the city, as the borders expanded, the field was flattened, given over to the construction of tall buildings. Her grave disappeared, and there was no place for him to pay his respects, foiling his desire to relocate her resting place. That was that.

In the afternoon, he boarded a high-speed train to return to Xi'an, arriving later that night. At home, Xiaomeng greeted him with a number of questions, all of which he answered. All but one, that is. He did not mention Hua Erniang coming to him in a dream, but that was fine since all her questions dealt with daily matters, not his dreams.

No more was said that night. The next morning, he was off to the original Marshal Tianpeng's.

Sun Erhuo's son showed up, and said, "My father asked you to come see him, Uncle."

"What about?"

"He heard you'd made a trip to Yanjin, and wants to know if you had his fortune told."

"How did he know about my trip?" Mingliang wondered aloud.

"I told him. I came with some friends for pigs' feet, and they told me there."

He was not sure he wanted to visit Sun. True, he'd gone to Yanjin, but Old Dong the fortune-teller was dead by then, so that was that. Sun had asked him to do that for him over a month before, but it had slipped his mind when he went to Yanjin. The tuft of the human Sun Erhuo's hair still lay at the bottom of canine Sun Erhuo's dog bed. The responsibility for the failed attempt rested on him, that was certain.

And he had just returned, and there was much to do in the cafe.

"I just got back, and I'm swamped here, I'll go see him in a couple of days."

"That would be OK if you hadn't gone to Yanjin. Since you did, my father's nearly gone crazy waiting for you."

So Mingliang had no choice but to go with Sun's son.

"Sihai," Sun said, skipping all pleasantries. "Did you go to Yanjin on my business?"

Mingliang did, of course, go to Yanjin, but not on Sun's business. However, this was no time to tell the truth.

"Yes, I did."

"Did you have the fortune-teller perform a live transmission for me?"

"Yes," Mingliang replied to keep the lie going.

"What did he do? What did he say I'd be in my next life?"

"According to his prediction, you'll be a good man next time, a charitable person."

"How's that?"

"You'll be a sutra-chanting vegetarian and leave the secular world in your twenties."

"Did he really say that?" Sun asked, unable to believe what he was hearing.

"Absolutely."

Sun's head wobbled like a toy. "Then he was wrong."

"How can you say that?"

"It's not what I had in mind."

"What did you have in mind?"

"Either a powerful man, or a rich one."

Mingliang chuckled at Sun's foolish response, surprised by the man's wild ambition.

"Why do you want to be powerful or rich?"

"So my word means something, so I can live like a man ought to live." Sun gestured animatedly. "Take now, for instance. Except for the mosquitos flying around, I'm the only occupant of this house. With power or wealth, would people drop by to see me, or wouldn't they?"

"I'm here, aren't I?"

"Sihai," Sun replied, "you're one of the world's few good-hearted men. If I had power or riches, you'd be well-treated."

Another chuckle. Mingliang thought of Guo Zikai's father, Guo Baochen, who'd been a prime minister in his previous life and was now one of Yanjin's street sweepers. He told this to Sun.

"There's nothing wrong with having no power or wealth. You can be rich and powerful this time around, and sweep streets next time."

He should have said, why worry about the next life instead of living a good life this time? Instead: "It's what Fortune-Teller Dong said. You can't just try to change your fate."

Sun smacked his own forehead. "Aiya, a monk in my next life, how could that be?"

That same evening, Mingliang received a phone call from the police substation in a southern suburb informing him that his son, Chen Hongzhi, had injured someone in a fight. He was told to come to the station to resolve the matter. When Hongzhi was still small, his parents had just opened the first Marshal Tianpeng's Cafe in a rented building. Their home was also a rental, which had kept them from firmly establishing a home for themselves. They hadn't had much money, so Hongzhi wasn't dressed as well as the other boys. In winter months, they didn't buy him new padded clothes and shoes in stores; instead, Xiaomeng sat up at night after closing sewing clothes for him. Since the family business was a cafe, the boy ate well, with meat on a daily basis. Mingliang still recalled how it was for him as a boy in the Wuhan railway dormitory, where he shared a room with his father. When his father was on a train somewhere, Mingliang went to the dining hall with his food bowl. Two options were available, vegetables only at five fen, meat and vegetables at fifteen fen. He bought only vegetables.

At school, Hongzhi often compared what he was given to wear with the other boys. Mingliang would give him a kick on his backside and say, "Don't ask for trouble. You're much better off than I was at your age."

When the boy started middle school, he moved into the school dormitory. By then, business at the diner was doing so well that they began opening Marshal Tianpeng's cafes in other locations. Their son's clothing was now on a par with other children, even better than some of the city boys.

Mingliang got into his car and drove to the police station, where the duty officer, a man in his thirties, sat at the desk. Hongzhi was in a chair in front of him, beside a forty-year-old man, who looked daggers at Mingliang.

"Are you Hongzhi's father?" the policeman asked.

With a nod, Mingliang pointed to his son. "What's he done?"

"This afternoon during a football match, Hongzhi got into a fight with a player on the other team over a free kick, knocking out three of his teeth. The boy was sent to the hospital, where he was found to have suffered a mild concussion. Given the consequences, it was considered serious enough to detain your son. Both fathers have come in. We'll try mediation. If that doesn't work, it will have to go to court."

Obviously, the man who'd just glared at him was the other boy's father.

"I'm OK with mediation," said Mingliang.

"Your boy slugged my son, so of course you'll agree to mediation."

"What he did was wrong, no doubt about it, but it's over now, so if you're in a forgiving mood, I'll do my best to make it up to you."

"Make it up how?"

"We'll pay for your son's dental bill. Take him to the finest dentist for implants. They can do wonderful things these days. I had one last year, and it's holding up perfectly. As for the concussion, take him to see the best doctor at the best hospital, and I'll pay all the medical costs."

"That's it?"

"If you want compensation, give me a number."

"I'll take a hundred thousand."

Hongzhi stood up to say something, but his father pushed him back down. "All right," he said to the other man. "We'll exchange text numbers, and I'll send it to you when I get home."

"We're still the loser," the man said. "The boy's lost three teeth and we don't know how serious the concussion is."

"Mr Li," the policeman said, "he's dealt with this fairly, it's a good offer. High school boys can be impulsive. We all went through the same stage, and he's offered to make it good. Don't be unreasonable."

The man scowled at Mingliang. "This isn't about you, but you need to watch this son of yours."

"I will, I definitely will."

After the fathers signed an agreement and exchanged addresses, Mingliang took Hongzhi out of the station. The boy was not happy.

"How could you give him a hundred thousand yuan? It's blackmail."

"So what? Would you rather remain in detention? That would be a stain you'd live with from now on. Fighting doesn't have to be a big deal, but why did you have to be so violent?"

"I didn't hit him."

"Those three teeth didn't fall out on their own. And he didn't give himself a concussion."

"I head-butted him."

That stopped Mingliang in his tracks. A single head-butt knocked out three teeth and caused a minor concussion.

"Do you have a head of steel?"

"Who knew he had such a soft head?"

"Why'd you do it?"

"They were three down and he lost his temper when I dribbled the ball towards his goal. So he tripped me and I was given a free kick. He came up, stuck his face right up to mine and said my ma had been a whore."

That stopped Mingliang. Xiaomeng had been a prostitute twenty years before, and that had been the cause of their move from Yanjin to Xi'an. As far as they were concerned, it was history, and they had re-established contact with their families, never expecting it to come back to haunt them after all those years – from Yanjin to Xi'an to their son's middle school. Mingliang was livid.

"The little bastard. He got off easy with a head-butt. You should have ripped his mouth open."

"Was Mama a whore when she was young, Papa?" Hongzhi asked.

"When your mother was nineteen, she stewed pigs' feet at Marshal Tianpeng's with me in Yanjin. Where could she have done that?"

"If he ever says that again, I will rip his mouth open."

"Right. But you don't really have to go that far. You could go to jail for that. Just hit him."

The surfacing of Xiaomeng's past was worrisome, although there were distinct differences between what happened then and what arose now. Back then, it was a provable situation; now, it was just talk. Twenty years before, there had been a printed ad as evidence, now nothing but a rumour. In that earlier time, Sun Erhuo had used it to blackmail Xiaomeng. Now, nobody would dare mention it to them. It was just tongues wagging behind their backs. When people tire of wagging their tongues, they stop doing it. He felt better after thinking it over.

"Don't say anything about this to your mother."

"I won't."

After dinner that night, Mingliang was on the sofa watching TV. He took a look at his phone and, feeling tired, went to his bedroom and got ready for bed. Before he turned off the light, Xiaomeng rushed in, still dressed.

"Bad news!" she announced.

Mingliang assumed she had heard about the talk that

had spread to Xi'an. Forcing himself to look calm, he said, "Whatever it is, we can deal with it. Slow down, tell me what it is."

"Remember the girl Xiangxiu?"

What a relief, it wasn't about Xiaomeng. Of course, Mingliang remembered Xiangxiu, the girl who had publicly revealed Xiaomeng's Beijing activity to the people of Yanjin. She had recently asked if she could bring a woman with a damaged face to their home. Concerned about the girl's friend, they had said no. "What's up with her?"

"She'd dead."

"What!" He sat up. "How did that happen?"

Xiaomeng was shaking. "About three months ago, she phoned to ask if she could come here and bring a friend with a damaged face. I said no. Remember?"

"I do. We talked it over."

"Today I learned that she was in fact the woman with the damaged face. She was sounding me out, seeing if I'd be willing to have a girl like that come."

Mingliang slapped his forehead, now that he saw what the woman had had in mind. "Was it the disease that killed her?"

"It had nothing to do with it. She hanged herself in Ulanqab. Anyone who does something that extreme has to have lost hope. I tried it myself, didn't I? If I'd told her she could visit for a few days of girl-talk, maybe she'd have felt good enough to not do what she did."

Mingliang had nothing to say to that, finding no reason to dispute her logic. After he'd saved her from trying to hang herself in the nick of time, he'd brought her with him to Xi'an.

"My aunt in Yanjin phoned me with the news, and all I could think was, I killed Xiangxiu."

She began to weep. "We'd once been terrible enemies, but then she called and said she'd like to visit. Just think how alone she must have been at that point. Why didn't I think of that at the time? Is it reasonable to say I killed her, Mingliang?"

He did not respond right away, for after his mother hanged herself, he felt responsible, believing it had something to do with his going out to buy a soft drink. In the garden outside the railway hospital in Wuhan, Chen Changjie said he'd been responsible. If Xiaomeng had indeed played a role in Xiangxiu's death, since they had talked over her request to visit them, which they had refused, he must have shared responsibility. He recalled the day twenty years earlier, when Xiangxiu had distributed the ad with Xiaomeng's name all over town, and he'd gone looking for her at her home the next day. She'd already left Yanjin. He'd seen her photo in the house, a girl with a round face, large eyes and a ready smile, with two dimples.

"There's no need to blame yourself at this point. She should have told you the truth."

"I feel terrible. I'm going to sleep here tonight."

"Of course. And try not to think about it. I should have given it more thought and had you ask more questions."

As Xiaomeng slept beside Mingliang, he lay awake thinking life is unpredictable.

At around three o'clock one afternoon two months later, as lunch diners at Marshal Tianpeng's were leaving and dinner guests would not start arriving until five o'clock, the cooks and waiters took advantage of the two-hour break to do some window shopping in the Great Wild Goose Tower retail district. Mingliang recalled how he had taken advantage of the free time when he and Xiaomeng were working at the Yanjin cafe to go out back and play his flute by the riverbank. Now, with the cafe empty, he brewed a cup of tea. Seeing what a nice, sunny day it was, he went to sit at a table outside the entrance to enjoy his tea, take in the sun and watch people go by. Starting to feel sleepy, he leaned back in his chair to take a nap, when he saw a man with a woven sack over his shoulder rush up. Thinking it could be someone coming into town from the countryside to find work, he paid him no attention. To his surprise, the man looked around and let his gaze fall on the Marshal Tianpeng's sign. He laid down his sack, wiped his sweaty brow and said to himself, This is the place.

Seeing someone sitting there, he asked, "Is this the place owned by Chen Mingliang, General Manager Chen of Henan?"

No longer in the mood to nap, Mingliang heard the Henan accent.

"Yes, it is. Can I help you with something?"

"I want to see him."

"For what, may I ask?"

"Something important."

That made Mingliang laugh. "What's so important? Tell me?"

"Not you. I'll only tell Mr Chen."

"That's me."

"Don't lie to me."

Switching to a Henan accent, Mingliang said, "Listen to me. Is this a Henan accent or a Yanjin one?"

The man cocked his ear and smiled. "So you're General Manager Chen."

He opened his sack, took out something wrapped in cloth and unwrapped it to reveal a heavy placard. Its condition showed its age. On it were carved four words: One Year Three Autumns.

Mingliang jumped out of his chair. Three months earlier he'd gone to Yanjin to move his ancestors' graves, where he'd heard that the date tree in his grandmother's garden had been turned into furniture by a man named Fan. When he went to see for himself, he was told that Fan's sons had cut it all up for firewood. He then learned, however, that a man named Jin had bought the heart of the tree's trunk and had it carved to hang over the gate of his home. But the building was sold to a man named Zhou, who razed it and built a Western-style building in its place. The one-time gatekeeper informed Mingliang that Zhou had thrown the placard away. Mingliang told the gatekeeper that a reward of a hundred thousand yuan awaited anyone who found and returned it to him. He'd left his contact information. He was surprised that someone would bring it to him three months later.

"Where did you find this?"

"I looked everywhere for it, and it just about fell into my lap."

"What does that mean?"

"I'm from the Tangyin countryside. When Zhou tore down the original house, my grandfather and others scavenged the abandoned materials. This placard was part of it. A few days ago, the old gatekeeper told me you said it was a valuable item and that you'd pay a lot of money to get it. I asked him how to contact you in Xi'an, and here I am." He pointed to the placard. "Pick it up, you'll see it's made of date wood. Carrying it all this way from Henan was tough. Go ahead, pick it up."

Mingliang tested its weight. It was heavy, all right.

"You said you'd give a hundred thousand yuan to whoever found and brought this to you. You're as good as your word, are you?"

As Mingliang looked at it, he thought back to his grandmother, who had made date cakes from its fruit.

"Don't worry. If it's genuine, you'll get your money."

That did not please the man. "Do you think I'd carry a phoney placard on my back all the way from Henan?"

"I also gave the gatekeeper my phone number. Why didn't you phone before you came?"

"How can you tell if something's phoney or not over the phone? Don't forget the saying, 'What you hear is false, what you see is true.'"

Mingliang couldn't dispute that. "May I ask your name?"

"No need to be so polite. My name's Cai."

Mingliang invited Cai to sit with him and have a cup of tea as he studied the placard. At first glance, it looked to be old, but the varnish had a new look about it. Not the varnish itself, but a slight smear of dried liquid that had left its mark after it was wiped off. Mingliang picked up the board to smell it. The smell of new varnish was unmistakable. Something didn't feel right, so he got up and went next door to the jewellery store to borrow an electric drill, which he used on a corner of the board.

"What are you doing?" an astonished Cai asked. He

jumped up to stop him. "You're going to ruin a historical relic."

Mingliang had by then drilled a hole in the wood. Sawdust from new wood emerged from the hole. Mingliang removed the drill and pointed to the sawdust for Cai's benefit.

"Take a good look. Did this come from a relic? A ten-year-old placard, wood from a two-hundred-year-old tree?"

Now what? Cai was thinking. With an embarrassed laugh, he said, "You're amazing. You caught me."

"I used to stew pigs' feet for a living. I could tell how well done they were by poking them with a chopstick. Drilling a hole in a piece of wood will give you its age. What are you trying to pull here?"

More embarrassed laughs. "Since you've spotted the trick, I'll come clean." He slapped his face a couple of times. "To be honest, the old gatekeeper for the Zhou family is my uncle. I was in Tangyin to look up a friend last month and stopped by to see my uncle, who told me about this, and thought it was a good way to make some money. So I went to Linzhou to get a man named Jin to carve another piece of wood to look like the original. He refused, saying it would damage his reputation. But his son said he'd do it, so the two of us went to a village where we bought a piece of date wood and air-dried it. After he carved it, we found someone to make it look old. That's why I came to Xi'an without a phone call ahead of time. That way you wouldn't have time to prepare yourself for what you'd see. I figured I'd hand it over, you'd pay me, and I'd be on my way. If you discovered the truth after that, it'd be too late. I didn't expect you'd see through the deception."

Despite knowing that Cai had planned to cheat him, Mingliang was impressed by the honest confession and had to laugh.

"If you'd managed to get me to pay you, how would you have split the money with Jin's son?"

"Fifty-fifty. I went to a lot of trouble and expense for this. It took me two weeks to get from Tangyin to Linzhou. There's the cost for the carving, and finding someone to make the board look old took time, and then I had to come all the way to Xi'an. You found me out, that's true, so we'll forget the original amount of money, but could you pay me something for what I spent and my travel expenses?"

"How much were you thinking of?"

"It'll have to be twenty thousand, ten thousand apiece for Jin and me. Even with that, when I get back, Jin might call me a dumb arse or something."

Mingliang took another look at the placard. Although the carving wasn't perfect, the characters themselves and the texture of the wood grain weren't bad. And he wouldn't have noticed the weathered look was faked if he hadn't studied it carefully.

"You came here to palm a phoney placard off on me, and you're lucky I'm not reporting you to the authorities. And now you want me to pay you for that!" He pointed to the teapot and cups. "Drink your tea and take that thing away with you."

"Fifteen thousand," Cai said, his eye on Mingliang.

Mingliang leaned back in his chair and ignored him.

"Ten thousand."

Nothing.

"Eight thousand."

Still nothing.

"Five thousand."

Stony silence.

"Three thousand."

"Leave it with me," Mingliang said as he sat up.

"You know how to hurt a guy," Cai said. "Three thousand won't even cover what I spent on travel." He sighed. "Whoever thought I'd be stuck with this by bringing it here? I guess three thousand is better than throwing it away."

Mingliang transferred three thousand yuan into his account by text on their phones. Cai walked off muttering to himself.

When his visitor was gone, Mingliang returned the drill to the jewellery store owner Jin.

"What was all that about?" Jin asked.

Mingliang told him all about the placard. "It's not the one I wanted, but the carving isn't bad. I'm just worried that the wood might be inferior."

"Bring it over, I'll take a look," said Jin. "I tell you, before I got into the jewellery business, I studied to be a carpenter with an uncle of mine. We can talk about my carpentry skills some other time, but I do know wood."

Mingliang returned to Marshal Tianpeng's, picked up the placard and brought it to show his neighbour. Jin tapped it, turned it over and over, and leaned up close to study the hole Mingliang had drilled.

"I don't know where they got this piece of date wood, but it's not bad. Most date wood isn't especially hard, but this one's as hard as sandalwood. They got a piece of wood as hard as sandalwood for the price of date wood, which wasn't too bad a deal. In terms of quality, this placard could last several hundred years. Sure, it isn't from the date tree in your grandmother's garden, but the best wood loses its value when it's turned into something fake."

"It's fake, all right, but like the dog Sun Erhuo, who came to me," Mingliang said, "with the twists and turns of his background, we were destined to be together."

"That's for sure."

At a little past four o'clock, the employees began drifting back from their window shopping. Mingliang told them to clean the placard and hang it in the centre of the diner's wall. When the dinner customers arrived, the regulars spotted the addition.

"What do those four words mean?"

"It's the Marshal Tianpeng's Cafe motto."

"Meaning?"

"If you miss eating pigs' feet even for one day, it'll be on your mind for three years."

Mingliang dreamt that night that his placard had turned back into a tree, his grandmother's two-hundred-year-old date tree. It grew not in her garden, but at the Yanjin ferry landing. Still dense with foliage, its leaves rustled in the wind. A group of people sat beneath the tree swapping stories: Mingliang's grandmother and grandfather, Old Dong the fortune-teller, characters in Granny's tales, the dog Sun Erhuo and the middle-aged monkey he'd encountered at the landing, all people and animals he thought about often, but could no longer see. The blind fortune-teller was no longer blind; the Pekingese dog that had never set paw in Yanjin was there; the monkey's wounds had scabbed over. Who was telling stories? Not the humans. It was the animals, the weasel, the stubborn ox, the dog and the monkey, taking turns to tell stories about what they'd seen and who they'd met, laughing uproariously one minute and shedding tears the next. The sights were an inspiration to Mingliang to pick up his flute again. He hadn't played it in a very long time. And there it was, lying in his hand again, as the thought occurred to him, and he longed to start playing. In times past, he'd played about his mother dancing beside the Yangtze; he wondered where Granny's date tree had gone, and he played his unfamiliarity with Yanjin. Now he wanted to play "One Day Three Autumns", but where was it? It was in the dream, in tales told by the animals. But when he picked up the flute to play, a voice behind him said, "Don't. None of it's real."

Mingliang turned to look. It was Hua Erniang, a basket hanging from the crook of her arm, filled with persimmons. Mingliang was not happy.

"Erniang, everything here is real, how can you say it's not?"

"The tree is not real, it comes from 'One Day Three Autumns', which itself is not real, so how can the tale be real? Do you plan to play a tune of hypocrisy?"

"I'll tell you something, Erniang. Dreams are unreal, everything in them is unreal, and since two negatives make a positive, doesn't that prove that the sentiment is real? People in dreams often wet their pillows with real tears. Is that real crying? People in dreams often laugh out loud. Is that real laughter? Sometimes that reality is even more real than tears and laughter outside of dreams."

Hua Erniang had no response, apparently won over by his reasoning. A look of hostility burst onto her face.

"I want you to understand a principle of mine. I come to people in search of jokes, not new principles."

A light went off in Mingliang's head.

"Erniang, you're here in search of a joke, which goes without saying, but you really shouldn't be coming to me."

"Here we go again. Last time you said you were a Xi'an resident, didn't you?"

"Last time when I was in Yanjin, I was a Xi'an resident, but counted as half a Yanjin person. This time I'm in Xi'an, but have come to Yanjin in a dream; since Yanjin is not real, you shouldn't treat it as real and come to me for a joke. Does that make sense to you?"

"Even though you haven't come back, you've returned to Yanjin in your dream, which is to say your soul is here. If you rub me the wrong way, I'll crush your soul under a mountain, separating body from soul, and we'll see how you survive in Xi'an. There are always ways to deal with the unreal."

Mingliang was exasperated. The last time he left Yanjin, he vowed never to return. Which is exactly what he was doing in a dream. Who was in control of one's own soul? he wondered. "One Day Three Autumns" was at the heart of his troubles.

"Cat got your tongue?" Hua Erniang said, obviously pleased with herself. "It's folly for anyone to try to delude me. You might as well delude yourself."

The flute in Mingliang's hand vanished. No flute could tell Hua Erniang a joke. As disaster was about to strike, he had an inspiration. "Since we're talking about reason, Erniang, I have a joke about it."

"Let's hear it."

"Reason can't delude you, that's for sure, but it can certainly delude plenty of other people. There's a lot of false reason in life, but every day there are people who call it the truth, which, over time, makes it the truth. If everyone believes that something is false, they need to act in accordance with that falsity, but pretend it's the truth. Don't you think that's funny? Better if the dream is the truth."

Hua Erniang figured this out and laughed. "That's an interesting detour, like telling a joke with a twist. Turning reason into a joke is boring. You did a lot better with your smutty joke last time."

The smutty joke Mingliang told, however, was a sore spot. He wouldn't be able to live through many more jokes like that. After telling a joke this time, Hua Erniang did not reward him with a persimmon.

"I know I'm inarticulate, Erniang, and coming up with jokes for you is hard. I've learned my lesson this time. I won't be back in Yanjin, not even in my dreams."

"If you mean what you say, then we're done with each other. There are half a million people in this city. One more or one less won't stop me."

"That goes without saying."

Mingliang turned to leave. He stopped after two steps. "There is something I'd like to ask you before we say goodbye."

"What is it?"

"I may be worrying about nothing, so don't take offence."

"Go ahead, say it, I won't be offended."

"You've been looking for jokes in Yanjin every day for

three thousand years. Are Yanjin jokes like fish in an aquarium that will run out one day?"

She laughed. "You underestimate Yanjin. It's nothing like that, more like a mighty river. Don't forget, the Yellow River runs past it. Water in a fish pond is static, river water never runs stale; as life continues, so do new jokes. Of course, speaking of the jokes I've collected, the majority have been like the one you just told, fluid but a little forced. But fluid jokes are in plentiful supply, like river water."

"In your three thousand years here, have any Yanjin residents told spectacular jokes?"

"Once in a while, a one-liner that breaks me up. But not every day, of course, which is why patience is so important. There are two kinds of people I'm grateful to."

"What are they?"

"One type says they'll come, but don't, like Hua Erlang. I've been waiting for him, but he doesn't come, and I don't dare leave, which has given me time to wait for good jokes. Another type leaves but doesn't come back, like your mother, Yingtao. I keep thinking, if she comes back one day, she might bring with her jokes from out there somewhere."

"Erniang, that's where you're wrong. Besides being grateful to people who say they'll come but don't, and people who leave but haven't come back, you give no thought to thanking the people in Yanjin who are always telling you jokes, even though their jokes may not always be worth telling. Quite a few Yanjin residents were flattened because they couldn't tell you a joke, so everyone has been on tenterhooks since you arrived in Yanjin."

"My hands are tied. Before coming to Yanjin, I was a pretty good joke-teller and didn't need to get jokes from people. Since coming, I've become a beggar. Most beggars ask for food, I ask for jokes. If I'm not fed any, I die. You think I want to enter people's dreams at nightfall to seek jokes, don't you? Well, you're wrong. It's not me. There's someone who has been attached to my body for all these three thousand years. He's the one who wants to convert life into jokes. I'd like to leave Yanjin, but I've already been turned into a mountain."

Mingliang was gobsmacked by the news. "What a horrible person he is to be so cruel to you."

"It's not all bad," she said.

"How's that?"

"Being with him, gobbling up jokes for three thousand years is what's kept me alive so long. Look at me. Wouldn't you say I look like a seventeen or eighteen-year-old girl?"

Mingliang could not believe his ears. "So that's how it is. Who is this person?"

"Celestial mysteries cannot be divulged. If they were, and he was gone, wouldn't I be gone too? He knows this is an illness that can be cured only by jokes, so he's kept me with him for three thousand years and got the people of Yanjin to go along with him for three thousand years, and still his illness hangs on. He feels shame over this, but he's not in control of his actions. I ask you, isn't this whole thing a joke in itself?"

Mingliang mulled that over for a moment, then laughed.

"I told you this because you said you want to sever your relationship with Yanjin," she said. "I wouldn't say that to the local people, so don't tell anyone. If you do, I'll go to Xi'an in your dream, the same way you return to Yanjin in your dream, and ask for spicy soup."

Mingliang awakened with a start. He looked out the window, where the moonbeams were like water. He recalled what Hua Erniang had said in his dream. Although he didn't learn the identity of the person who was attached to her body, he realised what the person's illness was, and that scared the hell out of him.

PART IV
HAND-PICKED JOKES AND NEGLECTED JOKES

Section The First
Hua Erniang's selection of Yanjin residents' top one-liners

1. Add ceramic tiles to the Great Wall
2. Add a reverse gear to airplanes
3. Install an escalator to the Himalayan peaks
4. Desilt the Pacific Ocean
5. Fill people's bellies with joke machines

(Recorded in Hua Erniang's notebook)

SECTION THE SECOND
A Selection of Jokes Not Told in Yanjin

ONE: HOW DID HUA ERNIANG DIE?

Among the minority groups in ancient Northwest China was a clan named Lengyou. Jokes were their life. They travelled to many countries, with no fixed abode. The best joke-teller among them was called Hua Daye. When he told a joke, people laughed, but not him. He'd ask, Was that funny? His favourite joke involved a sunflower that turned throughout the day to face the sun. But one day, it ceased turning. So the sun stopped and asked why it wasn't turning. "My neck's broken," said the sunflower. "It looks all right to me," said the sun. "The neck's all right, the shaft inside snapped in two," the sunflower replied. The sun was angry. "Are you a mechanical flower, a fake?" When he told jokes, Hua Daye was fond of the phrase "that's for sure". "The sunflower was a fake, that's for sure," he said. "The monkey did a 180,000 *li* somersault, that's for sure. The woman married a fox and had a litter of kits in a few years, that's for sure. The tough guy got angry and used his knife on the scoundrel, who dropped like a stone, that's for sure." The term "that's for sure" first turned up in Song and Yuan prompt books, that was its origin.

On this day, Hua Daye led his clan to Huopo Guo, or "Lively Country". They began telling jokes in the market square. Everyone laughed. They went into the palace. The king laughed and so did the gathered officials. The king invited them to his private quarters to tell jokes. The queen and consort laughed, so did the princes and their sons, especially Prince Number Four, who rocked back and forth.

"See how lively the people here are, Hua Daye? They love to hear jokes. You don't have to travel all around, you can live here. As they say, it's easy to tell jokes, hard to find someone to appreciate them. Settling down here will mean the Lengyou Clan can have a hometown."

Hua talked it over with his people. "This is a land of sunshine and gentle rains, the people live in harmony under wise leadership, and the king has invited us to stay. What do you all say?"

Exhausted by constant travel, the people agreed: "You decide, Hua Daye."

"Always someplace else, year in and year out, no beginning and no end."

"We should jump at this opportunity, for it will not come again."

And so, the Lengyou Clan settled down in Lively Country, building houses, creating families, no problem.

Ten years passed, as did the King of Lively Country. Prince Number Four ascended the throne. In truth, he did not like jokes and changed the national motto to "Be solemn".

Now seated on the throne, the new king proclaimed, "From today henceforth, it is Our wish that the people seek solemnity. Away with senseless frivolity."

An official stepped up to address the throne. "There is a Lengyou Clan that incites gaiety among the people. How shall we deal with them?"

"Unrestrained hee-hee ha-ha degrades the character of Our people," said the new king. "It is injurious to heart and mind. This is all part of an evil scheme by Shenchou Guo and Dahen Guo. Enmity Country and Great Hatred Country, a fifth column they have sent here."

He ordered the extermination of the clan. Troops encircled the clan overnight. More than a hundred clansmen and women, young and old, lost their heads, like harvested melons.

In the moments before his execution, Hua Daye said, "How could this have happened? Back when we told jokes to the king, no one laughed harder." The reference was to the new king.

"It was all made up, a phoney act by a master of deception. The old king would roll over in his grave. I've told jokes all my life, and this is the biggest joke of all."

Only two members of the Lengyou Clan, a man and a woman, escaped the massacre. They had not been home on the night of the extermination campaign. They had gone out into the wild to engage in illicit sex. Their sexual appetites sated, they returned to the city, where they heard talk on the street that their fellow clansfolk had all been killed. They dared not display their grief, but decided to flee. "Where to?"

she asked. "I met a storyteller in the marketplace a few days ago who knew how to crack a joke," he replied. "He was from Yanjin, so let's go there." While they were talking it over, a commotion broke out on the street. Soldiers who were engaged in a mopping-up operation charged the couple, forcing them to separate.

"Meet me at the Yanjin ferry landing," he shouted.

"See you there," she responded.

He was eighteen. His name was Hua Erlang. She was seventeen. Her name was Liu Yingying, but on that day, she changed it to Hua Erniang.

Putting aside talk of the difficult twists and turns that brought Hua Erniang to Yanjin, we turn to Hua Erlang, who travelled east, experiencing warfare, cholera, malaria and hives, taking three years, five months and twenty-three days to make it to Yanjin. He arrived at the ferry landing in the evening. Hua Erniang had already gone to rest at a roadside inn. There were no mobile phones back then, which meant that Hua Erlang did not know if Hua Erniang had made it to Yanjin, or if she had encountered mishaps over the three years. Dispirited, he looked out at the tumbling waters of the Yellow River. Wanting to get something to eat, he walked into a riverside cafe. The owner was sitting behind the counter, his face resting in one hand as he watched a pair of calico cats fight.

"What's good to eat, Boss?" Hua Erlang asked.

"Well, since you're here beside the Yellow River, I'd say one of its famous carp would be best."

He led Hua Erlang out back to the fish pond, where a dozen carp were swimming, and one was floating belly-up.

"How come that one died, while the others swam?"

"Anger."

"Over what?"

"It was in there for two weeks and no one picked it."

Hua Erlang laughed for the first time in five years, three months and twenty-three days.

While Hua Erlang was eating his fish with a flatbread, some more customers walked in the door. Inasmuch as there was considerable marshy land by the ferry landing, mosquitos were plentiful. With a loud smack, a customer at a nearby table killed a mosquito. "You won't be seeing your mama again, friend," the man said. A second mosquito flew off. "It went off with bad news to the friend's mama," the man said. Hua Erlang laughed again, and he knew he'd been right to come to Yanjin. Like the residents of Lively Country, the people here loved telling jokes. Another man entered. Diners at a nearby table asked him, "What are you doing here after finishing your meal? And you're not drinking." Hua Erlang knew this was friendly banter, but how to respond to this, as a member of Lengyou clan, he could not say, let alone think. To his surprise, the newcomer said, "I ate yesterday, and I don't drink ersatz alcohol." Erlang was mightily impressed. He clapped his hands and laughed lustily, forgetting that he was eating a fish, and got a barbed fish bone caught in his throat, one he could neither cough up nor swallow. It didn't take long for the stuck fish bone to take his life. Or maybe it was the laugh. No one could save him, and the panicked owner didn't know what to do. The culprit was a fish bone, but since the man had died in his cafe, the owner could not dodge responsibility. The accent made it clear he was an outsider, so the owner said to the patrons, "There's no time to lose, I'll rush him to a doctor."

He picked up Hua Erlang and went outside. He'd walked a short distance to the bank of the Yellow River, where he was alone. "Good brother, since laughter was your undoing, in the spirit of the jolly episode, I'll send you to the land of extreme joy." With a splash, he tossed Hua Erlang into the river.

For the next three thousand years, Hua Erniang assumed that, perhaps owing to the turbulence of war, Erlang had died somewhere other than in Yanjin. She stayed in Yanjin for a period of three thousand years and looked beyond the place, or she stayed in Yanjin and forgot what was beyond, while the person she sought or forgot was there in Yanjin. Not really in Yanjin, of course, but carried along in the Yellow River, all the way to the Eastern Ocean.

Many residents of Yanjin over those three thousand years were aware of what happened, but none of them dared tell Hua Erniang, and were especially wary of relating it as a joke in their dream.

That itself was Yanjin's most stupendous joke.

Two: Where Did Yingtao Reach Land?

Generations of fishermen around Jiujiang in Jiangxi Province had fished the Yangtze for a living. They went out in the morning and returned at dusk to sell their catch of fish and shrimp to fishmongers in the marketplace. A man named Chen Erge was bringing his boat in for the day when he noticed a disturbance in the water ahead, the whitecaps indicating a school of fish swimming into the ocean. He shouted, "I'm sorry, but I'm going to have to take you in." He cast his net into the wave, and when he brought it in, it felt heavier than usual, which delighted him, figuring it to be a big catch. Struggling to drag it out of the water, he was shocked to see that there were no fish, only a charming young woman. She looked closely at his attire, wiped the water from her face, and said, "Good brother, what era are you living in?"

"This is the Song dynasty. Who are you?"

"I'm called Yingtao," she said, realising she'd been carried back to the Song.

"Why did you jump into the river?"

"It's a long story."

The owner of a cafe on the riverbank, named Song, was married to a woman named Ma. Fisherman Chen rowed his boat to the bank and took Yingtao in with him. When wife Ma saw Chen walk in with a woman who was drenched from head to toe, she said, "Chen Erge, where did you snatch a wife for yourself?"

"I didn't snatch her, I pulled her out of the river."

People who are tired of living have existed in every dynastic period, and for people who lived by the river, watery suicides were commonplace.

"Well, since you've rescued her, she ought to come to the fire right away."

"Coming to the fire" meant, in the Song dynasty, to warm oneself. Before she "came to the fire", she was shown inside to put on a set of wife Ma's clothes. When she came out, she paid her respects: "Thank you, good sister."

While Yingtao was warming by the fire, Ma said, "I can tell by your accent that you are not from here."

"No, from far away, and now that I'm here, I hope you'll help me out."

"You're a charming young lady, shall I try to find you a

husband?"

"I leave that up to my good sister."

"Do you not miss your home?"

"I wouldn't have come here if I did."

"You don't miss it? Why?"

"It's a long story."

"Where is your home?"

"I'd rather not say."

The wife could see that the young woman was embarrassed about something. Why else would anyone jump into a river? She chose not to follow up, as something dawned on her.

"After all this time, you must be hungry."

"I had nothing to eat before I jumped."

"Pick out a live fish," she told her cook, "and prepare a fish soup for the girl. She needs to get warm before anything else."

Again, Yingtao expressed her gratitude: "Thank you, good sister."

The cook went out back to the vat to pick out a fish. Inside the cafe, a man dressed like a scholar strolled in. A page boy walked in behind him, carrying writing implements. The man was Ma's young cousin, a talented scholar in Jiujiang. Song and Ma were illiterate, so this cousin had come to create a pair of New Year's scrolls for them. The cook came in from the back with a live fish, promptly bumped into the page boy, and the fish flew into the page boy's face, who yelped and flung the inkstone right into the chest of Yingtao, who yelped and fell like a stone.

"Look what you've done, you clumsy fool!" Ma cursed the cook.

Then it was the page boy's turn. "An intelligent boy like you ought to be more careful."

She helped Yingtao to her feet.

"Are you badly hurt, Miss?"

Yingtao rubbed her flat chest. "Nothing serious, good sister. A little pain here is all."

Wife Ma took Yingtao into the bedroom so she could lie down and rest.

While she was resting, she heard the scholar and some fishermen discussing the seriousness of what the inkstone had done to her. Opinions flew. An inkstone hitting a flat chest could produce one of three results: it could make the chest even flatter; the chest might become concave; or the chest might expand a little.

That infuriated Yingtao. I've been injured, and it's just a joke to you people. How dare you! You Song people are tawdry. She thought about rushing out and having words with them. On second thought, this was a chain of jokes, one joke per sentence. Another thought: Yama's rule was one joke for every sentence, up to fifty. Now the chain, one joke at a time, with a chain on top of a chain, up to fifty jokes. Yingtao's anger turned to cheerfulness, and she committed this joke to memory, thinking she'd take it back to Yama, and she could be reborn. The choice between being the victim of a game or being reborn was a no-brainer. Master, I can't escape from your grasp, but I'll give you a joke. She breathed a sigh. I went from Yanjin to Wuhan and from there to Jiujiang, twists and turns, difficulties and hardships, never imagining the chance for rebirth would be at this spot, and never imagining that I'd owe my salvation to Song people.

That's for sure.

PART V
BEGINNING OF A BIOGRAPHY OF HUA ERNIANG

This is a book about laughter. It's also a book about tears. In the final analysis, it's a book about blood. A lot of people paying their lives for jokes, isn't that a book about blood?

(That's it, no more)

About the Author

Liu Zhenyun, born in 1958 in Yanjin, Henan Province, is one of the most famous writers in contemporary China. He graduated from the Chinese Department of Peking University and is now a professor at the School of Liberal Arts, Renmin University of China.

Liu has been awarded many prestigious prizes at home and abroad, including China's top literary accolade, the Mao Dun Literature Award in 2011, and the Knight of the Order of Arts and Letters in 2018 from the Minster of Culture in France. Liu's works have been translated into more than twenty languages, including English, French, German, Italian, Spanish and Swedish.

Many of Liu's books have been adapted into films, TV series and dramas, including *Remembering 1942* (2012) and *I Am Not Madame Bovary* (2016), for which Liu wrote the screenplays. Several of these adapted works have won awards at various film festivals, including the Taiwan Golden Horse Awards and the International Film Festivals of Toronto, San Sebastián, Berlin, Rome, Cairo, Busan and Hong Kong.

About the Translators

Howard Goldblatt is the translator of more than fifty works in Chinese, including the novels of Nobel laureate Mo Yan, for which he received a Guggenheim Fellowship. A former academic, his translations have won two Man Asia Literary Prizes. He has received two grants from the National Endowment of the Arts.

Sylvia Li-chun Lin is a retired professor, award-winning writer and Chinese to English translator of numerous bestselling novels. As a former professor at the University of Notre Dame, she is the recipient of a translation grant from the National Endowment of the Arts.

As a team, Goldblatt and Lin have translated more than a dozen novels and collections by writers from China and Taiwan, including *Notes of a Desolate Man* by Chu Tien-wen, chosen as 1999 Translation of the Year by the American Literary Translators Association, and *Three Sisters* by Bi Feiyu, which won the second annual Man Asia Literary Prize. They live, work and cycle in Lafayette, Colorado with their neurotic cat.